Making IT Governance
Work in a Sarbanes-Oxley World

'*Man is an animal that overestimates itself*'

—John Gray, Professor of European Thought,
Government Dept., London School of Economics

Making IT Governance
Work in a Sarbanes-Oxley World

JAAP BLOEM

MENNO VAN DOORN

PIYUSH MITTAL

WILEY

John Wiley & Sons, Inc.

For general information on our other products and services, or technical support, please contact our Customer Care Department within the United States at 800-762-2974, outside the United States at 317-572-3993 or fax 317-572-4002.

Wiley also publishes its books in a variety of electronic formats. Some content that appears in print may not be available in electronic books.

For more information about Wiley products, visit our Web site at http://www.wiley.com.

Library of Congress Cataloging-in-Publication Data:
Bloem, Jaap, 1957-
  Making IT governance work in a Sarbanes-Oxley world / Jaap Bloem,
Menno van Doorn, Piyush Mittal.
    p. cm.
  Includes index.
  ISBN-13: 978-0-471-74359-0 (cloth)
  ISBN-10: 0-471-74359-3 (cloth)
    1. Information technology—Management. 2. Corporate governance
—United States. 3. Corporations—Accounting—Law and legislation
—United States.   I. Doorn, Menno van, 1964- . II. Title.
HD30.2.B564 2005
658.4'038—dc22

                                        2005016636

Printed in the United States of America

10 9 8 7 6 5 4 3 2 1

Contents

CHAPTER 4
IT Portfolio Management   91

CHAPTER 5
Activity-Based Costing, Economic Value Added, and Applied Information Economics   137

Foreword

It may not be readily apparent, but IT is undergoing what may be its most significant revolution ever—a revolution driven by rapidly emerging new business models, the power of the customer, global operations, and radical new technologies at the edge of the Net. And this revolution is having as much impact on how technology gets managed as it does on what happens inside the datacenter.

Envision IT as an iceberg, the bulk of which is below the waterline. Below the IT waterline are commodity technologies like the wire in the wall, the network protocols, the servers, and storage—and even applications like the general ledger, payroll, and personnel. Above the IT waterline are those technologies that deliver competitive advantage. And when they achieve this stabilization, IT shops can focus on investments that drive competitive advantage—like cross-channel integration and optimization or demand-driven supply chain operations.

What does the Sarbanes-Oxley era have to do with this stabilization? IT begins to be focused on speed, span of activities beyond traditional regulatory boundaries, and the stabilization of technology management.

Those of us in IT caused things to be the way they are today. We set ourselves up as Queens and Kings of a magical world with heroic-like efforts by the knights of the roundtable. It was magic, the work we did. Sure, we needed funding, but we felt we didn't need to be accountable. Now all of this is changing.

"Making IT Governance Work in a Sarbanes-Oxley World" today requires consistency, predictability, and auditability—pushing more and more of the technology below the IT waterline so that we can focus where our businesses require us to focus.

Best practices learned from Forrester's CIO Group research supports this as in the following:

- **What are high-performance CIOs doing to optimize business impact?** CIOs in high performing IT shops—those in top performing businesses whose IT operations have a high correlation with their firms' business success—report that their success comes from focusing on business processes—not functions. And they use transparency of IT activities, resources, and spend to drive success.

- **How does Sarbanes-Oxley relate to high-performance IT's process focus and transparency?** Sarbanes-Oxley compliance will be significantly enhanced through IT's efforts at stabilization—not just from specific investments. The focus on creating consistent, predictable, and auditable IT operations will generate the track record that will ensure Sarbanes-Oxley compliance, through standards, shared services, and outsourcing.

- **What creates the required IT transparency?** It's all about portfolio management—the creation of information about all of IT-based activities in a single, enterprise-wide tool—maintained through common, IT-led processes—like prioritization, IT governance, and value realization management. This is a necessary but not sufficient condition—high-performance IT shops have some form of portfolio management in place, but just having a portfolio management process does not guarantee high performance.

Bobby Cameron
Vice President and Principal, The CIO Group
Forrester Research, Inc

Preface

This preface is both a summary explanation and an introduction to the subject explored here, the management of information and IT, which we call "IT governance." Although this expression has become increasingly common, those in the IT world will not be surprised to hear that not everyone uses it to mean the same thing. However, because everyone involved in IT governance has the same objective in mind—a response to the challenge of finding new ways to gain more business value from IT investments—a common understanding of what "IT governance" means needs to be reached.

MAKING IT GOVERNANCE WORK IN A SARBANES-OXLEY WORLD

Until recently, "Sarbanes-Oxley" meant nothing more than the last names of Senator Paul Sarbanes and Representative Michael Oxley. However, in July 2002 the U.S. Congress enacted a law—the Sarbanes-Oxley Act (SOX or Sarbox). This law imposes requirements on companies with respect to internal control and reporting and was a response to the extravagant conduct of managers and directors. The fall of WorldCom alone meant that the incredible amount of $180 billion of market value vanished. Investment banks and accountants had worked together to inflate market values, which no longer had any relation to reality. The resulting downslide in stock markets began in March 2000 and ultimately led to the failure of the New Economy. Enron, WorldCom, Arthur Andersen, and other companies no longer exist.

The Sarbanes-Oxley Act requires that companies make internal control a top priority, using wide-sweeping frameworks such as those formulated by The Committee of Sponsoring Organizations of the Treadway Commission (COSO) or laid out in *Guidance on Assessing Control*, published by the Canadian Institute of Chartered Accountants or *The Turnbull Report*, published by the Institute of Chartered Accountants in England and Wales.

The IT Governance Institute, established by the Information Systems Audit and Control Association (ISACA) in 1998, was the first organization to use the term "IT governance," thus giving the phrase some stature. The Institute also paved the way for good IT governance by introducing a COSO-based framework, the Control Objectives for Information and Related Technology (COBIT). COBIT is now being used as a tool to comply with the present more stringent reporting regulations. The need to use such frameworks sometimes gives rise to strange situations. Certain well-known businesses, after thorough consideration, rejected COBIT as a framework because it would be too impractical to implement. Some time later, the auditors had to declare that COBIT was in fact going to be used: It was mandatory.

This book discusses the tension between top-down governance directives and the challenge of functioning properly on a bottom-up basis. Making IT governance work does not simply mean adherence to an ABC such as (A) setting up more rules, (B) implementing a framework, and (C) registering good results. The book is not simply a guide to frameworks and compliance. It is our goal to describe an entire repertoire of resources that could be useful for arriving at better IT governance. COBIT is only one of these. Bottom-up governance principles such as distributed leadership constitute another. A third is called *portfolio management*.

It is a paradox, to say the least, that top-down control is given powerful legal reinforcement at the same time that businesses are simultaneously making every effort to teach people to think bottom up. Modern thinkers on organizational governance, such as Shoshana Zuboff and Claudio Ciborra, warn of the danger of excessive control and point to the possibility that we might move "from control to drift" if we do not allow the people actually doing the work to have their say.

In this book we attempt to do justice to the management dilemmas of current practice. The Sarbanes-Oxley world we speak is not a world in which internal control automatically leads to better governance. It is above all a world in which we must seek out new and better forms of governance in order to satisfy lawmakers, shareholders, and employees alike. In "making IT governance work," the emphasis is on the last of these four words: work. Although we need to reflect on the situation, seek advice, and incorporate frameworks, ultimately good IT governance must exercise some influence on the desired conduct of the people in an organization: It has to work.

GO DIRECTLY TO JAIL

The Sarbanes-Oxley Act is known officially as the U.S. Public Accounting Reform and Investor Protection Act. Investors needed to be protected, and therefore reform of accounting practices was necessary. Because of this stricter attitude, directors had a genuine fear of ending up in U.S. jails.

The Sarbanes-Oxley Act makes senior level executives responsible for the financial reporting of their company. A violation of these rules can lead to jail time, as seen in the case of Jamie Olis. Jamie was happily married, had a six-month-old daughter, and was working for a company called Dynegy, a U.S. energy supplier. Dynegy had gotten into financial trouble, and analysts discovered something awry in the operating cash flow accounts. Olis was responsible for project alpha, which Dynegy claimed was a long-term effort to secure gas supplies. According to the Securities and Exchange Commission (SEC), project alpha was nothing more than a coverup. Olis believed he had acted above board and pled not guilty in court. He claimed to have been acting in good faith and said he trusted his company advisors. The SEC was proved to be right, and Jamie Olis was sentenced to 24 years. He had trusted his advisors, but the analysts had mistrusted the figures.

The executives responsible are being pursued by the authorities. Kenneth Lay, CEO and founder of Enron, has claimed that he has no understanding of accounting and consequently is not, by definition, blameworthy in the Enron affair. He also pled not guilty. His trial is scheduled for January 2006. Andrew Fastow, former CFO of Enron has admitted to cooking Enron's books. He agreed cooperating in the trial and he will testify against Kenneth Lay and other Enron executives, in exchange for a ten-year sentence. Scott Sullivan, the former CFO at WorldCom, has entered a guilty plea in this $11 billion accounting scandal. He has testified that Bernie Ebbers, the CEO of WorldCom, also acted wrongly. Sullivan has said that Ebbers requested him to hide costs and pump up the revenue. Like Jamie Olis, Bernie Ebbers declared he was innocent. Ebbers was found guilty by a New York court. His lawyer immediately declared he would appeal. Four months later Ebbers was sentenced to 25 years in prison.

While these court cases are dominating the media, companies are busy introducing extra measures to ensure that their compliance with Sarbanes-Oxley is in order. Sometimes diligent work to satisfy the requirements of the act is done under such revealing project titles as "How to Keep the Boss out of the Clink."

Jamie Olis, Bernie Ebbers, Kenneth Lay, Scott Sullivan, and many others may have been the "dupes" of a system in which they were themselves collaborators. (Other organizations like banks and accountants participated in this system as we describe in more depth in Chapter 2.) They trusted the advice of others, and others trusted them in their business transactions. Such blind trust is no longer possible.

Shareholders had been duped and were angry; something had to be done. President George W. Bush stated in his corporate responsibility speech that "we refused to allow fear to undermine our economy, and we will not allow fraud to undermine it either." The war against terrorism began with the attack on the Twin Towers. The war on fraud began after the destruction of an unimaginable amount of capital on the stock market. Here the opponents are not terrorists but rather directors and managers who manipulate data to improve their own situations and to "manage" shareholder contentment by means of inflated market values.

LIVING IN A SARBANES-OXLEY WORLD

We are all living in a Sarbanes-Oxley world: Americans, Europeans, Asians, everyone. Although a U.S. law is involved, directors from other countries also run the risk of winding up in a U.S. prison. With a budget of $840 million, the SEC can easily afford the expense of visits to the head offices of multinationals in European capitals. Companies that fall under the immediate jurisdiction of the law are those listed on the U.S. stock exchanges and those with large capital interests in the United States. These companies must also require their suppliers to operate in conformity with Sarbanes-Oxley. Consequently, the law has had an immediate widespread effect, not, incidentally, with everyone's approval. Rijkman Groenink, CEO of ABN-AMRO, a bank of European origin, sees one possible scenario: the eventual sale of U.S. interests to escape the burdens of this U.S. law. French and English companies even threatened to withdraw from the U.S. stock market if implementation of Sarbanes-Oxley was not delayed. Thus implementation of the Act has been postponed to 2006 for all foreign companies and for U.S. companies having assets of less than $75 million.

INFORMATION GOVERNANCE

The most important weapons against data manipulation are transparency and personal responsibility. Clear business decisions based on accurate data under which directors' signatures appear will restore confidence in organizations.

We view Sarbanes-Oxley as a turning point in the governance of organizations, especially in regard to the direct involvement of management and the use of information technology. The corresponding demand for transparency runs parallel to social trends in which the events of September 11 have certainly played an important part. Fear reigns, and this fear can only be allayed by information. Lawmakers and shareholders require insight into the course of events, along with crystal-clear guarantees that the information they receive is accurate. The Sarbanes-Oxley world in which we find ourselves is, above all, a transparent world.

Nevertheless, a great deal of business information remains far from transparent. In this modern era, personal spreadsheets on an employee's own PC still play a crucial role. The use of such spreadsheets poses a risk. Data can be deliberately manipulated, and unintentional mistakes can creep in.

A possible breakthrough in this area is expected from the use of Extensible Business Reporting Language (XBRL). Although this technology has not yet taken off, its use may start to speed up; former SEC Chairman William Donaldson recently announced the acceptability of XBRL in financial reports. A great deal of progress has recently been made in establishing business standards for the meaning of a certain tag. Such standards are crucial for the success of XBRL. The acceptance of XBRL can be regarded as a wake-up call for the many companies that have long been bypassing such technology. (You can read the opinion of the SEC on the subject in its report "Spotlight on Tagged Data and XBRL Initiatives," at *www.sec.gov/spotlight/xbrl.htm.*)

MAKING A RETURN ON IT INVESTMENT

Directors are paying increasing attention to the returns yielded by IT investments. Presently, 50% of all capital investment goes into IT. Statistics published by IDC reveal that more than $1 trillion will be spent on IT worldwide in 2005. The notion that all this investment must yield something is more than reasonable.

Making IT governance work is a challenge for managers and directors. The management of IT now and in coming years is not the same as the management of IT ten years ago. The most important reasons for this change are the increased expenditures on IT, the (still) growing importance of IT, and the blurring of the boundaries between IT and business. For the sake of convenience, we speak about IT governance. However, in the many discussions we have conducted with IT and business leaders, we are confirmed in our conviction that, in fact, we are actually dealing with business governance. Because IT is everywhere and involves everyone, business and IT initiatives are becoming progressively more difficult to keep apart.

Making IT governance work means, above all, that such initiatives must result in success, so that investments on the technological side yield more than they cost. The proper decision-making structures, the clearer prioritization of projects, and commitments on the work floor required for success are crucial.

FIGHTING FOR IT GOVERNANCE SURVIVAL IN A SARBANES-OXLEY WORLD

For three main reasons "Making IT Governance Work in a Sarbanes-Oxley World" might well be one of the most relevant business issues for the coming years. First and foremost, business and IT have become extremely interwoven. Secondly, good IT governance practices still are lacking in many companies. And last but not least, it still remains unclear what this Sarbanes-Oxley World we are in actually looks like.

Internal and external auditors tried to figure this out themselves during the first year of SOX compliance, putting a heavy burden on company managers. "For every hour the auditor works, the managers are working 10," says Mark Beasley, who is an accounting professor at N.C. State University (*soxmonitoring.blogspot.com/ 2005_01_23_soxmonitoring_archive.html*).

For many executives, the discussion of auditing standards between internal and external auditors was the eye opener to the fact that SOX issues still very much need to be sorted out. In *CIO Magazine* of July 1, 2005 the VP of IT for Arch Chemicals was quoted as follows: "The auditors kept coming up with issues. It became time-consuming, well in excess of anything I've ever experienced." The magazine warned that the second SOX audit ironically could "take even more time, cost even more money, and cause even more pain," namely because the necessary automation tools are still pending (*www.cio.com/archive/070105/sox.html*).

Where does this leave IT governance? Well, chances are that SOX conformance pressure will hinder the further development of initial IT governance efforts so eagerly deployed after the Internet and IT bubble burst. CIOs need to take their own company-specific measures to stop this from happening. The challenge of "Making IT Governance Work in a Sarbanes-Oxley World" for many executives is that they very likely will start off with their backs against the wall, fighting for IT governance survival in this Sarbanes-Oxley World. This book will help them in this important struggle.

The rationale behind Sarbanes-Oxley of course is that "in an era where over 93 percent of all documents are produced electronically and 75 percent of those never make it to the printer, the 'smoking gun' evidence for litigation or compliance purposes is more likely to be found on a computer than buried in a filing cabinet" (*www.legal technology.com/digital/pdf/2004/lti163.pdf*). But with a proper focus on how you work—financials, decision mechanisms, people management, content management, and architecture included—SOX compliance will be(come) a by-product of your efforts. Overcoming conformance pressure by aiming for performance pleasure is one of the ultimate governance goals to which Sarbanes-Oxley is merely a means.

FROM COMPLIANCE PRESSURE TO PERFORMANCE PLEASURE

Making IT governance work in a Sarbanes-Oxley world presents us with an awful dilemma: How do we ensure that the money we devote toward compliance with the new legislation results in better governance of the organization in general and of IT in particular? AMR Research estimates that the costs of Sarbanes-Oxley compliance will be $6.1 billion in 2005. The August 14, 2003 issue of the SEC's *Final Rule* mentions a sum of $1.24 billion for compliance with the costly section 404 of Sarbanes-Oxley. Obviously such appraisals will have to be adjusted on the basis of experience.

The pressure to comply with the law is great. The challenge is to convert this compliance pressure into good performance. There is a great clamor to downsize Sarbanes-Oxley into manageable proportions, as many organizations nourish the ambition of changing compliance pressure into performance pleasure. As a result, businesses are no longer required to chase all the audit objectives of COBIT in order to become compliant with Sarbanes-Oxley.

The people in the organization who are busy satisfying the Sarbanes-Oxley regulations are, in many cases, not the same ones as those who are busy improving IT performance. The integration of compliance and performance is an ideal that we will only be able to achieve in small stages. If compliance becomes a goal in itself, the risk of "gaming the system" is just around the corner. On paper, everything appears fine, but the procedures that are instituted are astutely undermined by managers who set up rules to suit themselves. Gaming the system is, of course, an especially unproductive manner of taking up each other's time. The rules must be so well observed that they become a part of an organization's DNA structure, as it were. Former SEC Chairman William Donaldson made it clear:

> ...*simply complying with the rules is not enough. They should, as I have said before, make this approach part of their companies'*

DNA. *For companies that take this approach, most of the major concerns about compliance disappear. Moreover, if companies view the new laws as opportunities—opportunities to improve internal controls, improve the performance of the board, and improve their public reporting—they will ultimately be better run, more transparent, and therefore more attractive to investors.*[1]

Ideally, compliance leads to better run and more transparent organizations, which sits well with shareholders. According to Donaldson, such an effect will occur when compliance is made an integrated part of an organization's DNA; otherwise nothing will change.

Improving performance without frameworks, procedures, and approaches is impossible in any larger company. IT governance is something of an endurance test requiring repetitions and transparent decision-making processes. Frameworks are an aid in such a difficult task. Those who truly believe in Sarbanes-Oxley and the imposition of such frameworks as COBIT have no doubt about the need for them. The law will lead to better IT governance. Pragmatists will say that we must make the best of it, by grabbing onto the energy and momentum that governance now has and using it to work toward an optimum and transparent form of IT governance. Skeptics will continue to see Sarbanes-Oxley as a nuisance and will expend the smallest possible effort on formal compliance with its rules.

We believe that making IT governance work in a Sarbanes-Oxley world will only be effective if the conduct of people in organizations is in line with the objectives for which IT is striving. In an ideal sense, compliance and performance stand for the same thing: the creation of shareholder value.

The shareholder has a right to accurate information, as well as to good IT governance, which is nothing more or less than business governance in IT. It is therefore not without reason that the three parts of this book are entitled Management, Accountability, and Supervision. Together they comprise the ingredients needed to "get things done." Making IT governance work depends on good management, the revamping of practices to make them accountable and measurable, and supervision that does justice to the bottom-up dimension of control.

---

[1] W.H. Donaldson, "Speech by SEC Chairman: Remarks on the National Press Club," U.S. Securities and Exchange Commission, Washington, D.C., July 30, 2003. *www.sec.gov/news/speech/spch073003whd.htm*

EMPHASIS ON BUSINESS PERFORMANCE

Proper IT governance and good management of information and IT have only one standard of measure: the organization's success in the marketplace. It is therefore critical that we work to achieve a performance-oriented form of IT governance. Past difficulties with IT lead to this inevitable conclusion. An adequate mixture of management, accountability, and supervision must ensure that information and IT will actually result in improved business performance.

In the numerous interviews we conducted with those responsible for IT (portfolio managers, company directors, business developers, and architects), one issue was raised repeatedly. IT governance involves everyone; it occurs among human beings and encompasses an entire organization. Everyone is involved with IT and must do their bit to ensure that IT is successfully interwoven into the firm's business processes and adopted as everyday behavior by everyone in the organization.

The spirit of the age was also discussed in many interviews. The way we interact at the present time is different from what it was 15 years ago and will probably be just as different 15 years from now. In this sense, and quite importantly, IT governance is never "finished." Of course, although this is related to the changing role of IT in organizations, let us not overlook changes in society and the interactions between such social transformations and business cultures.

DEVELOPMENT OF IT GOVERNANCE

A great deal has already been said and written about effective management of IT; Chapter 3 deals with developing notions in this field. For a long time, we thought that IT governance would more or less occur on its own. As long as we concentrated on business/IT alignment and allowed the business itself to determine what needed to happen with IT, it was thought that everything would turn out all right. However, the actual business benefits realized from IT as a result of such attempted alignments remained far below expectations. Unfortunately, a fundamental crisis was required to activate the dialogue between business and IT in a meaningful fashion.

At the present time, IT is fully incorporated into business processes, and a great deal of money is devoted to IT needs, year in and year out. Consequently, IT must also contribute demonstrably to a business's competitive and financial performance. It was always intended that IT would have such an effect. However, for far too long, we have been content with the mere promise that technology would significantly contribute to business success. Furthermore, we are all too often confronted by disappointment and lowered expectations caused by our own misconceptions about the effects of IT.

What is needed to deal with this situation is "simply" the following: Ensure that our processes, our IT, our organization, and all other environmental factors (which together perform the company's work) are properly structured and well integrated. To achieve this goal, we must constantly keep our finger on the pulse of business and financial concerns and everything involving employee conduct. Only then will we be able to steer clear of difficulties.

It is essential that an organization's employees be capable of acts that positively influence a business's ability to perform according to plan. Whenever possible, this will preferably become second nature. Ultimately, the organization of people becomes an organic system, a well-oiled machine with as little friction as possible. Such an operation costs the least and yields the most. When we talk of making IT governance work, we are telling the story of how we have come to recognize this factor and how we are now beginning to act on it. In essence, this is a story that we already know, one that involves the choices and actions implicit in doing "business." Such actions consist of setting goals, estimating costs and benefits, assessing risks, protecting interests, and stimulating desirable behavior. These activities and their implications are of concern to the entire organization in all its facets.

CENTRAL IMPORTANCE OF BEHAVIOR

Is all the attention paid to IT governance overexaggerated? The phenomenon of "hype," or at least of unrealistic representation, appears to be inextricably linked to IT-related developments.

Previously, everyone focused on the content of IT, its processes, the age of systems (legacy), or the new possibilities that IT offered (e-business). Now we are more interested in behavior. This is the central component of IT governance: the human activity of managers and employees regarding IT. This behavior includes investment decisions, employee task assignments, leadership, self-interest, and the use-value of IT. Our attention in the coming years will be directed at the decision-making process and the IT outcomes we might expect. If this view of IT remains constant, then the end of all the hype could be at hand.

BECAUSE OVERSTATEMENT IS ALWAYS WAITING IN AMBUSH...

Operationalizing our performance focus entails the juggling of constructs, abstractions, and expectations. Models and projections are important elements in human thinking and action; the strongest example is provided by all that we have done and achieved "business-wise" with information and IT over the last decade, in addition to what we have thought about it over the same period. Operationalizing our performance has ranged from business process reengineering, e-business, e-tailing, and e-marketplaces to virtual organizations and collaborative commerce. Without really reflecting on the matter, we rattled blissfully on and have subsequently accomplished more harm than good.

When such a juggling act is going on, a few factors can mess up the works. To begin with, there is the complexity that might arise when simple ingredients from different domains are combined. Consider the need for connection among variously arranged business activities, information streams, and diverse software applications from various departments and organizations. At the same time, psychosocial factors (such as cultural differences) are part of the entire complex, as well as fanciful, self-willed, and sometimes politically motivated behavior.

Taking all these factors together, the chance becomes greater that clear objectives will unwittingly be transformed into other-worldly ideals. It is also not inconceivable that Babel-like communication about objectives will occur, with any financial/economic consequences set aside for the sake of convenience. It is a part of our nature to try to repair what is at hand, rather than change it, although we have to admit that reality does not always accommodate our ambitions. Instead of displaying heroic never-say-die behavior, it would often be better if we could discard an ideal at an early stage.

We can conclude that humans are little more than animals that constantly overestimate themselves. As long as we consciously limit this overestimation to merely "setting the bar as high as possible," that is, as a means of accelerating progress, it remains extremely useful. Unfortunately, in practice, we repeatedly hang on to outdated ambitions and, in so doing, cause damage.

We need to be more alert in appraising the impact of information and IT on business and people, as well as on the micro- and macroeconomy. As we look back on the last decade of our business/IT history, we see that the drift into overestimation has too often been the norm. John Gray wrote that "Man is an animal that overestimates itself," and it is not for nothing that we have chosen this provocative statement as the motto for this book.[2]

...THE HUMAN DIMENSION MUST SET THE STANDARD

As a result, an important message for IT governance is to keep the human dimension in mind and, above all else, keep it simple. In daily practice involving IT, this is often far from the case. We need to recognize that our capacities are limited and that our projections are not always as realistic as they should be. Furthermore, the human factor is often deliberately left out of the equation, even in the study of economics.

Fortunately, we are slowly but surely beginning to be convinced that it is counterproductive to ignore or minimize the human factor for the sake of convenience. A clear view of the impact of human behavior on organizations, in all its facets, needs to be formulated in order to construct a sound basis on which to compose and implement realistic plans.

We would strongly discourage any naïve faith in methodologies and tools. Somewhere in the large number of articles that we collected in writing this book, the expression "ITIL fetishism" appears. Not that we mean to denigrate ITIL (IT Infrastructure Library), but this

---

[2] "De Nieuwe Utopie," *De Volkskrant*, December 11 , 2004.

phrase accurately illustrates our message about the importance of the human dimension as a critical part of a healthy IT conceptualization.

MONEY IS THE UNIVERSAL LANGUAGE

This is also a financial book about IT governance. In organizations, money is the universal language that everyone speaks and understands. The economic performance of an organization is the ultimate measure of any governing practice. Costs, benefits, interests, risks, and business performance are the collective concern of portfolio management, a specialty that is given heavy emphasis in this book. Clear insight into the true costs of IT (and the cost categories to which they can be attributed) is necessary and critical for an organization's survival and success.

IT costs are usually identified as indirect costs. When these costs are apportioned, and all the money that went into supporting them is accounted for, undoubtedly one department ends up paying for another. For this reason alone, IT costs should be seen as direct costs and handled as such by an organization's accounting practices. As a result we should know in detail how cash is utilized within the organization, in order to determine the true cost paid by our profit centers for the IT services they consume. In addition, it is even more important to determine (on the basis of these real costs) the true *value* of IT for each of these profit centers. In our high-speed world, with its highly competitive pressures, such an accounting is the first requirement to begin establishing a sound basis for managing the business.

FULL-CYCLE GOVERNANCE

Most organizations have not yet reached a state of performance-oriented governance of IT. To help gauge and evaluate the performance orientation of IT, transparent measurement and control loops must be put in place and allowed to permeate the entire organization and its budgetary cycles. This is what we refer to as "full cycle," or, more precisely, "remaining both wide-reaching and performance-oriented (i.e., business performance oriented) at the same time."

Such a practice involves much more than just "management," in the sense of day-to-day tending or maintenance of business activities and concerns, which is why we purposely use the word "governance" in the title of this book. This full-cycle managerial posture implies a management style that, to be effective and efficient, needs to penetrate and permeate the entire organization. Because information and IT constitute an increasingly greater part of nearly every business, we must all do our part to ensure that information and IT are put to their most effective use within our respective organizations.

Launching performance-oriented governance of IT involves all of an organization's diverse interests. In particular, the financial interests of the organization and its departments must be considered when one is assessing the value that IT will provide.

It is our point that this is the concern of portfolio management, a method of making business performance-oriented IT decisions on the basis of costs, benefits, and risks. Portfolio management is a crucial component in answering the question: "How do we perform IT governance?" To answer this question, it may also be helpful to consider responses to such simple business-case questions as: "What are we going to do? What will be better as a result? How much is that worth to us? How are we going to measure that?"

We need good performance-oriented governance if we want to be seriously concerned with the costs and benefits of such an expensive performance creator as IT. What this subsequently entails is the operationalization of such governance throughout the entire business, mainly by means of a mix of management tools and skills consisting of accurate calculation, commitment, collaboration, leadership, accountability, and supervision. To be effective and successful, the associated processes must permeate the organization and comprise an element that is consistently present and included as a critical component in each budgetary round.

Consequently, the issue is not just *governance*. Instead, it involves a continuous practice in which an understanding of the true concrete value of the business—up or down—must always be the ultimate yardstick.

During our research, which involved reading many reports and books as well as discussing IT governance in organizations, we sought to deepen our understanding by consulting with a number of the leading thinkers in the field. We would like to mention two such people at this point: Claudio Ciborra, affiliated with the London School of Economics, and Bobby Cameron, from Forrester Research.

They have adopted interesting positions concerning IT management, both of which provide a sharp contrast with the objectives of this book. One concentrates on gathering perspectives, insights, and an understanding concerning what is happening now. The other seeks responses to the question of how we will have to operate in the future.

Ciborra focuses on the examination and understanding of present practice. He is not concerned with concrete tips for better governance. He claims that management has caused control to become a goal in itself and, consequently, IT performance is too often disappointing. Managers must abandon their urge to control.

Bobby Cameron constructively criticizes this view at several points, all in relation to IT portfolio management. Briefly stated, his objections involve the determination and consideration of the costs, benefits, and risks of IT projects in relation to business goals.

Much remains to be said about the governance of information and IT, but where action is concerned, portfolio management is the appropriate path to take. It was not just happenstance that our visit to Forrester Research in Boston coincided with the report in the *Financial Dagblad* that IT productivity in the United States is much higher than that in Europe. Jean Claude Trichet, president of the European Central Bank, agreed and added in his Euro Vision piece in the *Wall Street Journal* (February 24, 2005):

> *A large part of the productivity gap [between the United States and Europe over the past decade] seems to be attributed to capital deepening—in fact Information and Communication Technology (ICT) capital deepening—and total factor productivity associated with a better utilization of ICT. When analyzed sector by sector it is impressive to see that, on top of the ICT manufacturing productivity sector, it is the very rapid improvement in the ICT-using services sector (wholesale trade, retail trade, financial intermediation) that explains much of the difference.*

We have much to learn from the United States, which has formalized IT portfolio management by means of legislation and regulation.

TEN POINTS FOR FORMULATING ACTION PLANS

If we do not constantly consider management and handling of IT from an economic-based business perspective (one that penetrates the entire organization), squandering of money will continue and the credibility of IT will not be quickly secured.

All IT investments must be evaluated and monitored on the basis of the value they supply to business processes. Although so many people do not seem to understand this, it is the most normal thing in the world, because IT is how we code and operate our business. The interlinking of business and IT, an intertwining that will only further increase in breadth and volume, requires a form of management that branches out across the entire organization and at the same time is deeply rooted in it.

Effort is needed to put this form of management in place. To provide a basis for formulating sound and realistic action plans, the ten most important points that can be derived from this book are as follows:

1. Share leadership.
2. Realize that nearly any governance structure is good.
3. Stimulate desirable behavior.
4. Understand that people are allergic to excessive control.
5. Keep it simple: Simplicity is the mark of truth.
6. Recognize that in the end, the business determines the value of IT.
7. Allocate all IT funding to concrete business goals.
8. Continue to evaluate.
9. Cultivate maturity.
10. Stay tuned on Sarbanes-Oxley.

Share Leadership

We would all like to keep our IT and our IT investments under control. However, sometimes it seems that the more we strive for such control, the less we are able to achieve it. We need to refrain from any urge to engage in knee-jerk management and make a transition to "distributed leadership." This specifically involves the manner in which everyone in the organization deals with information and IT. When everyone knows what is desired, understands why it is desirable, and is subsequently willing to open themselves up to instruction about such issues as they clearly relate to business performance—only then will we be able to make IT second nature to everyone in business organizations.

Realize That Nearly Every Governance Structure Is Good

An IT governance structure is important for clarity, but it is only a tool for obtaining a better grasp of IT. Of course, IT steering committees, architectural councils, and sounding-board groups are needed. However, all this effort must be centered on a mechanism for arriving at good decisions. It is this mechanism that we call "IT portfolio management." The portfolio metaphor emphasizes that we must constantly make accountable investment choices to improve the competitive and financial nature of business performance.

Stimulate Desirable Behavior

In effect, management of information and IT is any effort to elicit desirable behavior in our IT-related actions. An arsenal of tools is available for this purpose. The possibility of people behaving in the ways that we would like depends on rules, leadership, legislation, and frameworks. Possible snags remain because of the high expectations we have regarding IT performance and what it is supposed to deliver. Effective performance-oriented governance of IT is possible only when the essential relationship between IT and business value is reflected in employee understanding and, subsequently, in employee conduct.

Understand That People Are Allergic to Excessive Control

Just let me do my work. Interference does not improve employee performance; improvement is accomplished by motivating, allowing freedom of action, and understanding the contributions that people make. As stated in the first point, the urge to manage in a knee-jerk manner inevitably causes work to get bogged down. Using IT as a control instrument when that happens tends to make matters even worse.

Keep It Simple: Simplicity Is the Mark of Truth

We can only cope with a limited quantity of information and, perhaps not surprisingly, in spite of the amount of information we have, we cannot look into the future. We make decisions on the basis of "best guesses" and continue to do so until a solution is determined that provides us with some satisfaction. This suboptimization does not result from laziness but from the need to perform on many fronts at the same time, while the mountain of information continues to grow and time remains short. We have to make use of our limited human capacities. Consequently, keep it as simple as possible by, among other things, accepting the principle that "good is good enough" to guide your IT management. IT is already complex enough and, moreover, works in complicating ways.

Recognize That, in the End, the Business Determines the Value of IT

It would be crazy to ask IT organizations about the contributions that their products and services make to processes. IT is inextricably entwined in the business and is, therefore, an essential part of the business. Investment decisions have to be taken in consultation and made with commitment. The same holds true for all evaluations and adjustments.

Allocate All IT Funding to Concrete Business Goals

By and large, we devote too little effort to making a clear assessment of what IT initiatives contribute to the business. One should be especially aware of one issue: Only on the basis of a sound, economically based business focus can we responsibly decide to locate certain aspects of the business outside the office or to stop projects. The services of internal and external accountants need to be enlisted for such an evaluation. Cost and benefit data must come from them and must be recorded in and made part of their systems.

Continue to Evaluate

We must describe and justify what we would like to do, what we wish to achieve, how we are going to measure the results, and how much those results are worth. Above all, we must maintain our positions on such issues. The interplay between measuring and then accepting the consequences is crucial. Measurement only makes sense when something is done with the results of the measurements. Moreover, the responsibilities for proper and adequate measurement must be properly delegated.

Cultivate Maturity

Establish sound IT administration and organize IT processes and responsibilities. Examine the real costs and benefits of IT in relation to concrete business goals, take risks into account, and make choices on this basis. If you continue to do this, then the first steps toward portfolio management will have been taken. Ensure that the entire organization knows why work is done in this or that way and what everyone's role is in its execution. You will then be engaging in performance-oriented management of information and IT.

Stay Tuned on Sarbanes-Oxley

Organizations have to act in order to comply with international legislation. Keep searching for ways to convert the compliance pressure into performance pleasure. Best practices can lead the way. It is certainly the case that much real and passionate work is being done in the United States to improve the management practices of its most competitive firms. However, in practical application, such practices need not be followed slavishly. Instead, each company should identify best practices among the global portfolio, choosing those that can benefit one's own business and adopting those that make the most sense, adapting them when necessary, and implementing them as unmodified best practices when doing so provides the greatest potential benefit.

Structure of This Book

To conclude this introduction, we will now present an outline of how the book is structured and which subjects are given attention in each individual part. Before letting the key exhibit speak for itself—an exhibit that will be repeated at the beginning of each part—the following three points should first be emphasized:

1. IT governance, the management of information and IT, is the field with which this book is concerned.
2. Full-cycle business governance of IT is the path leading to performance orientation.
3. The appropriate mixture of management, accountability, and supervision is the essence of each form of governance, as well as of the three parts of the book.

In Part One, we discuss the essence of governance and the important relationship between IT and corporate governance. We review the recent history of governance and show that the cycle of management, accountability, and supervision was not really effective. Misconceptions about the effects and benefits of IT were a result of this factor.

Part Two starts by clarifying the milestones and developments one should seek in the quest for a "well-oiled" form of management. It winds up with a discussion of portfolio management, which is given extensive consideration in Chapter 4. Part Two concludes by examining the financial metrics and tools that are well suited to portfolio management, in particular, activity-based costing and economic value added.

Part Three focuses on the organizational behavior we would like to obtain, including supervision and the role of leadership, along with frameworks, legislation, and accountancy as instruments for eliciting desirable behavior. In Chapter 7, we explore the differences in emphasis between Cameron and Ciborra that were already briefly mentioned here.

Management: Governance and Its Human Dimension

Part One: Management

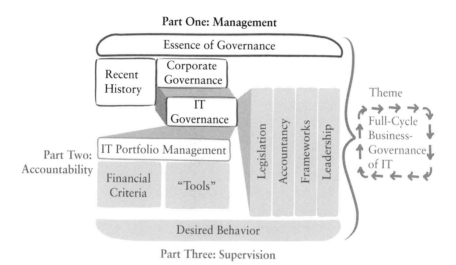

Part Two: Accountability

Essence of Governance

Recent History

Corporate Governance

IT Governance

IT Portfolio Management

Financial Criteria

"Tools"

Legislation

Accountancy

Frameworks

Leadership

Theme

Full-Cycle Business-Governance of IT

Desired Behavior

Part Three: Supervision

HIGHER FORMS OF MANAGEMENT, ACCOUNTABILITY, AND SUPERVISION

There are various types of governance, all of which are interrelated. The source of all these variants is corporate governance. It controls the interests of the various parties involved in a corporation. Business performance, understood in a competitive and financial sense, is the primary concern of corporate governance. The derived forms of governance, IT governance, for example, which should be regarded as the business governance of IT, must also contribute directly to business performance, for which we need to arrange, measure, and regulate everything. When done in combination, these governance factors quickly develop into an impressive system. However, common sense and the human dimension also have a leading role to play.

EXCESSIVE AMBITIONS AND MISCONCEPTIONS

It is never a good situation when confidence is undermined, but often such undermining is almost unavoidable. If large interests are involved, there is of course an increased chance of deceit, and overenthusiasm also easily leads to improper assessments and decisions. The combination of the economy, IT, and the financial markets at the end of the 1990s has provided us with some sterling examples of such practices. Since then, all kinds of measures have been taken, and we hope we have learned our lesson well enough so that in the future we will have more realistic expectations about IT, its (business) economic value, and the development of both.

CHAPTER 1

Types of Governance, Business Performance, and Common Sense

Choices and Adjustments

Governance is a heavily loaded term. It implies a rigorous approach to a concept that is grasped only with difficulty. It involves important strategic matters—the making of choices and adjustments.

IT Governance: A Condition of Credibility

Each form of governance, whether it is corporate, financial, or IT, has a direct relationship to business-economic performance. Because of the business value of IT, the high costs of technology, and the problems arising in the e-business experimental phase, IT is an outstanding example of a domain in which governance is necessary. Additionally, when a governance "catch-up" effort is needed to reestablish confidence in IT and to build credibility, IT must be reined in administratively.

Full-Cycle Business Governance of IT

Although the notion of IT governance has become well established, closer inspection reveals that this concept is misunderstood. The main focus should be on the business value of IT, a value that needs to be demonstrated.

"Full-cycle IT governance" means that governance processes and guidelines involve the entire organization and are appropriately applied everywhere within it. Processes and guidelines must influence behavior so that the organization performs better. This means that the same processes and guidelines must be evaluated over time in terms of the organization's competitive and financial performance, another cycle that has a direct impact on business.

■ ■ ■

FROM THE SEPARATION OF POWERS
TO SARBANES-OXLEY

Many different interests are involved in business-economic performance, i.e., those of employers, employees, financiers, business partners, government authorities, customers, environmental activists, IT suppliers, and others.

There is every chance that these interests will conflict or, at the very least, create frustration; such conflicts must be dealt with effectively. Ever since Charles de Secondat (1689–1755), better known as the Baron de Montesquieu,[1] discussed the separation of powers in the 18th century, it has been commonly acknowledged that absolute power must not be placed in the hands of any single institution or person. Montesquieu, who was the originator of this idea, hoped that conflict in the top echelons of society could be peacefully resolved by an evenly weighted system of power. In the business domain, to avoid conflicts among the various stakeholders, an objective system of issues, agreements, and processes has been constructed.

Management, accountability, and supervision—the three principle components of governance[2]—are explicitly separated in this system. If the system is constructed properly, all relevant interests can be weighed and protected effectively and efficiently. Such a system of fundamental protection of interests and their effects—designed to avoid unwanted entanglements of interests and to serve an organization's principle goals—this is *governance*.

When most people say "governance," they really mean "good governance." In general, this concept works for the fundamental protection of interests required to maintain a system and its various subsystems in harmony. Thus we are able to avoid frustrating relevant internal or external interests or inflicting damage on them. The practice of good governance requires good consultation and collaboration, as well as making accountable choices, while constantly paying attention to the principle objectives of the business over both the short and the long term. Governance begins with the separation of powers, in the *trias politica* of Montesquieu; such a separation is at the heart of Deming's model of corporate performance and has been the main issue in the recent Sarbanes-Oxley legislation (see Exhibit 1.1).

An example of how substantial damage can occur is the negative cascading effect that the overenthusiastic global embrace of IT had on business operations during the tech run-up of the late 1990s. The cascade had an enormous negative impact on financial markets and the global economy, creating a crisis of faith.

The current conviction is that a better (or more rigorously observed) form of governance among the full range of businesses operating in the late 1990s could have prevented this situation. In this

Governance

The separation of power and authority among special interests to achieve principal goals. This entails making choices and making them possible, recognizing progressive insights, and acting on their basis, that is, implementing continuous adjustment.

Montesquieu *Trias politica*	**Deming** TQM/Plan-Do-Check-Act	**Bush/Sarbanes-Oxley** Corporate Responsibility
The legislative, executive, and judicial powers	Measurement and control loops to attain better results	Make managers responsible for the accuracy of their written accounts

EXHIBIT 1.1   Governance: Three Exponents of the Separation of Powers and Their Concepts

sense, governance safeguards trust—trust that the statistics are correct, trust that the facts are accurate, and trust that the stakeholders in the organization are acting competently and in the best interest of the organization, free of self-interest and the desire for personal gain. The institutions, laws, and regulations to which businesses and other organizations should have remained attentive were fundamentally flawed. It was undoubtedly governance that failed. Ironically, if there is anything that has the potential to make things better, it is also governance. With better supervision and more effective widespread implementation of sound governance practices, perhaps the course of history would have been different. Therefore the well defined distribution of power and authority, as well as the proper supervision of both entities, is critical for avoiding the problems of the past, particularly in such a strategic and expensive endeavor as IT.

The separation of power and authority is absolutely crucial for the proper promotion of special interests oriented toward the accomplishment of the principle goals. This entails making choices and making such choices possible in the first place, recognizing progressive attitudes and insight, while also acting on their basis—in other words, implementing a program of continuous adjustment and improvement.

Because IT consumes large quantities of money and because disappointing experiences have surrounded IT in the past, reliable reporting to owners of the current status and state of IT is a critical concern. The American Public Company Accounting Reform and Investor Protection Act, otherwise known as the Sarbanes-Oxley Act (which was implemented in 2002 after the billion-dollar frauds at Enron and WorldCom became known), makes management responsible for a company's reported results and reporting procedures,[3] including reports about the status of IT.

The intent of the legislators had already been established in legislation such as the IT Management Reform Act of 1996, better known as the Clinger-Cohen Act. Since the implementation of this act, IT performance management using a portfolio management approach has become mandatory in all government departments. Amendments to the Clinger-Cohen Act enacted in 2003 affect the design and use of IT-related architecture. It is not expected that IT performance management in business will deviate from that of government departments. In fact, the legislation just described for the regulation of government was established in consultation with private sector organizations.

Rules for the management and reporting of IT have been legally determined in laws that apply to all businesses with large interests in the United States. According to the Sarbanes-Oxley Act, a maximum $5 million fine and up to 20 years in prison are the penalties for deliberately issuing a misleading report. One would thus expect that reporting standards will be improved all over the world.

CORPORATE GOVERNANCE IS GOOD MANAGEMENT

Although corporate governance is different from other types of governance within organizations (such as financial or IT governance), most people think of corporate governance when the term "governance" is used.

For this reason, a brief survey of a number of central issues involving corporate governance is given here. Corporate governance must be regarded as the principle form of governance. The governance of divisions within organizations should contribute to more competitive and better financial business performance. Ultimately corporate governance involves the return of money to those who invest in and own the corporation. Hence, governance is specifically concerned with real profits, the return of invested capital, and the maximizing of profits for shareholders.

Corporate governance is the system that manages and controls organizations. The idea of corporate governance stands for a coherent and cohesive whole comprising organizational management, its supervision and accountability for policy, and its management. Although corporate governance is a complex notion, at its most simplistic level it involves *good* or *sound* management.

First, corporate governance is specifically concerned with accountability to shareholders, the owners of the business, and the avoidance of self-interested activity by management. The notion of corporate governance has been extended to include responsibility to the various stakeholders in a business. In addition to the attainment of financial goals, such responsibility includes the vision, mission, and social standing of the business.

Corporate governance is an extremely broad field. Political and economic structures are involved in its manifestations, laws, practices, and processes. Taken together, these establish contexts for a business's boundaries, concrete goals, and underlying strategies.

Despite many conceptual and operational differences, legal, financial, and business experts in the world's business centers agree on one thing: Corporate governance is a collection of formal and informal mechanisms that must bring managerial behavior in line with the interests of the company owners. The idea is that business managers should strive to achieve agreed-on business and operational goals, whereas corporate owners—especially when they are quite distant from the operation, as is the case with shareholders—should primarily seek (and expect) a good return on their investment. Boards of directors must therefore always explain to the shareholders why certain decisions affecting the business's performance and the shareholders' investment were made.

Articles of incorporation, legal provisions, or self-selected regulations and institutions establish the practices of corporate governance, which are the key processes of supervision, management, and accountability. Directors, for example, can be legally obligated to run the business in a proper manner and must be accountable to the shareholders. In the context of governance, the shareholders have a full scale of rights and roles, e.g., the appointment of a board of directors, the assignment of voting rights at shareholder meetings, and the right to obtain diverse information about the company.

Others, inside and outside the company, do not actually have any formal roles, although such relationships and responsibilities have been hotly debated over the past ten years, especially in the European Union, as well as because of the stakeholder issue noted above ("stakeholders" being deemed "interested parties" in a broader sense than merely financial).

The economic dimensions of governance complicate the issue even further; for example, think of the range of structures of corporate ownership and the divergent effects on the market each type of structure can potentially have.

As a result, guidelines for governance must involve the following three important elements:

1. The structure, role, and duties of the directors.
2. The role and rights of the shareholders.
3. The regime for disseminating information, accounting, and auditing.

These issues can be determined collectively or imposed by the appropriate governance authorities.

Historically, there have been significant differences between continental European corporate governance, in particular the German model, and the Anglo-American approach. Characteristic of the continental European type are the close and stable relationships between suppliers of capital and management, concentrated ownership, and explicit considerations given stakeholders (especially company employees). The Anglo-American type is oriented toward various markets, shareholders, and the formal exclusion of other stakeholders.

The European type of corporate governance is called *insider* friendly, and the Anglo-American type is considered *outsider* friendly. The position of a business's employees is a controversial issue in the Anglo-American model, less so in the European type. In the Anglo-American view, a larger role for employees is, to some people, a threat to a company's competitive position; others would like to strengthen the status of employees so that the democratic quality of corporate governance can be increased.

Although there is a trend toward the Anglo-American model of corporate governance worldwide, the position of the shareholders, the information they receive, and the quality of that information remain problematic.

In 1994, Mark Roe examined this problem in his book, *Strong Managers, Weak Owners*.[4] Despite good corporate intentions, guidelines and processes, pragmatic business-economic thinking remains prevalent. As a starting point, every business must, of course, operate in a sound manner on a daily basis, unhindered by fundamental or indirectly relevant issues. Thus it is of the utmost importance to avoid problems by practicing good governance on a daily basis.

GOVERNANCE IN CORPORATIONS: ALL ABOUT BUSINESS PERFORMANCE

Each type of governance in business (e.g., financial and IT) is also a system of management, accountability, and supervision. Governance in business must guarantee a constantly adequate and objective assessment and promotion of the business's domain-specific interests that have an essential relationship with business performance, and ultimately with economic performance. The primary goal is to improve the competitive and financial performance of the business.

In practice, an "essential relationship with business performance" often means that large intrinsic risks and unavoidable complexity are directly associated with the interests in question. Organizations are not confronted with easy choices, yet they still want to progress rapidly. This substantially increases the chance of economic and organizational damage and the frustration of strategic interests.

Governance can be also be seen as the measurement and control system of management, accountability, and supervision that is necessary when interests, risks, and complexity exceed the competence of the firm's various management lines of authority and organizational layers. In the context of governance, everything must be defined, controlled, and designed so that it is possible to examine what is happening objectively—and to formulate an appropriate way of acting accordingly.

Consequently, governance has a sky-high level of ambition. Unfortunately, governance in daily practice is too frequently regarded as "the rules and provisions that people have to obey." Such a pragmatic qualification is a significant underestimation (and lack of appreciation) of what governance should be.

It is therefore important to discuss effectively the different tasks and responsibilities that come under the head of management, accountability, and supervision, as outlined below.

1. **Management.** The manner in which plans, decisions, and initiatives are formulated and how the results are measured.
2. **Accountability.** The justification of plans based on business value, expressed in terms of financial metrics.
3. **Supervision.** How we make sure that plans are executed and how we intervene when the results **are not according to plan.**

ESSENTIALS OF IT GOVERNANCE

In the case of information and IT, we stand at the threshold of a coherent ordering of processes, rules, and testing criteria (key performance indicators [KPIs]), frameworks, and tools, which must form and further facilitate objective management, accountability, and supervision.

Some examples of IT governance essentials include:

- **Legislation and Regulation.** Clinger-Cohen Act, Sarbanes-Oxley Act, Generally Accepted Accounting Principles (GAAP), International Accounting Standards (IAS).
- **Frameworks and Tools.** Control Objectives for Information and Related Technology (COBIT), maturity models (Capability Maturity Model [CMM] and others), Information Services Procurement Library (ISPL), Information Technology Infrastructure Library (ITIL), Total Quality Management (TQM), balanced scorecards.
- **Metrics and Methodologies.** Activity-Based Costing (ABC), Economic Value Added (EVA), Internal Return Rate (IRR), Net Present Value (NPV), portfolio management, Applied Information Economics.
- **Leadership.** Distributed leadership instead of traditional management. At present, work is being done to consolidate the current situation of leadership, with its gaps and overlaps, around full-cycle business governance of IT, power-boosted by portfolio management.

Exhibit 1.2 represents schematically the *perpetuum mobile*, an ongoing, self-sustaining, and never-ending process by which an organization interacts with various stakeholders by means of full-cycle governance mechanisms. This involves governance of information and IT, in short *IT governance*. Given the high amount of investment and risk, as well as the central role of employees, IT governance is an important component of corporate governance. Governance mechanisms (bottom of Exhibit 1.2) have to ensure that all parties are satisfied. At the center are the stated business goals and the associated performance, along with the behavior that will create these goals and realize this performance (upper left and right in the circle). Information and IT are key assets because of their importance for business performance and the money involved. Paul Strassmann, former CIO of NASA and President of the Information Economics Press, for example, regards information and knowledge as the only factors that can ensure that an organization is distinctive. Full-cycle

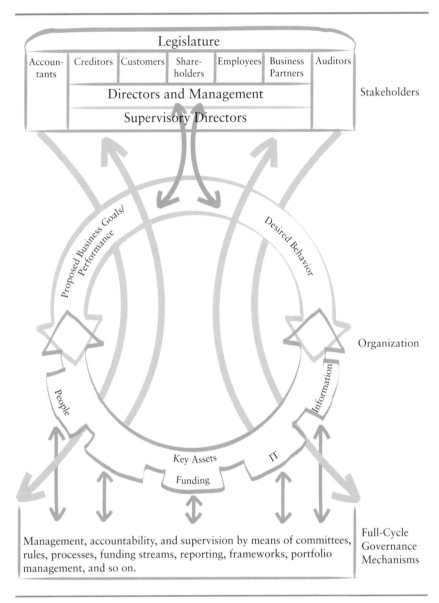

EXHIBIT 1.2 *Perpetuum Mobile* of Stakeholders: Organization and Full-Cycle Governance

IT governance is not only the governance of information and technology in relation to business processes and other key assets, it is also in particular the governance of organizational structures and desirable behavior within the organization.

IT governance has the task of realizing and securing appropriate employee behavior concerning information and IT. This gives rise to certain questions concerning correction and supervision. For example, how much should the current situation be changed? What is the best way to implement change? How much supervision is required? And when should management intervene so that everyone in the organization continues to display desirable behavior—in the most natural and motivated manner possible? As for leadership (which remains a critical human characteristic), how does this relate to all the factors involved in making and implementing plans? From this perspective, the relatively young discipline of IT governance (the IT Governance Institute having only existed since 1998) has begun to find its place at the heart of corporate governance.

Information and IT are as indispensable to organizations as electricity, the telephone, and the coffee machine, provided that IT is properly integrated into business processes. Slowly but surely the full scope of IT governance is beginning to be realized.

The first objective of IT governance is crystal clear: the most adequate, the clearest, and the most smoothly running measurement and control system possible—based on plan/do/check/act.

In the context of the key function that IT fulfills, and keeping an eye on the complex protection of interests that is associated with it, this system—*full-cycle governance*—can, over time, realize the essential relationship between strategy and business-economic performance on the one hand and the desired IT behavior on the other.

Operating between the mechanisms of financial governance and IT governance are the cogwheels of management, accountability, and supervision. They may be supported by everything available within the organization for such a purpose, from frameworks and calculations of value to "more human" elements such as leadership.

PLAIN COMMON SENSE

In the context of IT governance, we must be especially careful not to:

- Act in a too high-flown or academic manner.
- Give too much consideration to such questions as "central or federal."
- Overshoot the mark in implementing a measurement and control system like COBIT when the organization has not yet established the elements that must be measured.

To begin, we must aim for some easy wins! Given the limited maturity of IT governance, there is (fortunately or unfortunately, as the case may be) an overabundance of these. We encounter them, for example, in dealing with the redundancy of systems, platforms, and projects, as well as the proper handling of information. IT must be dealt with in a frugal manner, insofar as costs and resources are concerned, first of all by making an inventory of all systems and projects and then garnishing it with goals and figures.

Costly and unmanageable situations are usually revealed in this way, frequently those with which we have already had sufficient experience.

Second, supervision, control, and management cost money. If we could, without reservation, believe that everything will go well and everyone will "do the right thing," we would then be fine. Although trust is cheap, governance is extremely expensive. With an insufficient foundation, trust without control mechanisms is of course ultimately much more expensive.

Common sense must be our guide; common sense can tell us where an extra supervisory stimulus is still needed, where accountability gaps must be closed, and which well-intentioned schemes for better control must be transformed into a more compelling regulatory system.

The questions posed and the achievement of good solutions is irrevocably associated with the balance between ambition and constraint that is characteristic of the human factor of IT governance. Focus on quick wins—certainly—but also unleash the three IT governance elements of management, accountability, and supervision onto one another. Doing this effectively and efficiently is the trick.

As yardsticks, the following five rules should be considered:

1. IT governance involves the information, technology, people, and processes in organizations.
2. The relationship between economic performance and behavior must be emphasized.
3. Aim for the collective perception and appraisal of interests.
4. Guard against overregulation.
5. Organize for the purpose of creating an *organic* situation, in which it is second nature to strive for goals.

ENDNOTES

1. C. de Secondat (Baron de Montesquieu), *De l'Esprit desLois*, 1748, Barillot & Fils Genève. *www.constitution.org/cm/sol.htm*
2. Peters Committee, "Corporate Governance in Nederland. De veertig aanbevelingen," 1997. *www.nivra.nl/corporate%20 governance/Corporate%20GovernanceNL%20_JPR_.pdf*
3. Sarbanes-Oxley Act, 2002 (*www.sarbanes-oxley.com*). *www .thecorporatelibrary.com/spotlight/regulatory/bush-corpres.html*
4. Mark Roe, *Strong Managers, Weak Owners: The Political Roots of American Corporate Finance*, Princeton, NJ, Princeton University Press, 1994. *www.law.harvard.edu/news/2001/03/ 13_roe.php*

CHAPTER 2

Impact and Challenges
of Betrayed Trust

Failure of the Separation of Powers

Despite Montesquieu's elegant body of thought, in recent years it has seemed that the concept of separation of powers had gone into oblivion. Although Alan Greenspan, chairman of the U.S. Federal Reserve, warned as early as 1996 about "irrational exuberance," the free reign of greed continued, and a blind faith in progress persisted. Norms of governance were trampled under foot. The Sarbanes-Oxley Act[1] now makes senior executives personally liable for their managerial responsibilities under penalty of heavy fines and imprisonment. This act has had direct consequences for the full-cycle business governance of IT.

Deception and Blind Faith

The history of IT is paved with illusions and miscalculations. The belief in what IT would yield has not been in step with reality since 1968. In addition, the collapse of the New Economy has revealed the extent to which IT has been misused, giving the illusion of a healthy economy. It is no coincidence that Enron and WorldCom—one the e-business flagship and the other the literal backbone of the Internet (currently operating as MCI)—engaged in such practices as the misleading of shareholders. Rules were flouted in the blind faith that all the debts a business or person assumed would, in the new economic order of unbridled growth, be reduced to nothing by the enormous and sustained profits that were expected. Everyone jumped on the bandwagon: companies, banks, accountants, auditors, and consultants. A rigorous clean sweep has since been made in the worlds of accountancy and consultancy, and corporate and IT governance is now given high priority.

Realists at the Helm

IT was not used realistically. The financial markets, the economy, and our IT experience first had to reach a critical point before the awareness finally hit home that an overarching management (governance) was needed to redress the situation. Information and IT were found in every nook and cranny of our culture, and their challenges were given too little consideration. This soon led to an enormous series of miscalculations that tarnished the image of IT. We are currently attempting to deal with IT and its management in a more realistic manner in order to regain trust and increase credibility on the basis of such trust.

■　■　■

PROGRESS AND ITS CRISIS OF FAITH

In periods of prosperity, we often find that rules can be restrictive. They cramp innovation or nip it in the bud. However, both the power and the impact of innovations are often greatly overestimated. In the 1990s, this very situation occurred with IT—in its e-business and Internet capacities. Expectations were exaggerated and complexity too little understood. To make matters worse, some boards of directors, bankers, and accountants played fast and loose with the rules in the reckless belief that enormous profits lay just around the corner. The idea was that creative accounting was required to keep the voyage to innovation on course. We now know that this was a disastrous miscalculation.

When the Internet recession was at an end, the real homework was still to be done. We have now begun to do this work by developing finely honed practices of corporate governance—placing controls on the salaries paid senior executives, improving standards of reporting (particularly as a result of the Sarbanes-Oxley Act), and establishing full-cycle business governance of IT.

Let us consider the historic speech made by Alan Greenspan on December 5, 1996. Employing the now famous term "irrational exuberance," Greenspan expressed his uneasy feeling that share prices were no longer related to the true value of businesses.[2] An enormous bubble had been created. By making this statement, Greenspan did something considered very risky in 1996. Since 1982, stock prices had been rising markedly; they could fall at any moment. Stock market crashes like Black Monday in 1987, which actually had only slightly negative consequences for the real economy, are exceptional. The complex and fickle interaction between financial markets and the real economy of consumer confidence and unemployment must not be underestimated. In any future crash, we will probably not get off so easily.

Greenspan was also a man who constantly praised the economic virtues of IT. The Federal Reserve chairman now found himself in a ticklish situation. He saw trouble on the horizon (which everyone else also saw), but if he expressed a pessimistic view of the future, a self-fulfilling prophecy could be the result. His words are a gold standard. Moreover, as just noted, the relation between the share market and the real economy is complex and often contradictory, as is the relationship between IT investments and the state of the economy. The image of Greenspan, placed against a background of steeply declining markets, is a powerful representation of the crisis of faith in which we have landed.

In Exhibit 2.1, Greenspan is confronted with his own contradiction: using the term "irrational exuberance" while forecasting sustained, healthy economic growth, at a time when the NASDAQ technology list and the New York Stock Exchange continued to fall steadily.

On the subject of greed, the *Wall Street Journal Europe* had this to say in 2002:

> *The "irrational exuberance" of which Federal Reserve Chairman Alan Greenspan so famously warned in 1996 is an essential part of explaining the 1990s. The greediness of human beings didn't increase in the 1990s, Mr. Greenspan observes when he talks informally with business and other groups. What increased, he says, were the number of opportunities to satisfy that greed. The run-up in stock prices meant there was more to grab.[3]*

EXHIBIT 2.1   Irrational Exuberance

Ultimately, an end only came to the dotcom hype and the unrealistic IT and telecom expectations in March 2000. The "irrational exuberance" of 1996 had then taken many extravagant forms. This time, in fact, with a lasting effect on the actual economy: We have truly entered a "creeping crash." No end appears to have yet come to the decline in the stock market. Modern business practices using the Internet, IT and telecom were, all at once, at a full stop. More than one year later, it was recognized that, in addition to a limitless and naïve confidence, the years of hype before the change of millennium were marked by a tampering with the books, which had, in fact, been occurring on an unprecedented scale. This is perhaps not so surprising, for one reckless action calls forth another. And the transitions between rock-solid belief, wishful thinking, legal loopholes and criminal activity are, indeed, shifting. As is well known, Enron and WorldCom take the cake.

Enron and the Rest

Since the fall of the energy giant Enron's worldwide business empire at the end of 2001, tinkering with the books and other forms of mismanagement have been at center stage. Enron is the worst example of a series of scandals: Tyco, Omnicom, Xerox, WorldCom, and many others. According to Stanley Sporkin, a retired federal judge and former head of the U.S. Securities and Exchange Commission (SEC), these were not exceptions: "A few bad apples? Looks like we've got the whole peck here."[4]

The accounting, auditing, and consulting world has been thrown into a commotion. The rearrangement of these sectors is being undertaken with increased intensity: Arthur Andersen, Enron's external auditor, was swept away, KPMG was broken up, and the consulting division of PricewaterhouseCoopers, which was going to be renamed "Monday," was, in the end, acquired by IBM. The reputation of accountants and consultants has been irreversibly damaged, and the trust of shareholders and other stakeholders in businesses and those overseeing them has reached an all-time low. Some experts think that the resulting insecurity might last a decade, along with all the economic consequences of such a state of affairs. In this regard, the *Wall Street Journal* cited the renowned professor John Coffee on June 20, 2002:

> *Enron is the private sector's Watergate [...]. Although not all politicians were crooks, Watergate bred a virulent cynicism about government among the public, the media and even some politicians. That cynicism persists 30 years after the White House-blessed burglary of the Democratic National Committee's office. Enron and all that followed threaten to do the same to American business.*[5]

What exactly had happened? At a time when the peer index was lagging by more than half, Enron shares achieved their peak of nearly $91. By the summer of 2000, business writers were already perceiving a strong rebound in the New Economy, which is why the success of Enron, with its flourishing e-marketplace, received a great deal of extra publicity. Such trend watchers as Forrester Research held Enron up as a model of what was possible given the energetic use of IT and the Internet, despite strong countervailing tendencies. This observation was correct, but Enron was the wrong example.

Two years earlier, the price of Enron shares was the same as other, similar shares—somewhere between $20 and $30. Enron appeared to typify the American Dream: new markets, new business, internationalization, and towering profits on the horizon. Such future value was greatly overestimated, however. More than two years after its historical stock market high, the energy giant suffered a straightforward business failure, and on December 2, 2001, only a radical reorganization could save the remnants. In subsequent months, the leadership of Enron, its accountants, its legal advisors, and the banks involved were placed on trial. This completed the downward spiral; Enron's fraudulent transactions had cost shareholders more than $25 billion.[6]

Enron's story illustrates the consequences of creative accounting in combination with overexuberant business practices. It is perhaps notable that the scandal occurred in the United States, the country with the strongest regulations governing reporting to shareholders. This strongly mandated system of rules and regulations should have led to the desired behavior of the people in the organization. But reporting to the shareholders and management ethics has shown to be two separate things. At Enron, an internal auditor sounded the alarm. The Sarbanes-Oxley Act now offers protection to whistle blowers.

This act is therefore not really a response to regulations, such as those constituting the U.S. Generally Accepted Accounting Principles (U.S. GAAP). The intent was more to expand on existing rules, in order to control the practices laid bare by the Enron saga. Such controls are usually put into place after the damage has been done. Greed, however, a close cousin to ambition, is one of the seven deadly sins and is therefore ineradicable. The Enron failure was the result of the collective fanaticism of Enron, Arthur Andersen, JPMorgan Chase, Citigroup, Merrill Lynch, Credit Suisse First Boston, Barclays Bank, Deutsche Bank, and Lehman Brothers, to name just a few of the most important players.

Because of the Enron debacle (among other factors), at the end of March 2002, Greenspan emphasized that the establishment and observation of good guidelines for responsible business practices were crucial economic pillars. Impeccable long-term financial status—not the share price—should represent the highest value, as in previous decades.

The Power of Investment Counselors

At the end of April 2003, the world of investment counseling was being put back in order. In particular, it had become clear that investment counselors had contributed enormously to the crisis of faith that is being discussed here. A sum amounting to $1.4 billion was paid out in compensation for misleading advice. What had been happening is revealed by the Internal e-mail correspondence at Merrill Lynch. "Beautiful, f*** 'em" is what senior analyst Henry Blodget wrote when the Internet company GoTo.com switched to Credit Suisse. Subsequently, buyers were dissuaded from purchasing its shares, which had originally been highly recommended. Such an unscrupulous practice was not unprecedented. The ten largest financial consultant companies have all more or less admitted their guilt. Some, such as Lehman Brothers and Goldman Sachs, got away with the admission that they had often publicized "exaggerated and unsupported claims." Salomon Brothers, Merrill Lynch, and Credit Suisse First Boston had to accept the term "fraudulent" as part of their settlement. William Donaldson, then head of the SEC, the U.S. stock-market watchdog, said that his predecessor's degree of tolerance could no longer be maintained—he was disappointed and angry that the banks were engaging in "spin"(the practice of recommending worthless stocks), as was made clear in the e-mail correspondence among analysts.[7]

And Europe? The Same Medicine

In Europe, investors are often less well equipped to expose fraud and take successful action against it. The public ministries simply do not have sufficient expertise at their disposal. However, the effects of the crisis of faith and the failure of full-cycle governance have been felt everywhere. Gerhard Schmid, CEO of MobilCom, a German mobile telephone provider, transferred 70.9 million from MobilCom to a company owned by his rich and powerful wife, without informing his fellow executives.

Schmid, who together with his wife owns half of all MobilCom shares, responded flippantly in a newspaper interview: "It's like you're going too fast on the street, but no accident happens. You learned that you should not go too fast, but no one got hurt." Given the fact that the share prices have decreased 97 percent since his company reached its highest stock market value (13 billion in March 2000), the time chosen to withdraw these millions was unfortunate, to say the least.[8]

THE ROLE OF IT AND THE INTERNET

Two days before Greenspan's memorable speech on December 5, 1996 in which he let slip the expression "irrational exuberance," top economist Robert Shiller testified to the irrationality of the stock exchange in a public hearing attended by the Reserve chairman. In his book on the subject, coincidentally entitled *Irrational Exuberance*, Shiller gives a number of reasons for the enormous differences between the financial markets and the real economy.[9]

To begin with, we were confronted with all sorts of reinforcement mechanisms. Then the baby-boomers entered the share market all at the same time, bringing into play the well-known herding factor. However, Shiller places his greatest emphasis on a blind faith in progress based on IT and the Internet, as does the Rabobank economist Henry Berendsen: "The miracle of the New Economy no longer exists. There is just an old-fashioned cyclical decline resulting from over-investment in information technology."[10]

In the mania of the last five years of the preceding century, IT was considered a necessary—and often (nearly) sufficient—condition for a successful business. The rise in value of Internet, IT, and telecommunications stock was the most evident outgrowth of the unfounded overactivity that we have come to know as the dotcom hype or the Internet bubble. We lived with the millennium bug, which turned out to be nothing, and the new economic order (inflationless, with a minimum of three percent annual growth, and without cyclical swings), which turned out to have no resemblance to reality, but we cannot live with the practices that produced the Enron scandal.

History repeats itself. If we want to grow in prosperity and well-being, then pitfalls like the irrational exuberance of the recent New Economy must be avoided. The British Railway craze, with the subsequent stock market crash of 1845, bears a strong resemblance to the IT and Internet hype of the present day.

Nineteenth-Century Railways and the Age of the Internet

It was a technological revolution that transformed and powered national economies. It gave rise to excitable stock markets, a flurry of start-ups, fraud and new modes of management. The technological revolution being referred to here is not the informa-tion and communication technologies or dotcom boom but the rail-way mania of 19th century Britain. There was huge speculation in railway shares followed by a spectacular crash in 1845 even in the shares of those companies that would become giants of the industry in later decades. Then as now, stock markets found that pricing shares associated with an exciting new technology is extremely dif-ficult, reflecting the considerable uncertainty about the value of the technology, both to the economy as a whole and to the sharehold-ers. An important implication is that the crash in technology shares in the spring of 2000 does not necessarily imply that economists who believe that ICT has raised sustainable growth in the American economy are wrong.[11]

McKinsey Comes under the Gun

Managers, gurus, consultants, accountants, auditors, financiers, reg-ulators, and the press—we all have egg on our faces or have been, to say the least, extremely shortsighted in our appraisals of what IT and the Internet had to offer us in the short term. The McKinsey consult-ing agency has been a particular target of criticism. At the beginning of August 1998, Arnold Kling, an Internet skeptic, was already pillo-rying the popular dotcom concept" of "stuffing substantial money in a good idea and then having the business sprout up by itself within a period of days." Such "self-generating" businesses were necessary to bring about the new economic "long boom."[12]

McKinsey has fought back. In an article entitled "Eperformance: The Path to Rational Exuberance," appearing in the first issue of the *McKinsey Quarterly* in 2001, the agency tried to correct its earlier naïve optimism.[13] Successful Internet activities, the article says, are based on the following fundamental rules of business:

- Target value proposals at specific market segments.
- Exert strict control over the expansion of product lines and busi-ness models.
- Do not embark on an enterprise with immature IT.

This requires iterations based on the following elements: an elab-orate long- and medium-term strategy, an incremental fleshing out of

QUICKLY RECOUP INVESTMENTS AND CONTINUE...

"A McKinsey business plan is a plan that starts out with costs much larger than revenues for one or two years, and then has revenues grow much more rapidly than costs forever. The result—on paper—is that once the business has reached the breakeven point, it is on a trajectory to earn ever-increasing profits."

Source: A. Kling, *Deconstructing McKinsey*, 1998. *arnoldkling .com/~arnoldsk/aimst19.htm*

this strategy, effective management, frank accountability, and good harmony of business with IT, as well as the inverse. This is directly related to the communication of the appropriate information, leadership, vision, prudent investment, and frank accountability to all stakeholders. These are, indeed, the current, politically correct views, if one wants to appear spic and span.

The Enron Failure and Its Link to IT

As we have seen, Enron had a prominent and positive new economic reputation because of its trail-blazing e-marketplace activities. Enron appeared ready to surpass the shining example that it took as a guide: General Electric's "Global eXchange Services." The drive and euphoria of those involved were legendary. Being world leader in the energy market was no longer sufficient; making deals is making deals and therefore no market was unassailable.

In 2001, Enron was the last proud example of what IT and the Internet could mean on a large scale. Then we suddenly found that megafraud was involved. It was annoying that we could have known this much earlier. Enron acted as both seller and buyer on the market and counted each side of the deal. And that was far from honest, to say the very least.[14]

WLEC: WORLD'S LEADING ENERGY COMPANY

"Enron's 1990s mandate, to be the World's Leading Energy Company, is passé now that the company is applying its E-trading model to all manner of commodities: telecom bandwidth, paper, metal—even financial instruments that let snowmobile makers hedge against mild winters. While chairman Ken Lay says Enron is evolving into 'an energy and broadband company,' president and chief operating officer Jeff Skilling (whose license plate still reads WLEC) suggests a wholly new moniker: We Make Markets. Enron doesn't just make markets; it assaults them. The company's main E-marketplace, EnronOnline, has logged close to $200 billion on 380,000 transactions since its launch just a year ago, making it the world's largest E-commerce site in terms of dollar volume."

Source: R. Preston and M. Koller, "Enron Surges into E-Markets," 2000. *www.informationweek.com/811/enron.htm*

THE AMERICAN PRESIDENT INTERVENES

The last "bubble," which built up from 1996 to March 2000, was beyond a doubt related to IT and the Internet. Enormous expectations about the share market and the real economy existed. What makes this so distressing is that these expectations were also justified. We use IT to give form to our world, and we do so in an unparalleled manner. However, we still engage in simplistic thinking about the hurdles and range of necessary conditions that are directly related to the desired innovations.

Extreme fraud or not—we repeatedly try to get the mechanism of self-fulfilling prophecy to work in our favor. In itself, this is sensible; we exhibit commitment and stand up for our business. However, in our naïvely blind faith, we were defeated.

Where do the boundaries lie? Definitely on this side of Enron- and WorldCom-style *mala fide* practices. After the terrorist attack that leveled the Twin Towers of New York's World Trade Center on September 11, 2001 and the Enron affair, the Bush administration found itself confronted by the WorldCom scandal and the serious challenges to the American economy that it represented. On July 9, 2002, the president urgently lectured the U.S. business community on its responsibilities and signed the Sarbanes-Oxley Act (intended to make creative bookkeeping less attractive) at the end of the same month.

Corporate Responsibility: The Sarbanes-Oxley Act

Sarbanes-Oxley created a federal accounting oversight board, making it easier to prosecute executives who shredded documents, set up criminal liability for executives who knowingly filed false financial reports, and added a felony penalty of 25 years in prison for securities fraud. "Corporate corruption has struck at investor confidence, offending the conscience of our nation," President Bush said at the signing ceremony, "yet, in the aftermath of September the 11th, we refused to allow fear to undermine our economy, and we will not allow fraud to undermine it, either."[15]

Corporate responsibility, which has a long history in the United States, involves the environment and ethics. In other nations such as the Netherlands, these concepts are known as "socially responsible business" and "sustainable" business practices and are associated with the slogan "People, Planet, Profit." Many U.S. businesses have a Corporate Responsibility Office (CRO), with, at its head, a similarly named Officer. The CRO determines whether a business is (ethically) responsible in its dealings with its employees, customers, and society. In response to the fraudulent practices at Enron and WorldCom, among others, the Bush administration saw the need to shift the focus of "corporate responsibility" from one concerned with ethical "side issues" to one emphasizing fundamental responsibilities. The message was that if top management did not drastically alter its practices, the nation and the world along with it would then suffer a great deal of damage.

President Bush was also afraid of the Watergate effect (which John Coffee described earlier in this chapter). Up to now, Bush has fended off such an effect by quickly signing a law with more severe consequences for fraud.

The new law attaches managerial responsibility to the actual physical person in question. The CEO and the CFO are specifically named in the law, but in reality the entire CxO organization is now held to be personally liable for the provision of reliable information. On the basis of the Sarbanes-Oxley Act, managers will now have to assume personal responsibility.

EIGHT CHALLENGES PLUS THE MILLENNIUM PROBLEM

Over and over again, we have seen that it is difficult to pinpoint the operations and results of IT. It appears that we crave progress while simultaneously underestimating the challenges we face—perhaps we are setting our expectations too high. Once again, we need to give the issue its proper dimension: our own human dimension. All our misconceptions reveal how poorly we are able to give IT its appropriate dimension. However, we first must fail before we learn our lesson.

The IT investment spiral has been enormous, and we now spend more than $1 billion annually, worldwide, on IT. Given the uncertain business value of IT, the enormous losses on the financial markets since March 2000, and the economic recession in which we find ourselves, we are now paying a substantial price for our lesson.

The Aberdeen Group's global IT spending forecast for 2003 puts total worldwide IT spending at $1.26 trillion and projects that it will reach $1.44 trillion by 2006. Worldwide hardware expenditures are expected to increase a total of only 8.3 percent from 2002 to 2006; software and services may increase 27.2 and 17.7 percent, respectively, over the same period.

New Slogans, New Chances

In the mid-1990s, expansive, business-oriented IT was in the spotlight. At that time, such emotionally charged terms as IT and automation faded into the background, the Internet and "e-commerce" came to the forefront, and a sense of comfort was reached. In 1997, we began to speak about "e-business."[16]

e-business was IBM's distinctive response to "e-commerce." Within a few years, the notion developed into the generic label for an example of technological newspeak jargon. In addition to "e-commerce" and "e-business," a great deal of noise was made about "business transformation" and the "virtual organization." Somewhat later, the emphasis came to be placed on "collaborative commerce" and "e-marketplaces." After the fall of the dotcoms, the telecom industry, and IT in general, this jargon was exchanged for other terms, which constituted promises and were no less weighty, for example, "service provisioning," "web services," and "utility computing." The latest state of affairs in the field of undiminished optimism can still be found on the Internet. Once again we need to work through new terms and concepts to understand the essential. We need to evaluate the new terms to avoid entering the realm of unrealistic expectations. Again, concepts, intentions, and meanings have made IT more cumbersome and confusing.

We are in danger of being led astray by our expectations for IT. The connecting thread winding though these misconceptions consists of complexity and productivity. The personal productivity, business productivity, and various sorts of macroeconomic productivity of IT constantly fall short of our expectations. In addition, the lack of a simple, fast, and easily applicable IT system is more than apparent.

In the following discussion, we provide eight examples of IT and IT-related problems, some long standing, that have not been corrected. Consideration of these issues cuts to the core of IT management, challenging the ways in which we deal with IT.

Challenge 1. Software Is Not Compatible: The Software Crisis (1968)

If we were to program more cleverly, we could manufacture IT systems much more cheaply and provide quicker delivery. However, because of all the deadlines and budgets that have been exceeded, we find ourselves in a permanent software crisis. Software projects are not meeting the expectations over and over again. They deliver late and are above budget. We have known about this problem for 35 years; in

1968, software engineering and the use of reliable standard parts and components were first discussed at a NATO-sponsored conference. Although theoretically we should be able to achieve compatibility, because of free competition in the IT sector as well as the rigorous nature of language programming. Working with reliable standard parts and components can improve the predictability of software engineering projects. Such a manufacture-based approach to software development has never been seriously undertaken. At the most, we can speak of "development lines" within a certain programming environment.

Challenge 2. Macroeconomic Productivity Leaves Something to Be Desired: Solow's Productivity Paradox (1987)

In 1987, Nobel Prize winner Robert Solow spoke out about the productivity paradox. He had noticed that the prominent use of computers was not reflected in productivity statistics,[17] whereas Federal Reserve chairman Alan Greenspan has always maintained that IT has made a positive contribution to economic growth. This factor can be considered from several angles. We are not, for example, so concerned about the contribution of the IT sector itself to growth. We are more interested in a positive relationship between the implementation of IT and the performance of business departments. (The productivity of IT in the American context can be demonstrated more clearly; see "Where Are We in Terms of the Micro- and Macro-Economics of E-Business?" in Chapter 3. Europe has clearly fallen behind in IT productivity.) "It took a while for businesses to learn not only how to use information technology, but how they needed to organize themselves.... It is very likely that we are seeing those benefits at last," says Solow.[18]

Challenge 3. There Is No Relationship between Investment in IT and Business Performance: Strassmann's Computer Paradox (1993)

On the microeconomic level, it was the renowned IT chief executive and analyst Paul Strassmann who has hammered home year in and year out his notion of the absence of any correlation between IT investment and the performance of organizations. He is still actively preoccupied with this phenomenon,[19] which he calls "the computer paradox."

Challenge 4. The Percentage of Successful IT Projects Is Much Too Low: The Standish Group's CHAOS Research

It is quite plausible that business on any scale has now become unfeasible without IT. However, in practice what is plausible often does not correspond with reality. We run the risk of missing the benefits of IT endeavors or even of unleashing them in a counterproductive manner, because of a range of interfering factors. The best-known longitudinal study of these factors is the one conducted by The Standish Group.[20]

Although increasingly more IT projects are successful, the situation remains far from ideal. As shown in Exhibit 2.2, in the nine years from 1994 to 2002, the number of successful projects more than doubled; however, nearly two-thirds of the projects investigated in 2002 had still failed, or failure was threatening. The year of greatest improvement since the second survey in 1996 was 2002. Over the entire research period, The Standish Group reviewed nearly 45,000 IT projects in large, medium, and small American businesses.

In 2002, success factors for IT projects were weighted as indicated in Exhibit 2.3. In general, the more points a project has, the greater its chances of success.

Discernible commitment throughout the organization coupled with good project management would produce a score of 48 (out of

EXHIBIT 2.2 Percentages of Successful, Failed, and Challenged IT Projects: 1994–2002

	1994	1996	1998	2000	2002
% Succeeded	16	27	26	28	34
% Failed	31	40	28	23	15
% Challenged	53	33	46	49	51

Source: J.H. Johnson, "Micro Projects Cause Constant Change," The Standish Group, 2001. *www.xp2003.org/conference/papers/Chapter30-Johnson.pdf*

EXHIBIT 2.3   Success Factors for IT Projects

Executive Support	18
User Involvement	16
Experienced Project Manager	14
Clear Business Objectives	12
Minimized Scope	10
Standard Software Infrastructure	8
Firm Basic Requirements	6
Formal Methodology	6
Reliable Estimates	5
Other	5

Source: J.H. Johnson, "Micro Projects Cause Constant Change, The Standish Group, 2001. *www.xp2003.org/conference/papers/Chapter30-Johnson.pdf*

100). When we add clear business goals and limited project ambition, we get 70 points. Good governance and consideration of the human dimension are once again shown to be decisively important factors.

Challenge 5. IT Costs Are Going through the Roof: Schrage's Investment Spiral (1999)

In terms of income, the investment spiral has proved to be unsustainable. In the first half of the 1990s, IT investments rose 11 percent annually in the United States; in the second half, growth increased to 26 percent annually.[21] Over the whole second half, Robert Samuelson, columnist for *Newsweek*, the *Washington Post,* and other publications, reported an increase in annual IT spending from 20 to 40 percent). MIT scholar Michael Schrage estimated at the turn of the century that "more than half of each investment dollar" went to IT. Schrage called this the "great lie of the information age.... In 1990, company purchases of high-tech equipment (computers, communication gear, instruments) was 20 percent of all business investment, which includes everything from office buildings to industrial machinery.... By 1998, it was 40 percent."[22] "Business worldwide ... has wasted billions of dollars believing the big lie of the information age. For almost two decades, that lie has encouraged a massive spending binge, absorbing over half of every dollar that U.S. business has invested in itself."[23] Such statements clearly express a lack of confidence in the possibility that investment in IT would pay a good return in hard cash. Investing in IT and obtaining revenue from IT were, so it seemed, completely separate from each other.

Challenge 6. Faster, More Complex, and Better Software Has to Be Developed: The Software Development Paradox of Booch, Jacobson, and Rumbaugh (2000)

What businesses want is to produce faster, better quality applications that provide more return on investment. The software development paradox, as stated by the Rational "amigos" (i.e., Booch,[24] Jacobson, and Rumbaugh; Rational has now become a subsidiary of IBM), confronts us with the cold hard facts. Building quality software that functionally satisfies ever higher expectations is extremely difficult. The time is always too short to create a quality product. In addition, because of technical, business, or financial objections, not everything we would like to have built can, in fact, be built. One last important point is that not everything we want should actually be built.

Challenge 7. We Need to Automate Many More Functions: Autonomic Computing (2001)

Only by equipping our computer systems with an autonomous human nervous system that regulates all of the reflex activities, such as our heartbeat, breathing, speech, and senses, can we perform the gigantic and increasing burden of maintenance and coordination that our information systems currently require. We need to ensure that as many of the technical devices as possible operate on their own, or else the system will collapse in on itself in a jumble of wires, buttons, and knobs. IBM knows that if they increase processor strength, storage capacity, and network connectivity, some kind of systemic authority must be put into place if we expect to take advantage of the potential. The human body's self-regulating nervous system presents an excellent model for creating the next generation of computing—autonomic computing.[25]

Otherwise, we immediately find ourselves in an impossible situation. The number of people that all the IT systems can keep busy will, because of the complexity that we ourselves have developed, soon become so great that the entire population of the United States will have to sit at the controls. As IBM describes the situation, "At the current rate of expansion, there will not be enough skilled IT people to keep the world's computing systems running.... Some estimates for the number of IT workers required globally to support a billion people and millions of businesses connected via the Internet—a situation we could reach in the next decade—put it at over 200 million, or close to the population of the entire United States. [But] even if we could somehow come up with enough skilled people, the complexity is growing beyond human ability to manage it."[26]

Challenge 8. The Reliability of Our IT System Must Be Drastically Increased: The Trustworthy Computing Memo from Bill Gates (2002)

In a personal memorandum, Bill Gates noted that the reliability of IT was the number one priority. Gates forecasts that, within 10 years, IT will be such an integral and indispensable element in our lives that the reliability of systems will become the most important factor in choosing a provider or supplier. Gates states:

> *Trustworthy Computing is more important than any other part of our work. If we don't do this, people simply won't be willing—or able—to take advantage of all the other great work we do.... Trustworthy Computing is computing that is as available, reliable and secure as electricity, water services and telephony.... With telephony, we rely both on its availability and its security for conducting highly confidential business transactions without worrying that information about who we call or what we say will be compromised. Computing falls well short of this, ranging from the individual user who isn't willing to add a new application because it might destabilize their system, to a corporation that moves slowly to embrace e-business because today's platforms don't make the grade.*[27]

For various reasons, which reinforce each other, the credibility of IT has suffered enormous damage in recent years. Obviously, there was something fundamentally wrong with IT management, and the situation in terms of as money, functionality, complexity, and productivity had gotten completely out of hand. There was a need to clamp down hard, especially when the economic "creeping crash" hit.

The Millennium Problem: "The Bug That Didn't Bite"

In the midst of the eight challenges just described, all of which strongly affect the credibility of IT, the millennium problem added more fuel to the fire. It is a story of extremely impractical but predictable thrift. What actually happened?

In the period when computer memory was scarce, as little memory as possible was reserved for the date. It was easier, for example, to register 77 rather than the four-digit 1977. The fear that computer systems would thus behave unpredictably led to real panic. The possibility of computer-controlled missiles being launched was one of the concerns that were floating around. People would be stuck in elevators, or complete meltdowns would occur in Russian or Ukrainian nuclear plants.

None of this happened. In fact, between December 31, 1999 and January 1, 2000 (and even a few months later), almost nothing happened. Did we, thanks to all our efforts, manage to avoid a disaster in time, or was there no great danger at all? As we now know, it was the latter.

However, ensuring against possible problems cost a great deal of money. Cap Gemini America estimates that $858 billion were spent worldwide on the possibility of a millennium bug. The Gartner Group limits the amount to $600 billion, but it is certain that at least $100 billion was spent in the United States. In Russia, however, only $200 million was spent.[28]

INSIGHT AS THE BASIS OF REALISM

In the previous two sections, we have seen that the desire to utilize IT and its reality are not always in line. Additionally, we have seen that chaos and complexity are the principle causes for the failure to meet expectations and the overshooting of budgets and deadlines. We have also seen that greater dependence on computers in the future will require reliability and simplicity of systems and applications and that we are far from such a state.

The first step toward simplicity is undoubtedly the recognition of complexity, but action is required as well. For organizations, such efforts come under the heading of IT governance. IT management must be given a better form. We need to critically examine the ways in which we make IT decisions and account for them. Peter Weill and Richard Woodham brought this point to our attention with their much-cited statement: "An effective IT Governance structure is the single most important predictor of getting value from IT."[29] The decision-making process, which is linked to the structure, is also a key factor. In the e-business years of irrational exuberance, it became patently obvious that there was a lack of IT management, as witnessed by the absence of a relationship between IT investment and income, which Michael Schrage calls the "big lie of the information age" (discussed earlier in this chapter). How this management has finally been developed and where we find ourselves now will be discussed in Part Two.

"From Control to Drift": Knee-Jerk Management Does Not Work

We can see that real control over IT is becoming increasingly more difficult. IT applications are pushing their way further into our lives, outside the contexts already familiar to businesses and institutions. We see implementations and uses of IT appearing in all parts of our culture. The "always on society" (continuous Internet access everywhere) is slowly emerging, and in time we may reach a crisis point. We also see that, by outsourcing our IT requirements, control is shifted from inside to outside the organization.

In *From Control to Drift*, Claudio Ciborra, who is affiliated with the London School of Economics, warns us that it may turn out to be impossible to steer the ship.[30] He also says that the people who work with IT should be left to their own devices, as far as possible. If the IT workers are sufficiently integrated into the organization and if full-cycle business governance is functioning properly, this should be possible.

According to Ciborra, we will never have complete control over IT, and thus there is no need for such control to be a goal. It would be better to resign ourselves to the notion that IT and its management are and remain DIY—do it yourself ("bricolage")—and that improvement can come one step at a time.

This should be apparent to anyone who has extensively researched IT use and the decision-making processes affecting IT in large business organizations. Ciborra concludes that we would be better off redirecting our aspirations regarding control (see "People No Longer Put up with Control" in Chapter 7).

Because our use of information and IT influences the shape of our world, Ciborra proposes that our limitations be placed at the center of our quest for improvement. This appears to be strongly related to the challenges of managing IT and the slow pace of the e-business developments and therefore the focus on the human dimension, which constitutes an initial movement toward a realistic view of the world.

What we want is a better use of information and technology, linked to business processes, strongly embedded in the organization, and having the goal of better competitive and financial business performance.

To reach this goal, we must remain specifically devoted to the following four aims:

1. A quantitative approach
2. Proper measurement and control loops
3. Keeping the costs and benefits of IT in hand
4. Full-cycle business governance as a mechanism enabling us to maintain the relationship between desirable behavior and business economic performance

ENDNOTES

1. Sarbanes-Oxley Act, 2002 (*www.sarbanes-oxley.com*). *www.thecorporatelibrary.com/spotlight/regulatory/bush-corpres.html*
2. The Federal Reserve Board, "Remarks by Chairman Alan Greenspan," 1996. *www.federalreserve.gov/boarddocs/speeches/1996/19961205.htm*
3. "Events That Produced Enron Festered for Years," *Wall Street Journal Europe*, June 20, 2002, A12.

4. David Wessel, "Why Boardroom Bad Guys Have Now Emerged En Masse," *Wall Street Journal,* June 20, 2002, A1.
5. J.C. Coffee, "The Enron Debacle and Gatekeeper Liability: Why Would the Gatekeepers Remain Silent?" Testimony of Professor John C. Coffee, Jr., Adolf A. Berle, Professor of Law, Columbia University Law School and Joseph Flom, Visiting Professor of Law, Harvard University Law School before the Senate Committee on Commerce, Science and Transportation December 18, 2001. *www.senate.gov/~commerce/hearings/121801Coffee.pdf*
6. Milberg Weiss, "The Enron Lawsuit." *www.enronfraud.com*
7. *De Volkskrant,* "Bedriegende analisten liepen in val eigen e-mail," April 30, 2003.
8. A. Latour and K. Delaney, "Foreign Business Scofflaws Aren't Hurting Much at All," *Wall Street Journal,* August 16, 2002. *www.happinessonline.org/InfectiousGreed/p25.htm*
9. R. Shiller, *Irrational Exuberance,* Princeton, New Jersey: Princeton University Press, 2000. *pup.princeton.edu/chapters/s6779.pdf*
10. *De Volkskrant,* "Overheid moet herstel VS brengen," November 11, 2001.
11. Crafts, et al., "Railways and the Electronic Age." *www.fathom.com/feature/122057*
12. P. Schwartz and P. Leyden, "The Long Boom: A History of the Future, 1980–2020," *Wired 5.07, 1997. www.wired.com/wired/archive/5.07/longboom_pr.html*
13. V. Argawal, L.D. Arjona, and R. Lemmens, "Eperformance: The Path to Rational Exuberance," *McKinsey Quarterly,* 2001. *www.mckinseyquarterly.com/article_page.asp?ar=975&L2=24&L3=45*
14. Ibid.
15. J. Block, "Bush Signs Corporate Responsibility Law," 2002. *www.cato.org/dispatch/07-31-02d.html*
16. IBM, "Year 1997." *www.ibm.com/ibm/history/history/year_1997.html*
17. R.M. Solow, "We'd Better Watch Out," *New York Times Book Review,* July 12, 1987. *cisnet.baruch.cuny.edu/phd/altschuller/CIS840/ISProductivity.doc*
18. J.E. Hilsenrath, "Data Show Technology Investments Are Paying Off for the Service Sector," *Wall Street Journal* November 7, 2003.

19. *www.strassmann.com*
20. J.H. Johnson, "Micro Projects Cause Constant Change," The Standish Group, 2001. *www.xp2003.org/conference/papers/ Chapter30-Johnson.pdf*
21. B. Laurence, "The Mail on Sunday's City Editor on Prospects for the IT Revolution," *Mail on Sunday,* October 22, 2000. *www.thisismoney.com/20001022/n m22431.html*
22. R.J. Samuelson, "The PC Boom—And Now Bust?" *Newsweek,* April 5, 1999.
23. Esolutionsworld, 2000. *www.esolutionsworld.com/conference/ es2000/proceedings/15000/15003/15003.pdf*
24. G. Booch, "The Limits of Technology: What We Can and Cannot Do with Software." *www.rational.com/media/corpinfo/ limits. pdf*
25. IBM, "Autonomic Computing: IBM's Perspective on the State of Information Technology," 2001. *www.research.ibm.com/ autonomic/manifesto/autonomic_computing.pdf*
26. Ibid.
27. Bill Gates, "Trustworthy Computing," *Wired News,* February 21, 2002.
28. "The Millennium Bug: Special Report," *The Guardian,* 2000. *www.guardian.co.uk/Y2K*
29. P. Weill and R. Woodham, "Don't Just Lead, Govern: Implementing Effective IT Governance," 2002. *hpds 1.mit .edu/retrieve/1451/4237-02.pdf*
30. C.U. Ciborra, et al., *From Control to Drift: The Dynamics of Corporate Information Infrastructures,* Oxford, Oxford University Press, 2000.

PART TWO

Accountability: An Economic-Based Business Focus for IT

Part One: Management

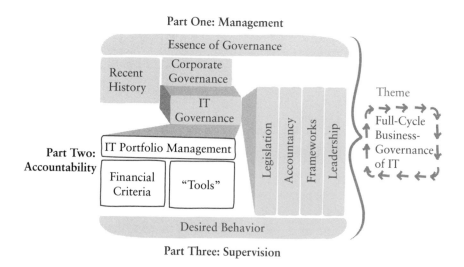

Part Three: Supervision

CONCEPTS AND PROMISES

The view that the introduction of IT into organizations is necessary and valuable is one that corporations have always wanted to substantiate. For years, corporations sought support in abstract concepts, including business process reengineering (BPR) and e-business. A constant central theme was "alignment"—the integration of business and IT. Indeed, although this ensured for dialogue, concrete metrics and techniques have long been underemphasized.

MANAGEMENT OF IT

Implementation of IT was not easy for two reasons: Projects became bogged down, and predicted results remained out of reach. Year in and year out, excessive amounts of money were spent on IT. In the second half of the 1990s, when business and IT were intrinsically interlinked, we began to understand that IT management must be improved. The dialogue between business and IT must be accurately and thoroughly tested according to performance standards that are valid throughout the entire organization.

In Chapter 3, we discuss the milestones and developments in our quest for the mechanisms that could lead to a well-oiled system of IT management. We follow the body of thought developed by Forrester Research and reflect on such studies as the one recently conducted by MIT professor Peter Weil in collaboration with Marianne Broadbent. She heads the executive program at Gartner, in which scores of CIOs from around the world are participants.

PROCESSES AND MONEY

Given the great investment in IT and the accompanying value claim associated with it, at the end of 2001 Forrester Research proclaimed the need for a new professionalism and proposed that the vague term "alignment" (the lining up of business activities, information, and IT) should be abandoned once and for all. The new focus had to be a complete economic valuation of IT oriented toward business processes, with primary emphasis on business value. This dialogue should ease the transition to accountable applications of IT based on a business perspective. Although everyone has now come to share this point of view, actual practice is lagging far behind in this respect.

DISCUSS, REGULATE, AND MEASURE

In the recent past, adequate control over IT has much more frequently involved abstract discussion rather than the concrete factors that need to be controlled, not to mention measured. This failure of development occurred even though (as we now begin to recognize) control actually requires that three things happen together: discussion, regulation, and measurement. Whenever this combination occurs throughout the organization, we are then able to speak of *full-cycle governance*: a system of measurement and control loops based on three categories of action (management, accountability, and supervision).

In the context of our quest for a well-oiled system of IT management and the development of IT measurement, at the end of Chapter 3 we explore Microsoft's Rapid Economic Justification Framework and the Total Economic Impact framework developed by the Giga Group (now a subsidiary of Forrester Research).

DESIRABLE BEHAVIOR

In addition to the process-oriented financial justification of IT, the stimulation of desirable behavior among employees in the organization is of crucial importance (see Part Three for a complete discussion).

BUSINESS RESPONSIBILITY AND PROFESSIONALISM

It is increasingly the case that the complete economic valuation of IT oriented toward business processes is insufficiently standardized and that there is little notion of the proper cohesion involved. Without the professionalism resulting from an emphasis on value, business responsibility, good metrics, consolidation, and standardization, a well-oiled system of IT management will remain beyond our grasp. Matters are slowly changing in this regard, however. The most important elements of this new development are IT portfolio management, Activity-Based Costing (ABC), and Economic Value Added (EVA).

IT PORTFOLIO, COHERENCE, AND NET PROFIT

In addition to costs and benefits, IT portfolio management specifically focuses on risks and prioritization (see Chapter 4). At the forefront of this new practice are ABC, which contributes enormously to a clear linking of business and IT, and EVA, which forces us to face issues concerning net value (see Chapter 5). Other developments in the direction of standardized and consolidated systems, which would provide some insight into costs, benefits, risks, prioritization, and flexibility, are encountered as parts of the concept of Total Economic Impact.

CHAPTER 3

A Basis for IT Management

Urgent Need

In recent years the need for good IT management has become blatantly obvious, especially after IT was implemented as *e-business*, a use that ultimately required an intensive integration of IT into our business processes. The large role that money plays (through IT investment) became subordinate; if we thought about the cost, we might miss the chance of enormous economic growth. For some time, such fears dominated practice.

Promotion of Dialogue

The 1990s were years of enthusiastic experiments without real reflection and with the spotlight shining steadily on innovation. Dialogue was needed, with three aims in mind: a clearer cost-benefit analysis, an estimate of the risks, and the setting of priorities. Such a dialogue was not "small talk" but rather a continuous, structured interaction among the financial experts, businessmen, and IT professionals in the organization. Ultimately, this dialogue resulted in what we now know as IT portfolio management, the subject of Chapter 4.

Ensuring that IT Measurement Occurs

For years, we have primarily sought our advantage through the most diverse abstract concepts, including Business Process Reengineering and e-business. The central theme of such notions is *alignment*—the synchronization of business and IT. We did not trouble ourselves about economic accountability or good measurement methods and techniques. In short, we did not bother with *IT measurement.* Nowadays, although everyone admits to the necessity of such measurements, they have not always been put into practice. As we shall see, given the pressure to make IT measurable, the CIO continues to play an unenviable role.

■　■　■

IT MEASUREMENT: TURNING A THREE-LEAF INTO A FOUR-LEAF CLOVER

The notions of management, strategy, and governance have been well known in the IT world for some time. ITers understand the integration of business, information, and digital technologies. This strategic interlinking requires an adequate line of attack. We thought we had found this in business/IT alignment—but IT measurement (i.e., concrete measurement and prioritization) was either missing or undergoing vigorous development. In combination with IT measurement, the *alignment* process, which is unclear, can be replaced by an economic dialogue oriented toward business processes. This need for a new professionalism, stemming from the great investment in IT and the accompanying claims for the value of such technology, was expressed by Forrester Research at the end of 2001 in the form of a proposal to ban the vague term *alignment.*[1]

This development has had a reinvigorating effect on IT management, governance, and strategy. Our three-leaf clover of IT management has been transformed into a four-leaf clover (see Exhibit 3.1). IT measurement reinforces the trio of IT management, IT governance, and IT strategy; a process-oriented, economic dialogue replaces the vague process of business/IT alignment—or at least makes it more concrete. We are in the process of quickly evolving from the use of a primarily strategy-oriented frame of reference (characterized by Business Process Reengineering and the recklessness of the initial e-business phase, as well as weak measurement and control loops) into a new and integral professionalism. In this transformation, attention is paid to innovative ambitions, as well as to a broad and lofty system of well defined business-related metrics for IT.

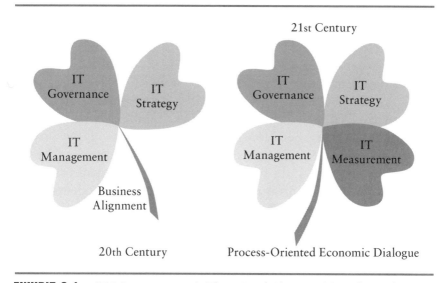

21st Century

20th Century   Process-Oriented Economic Dialogue

EXHIBIT 3.1   IT Management: A Three-Leaf Clover Is Transformed into a Four-Leaf Clover

Fragmented support for "new economic" ideals will not lead to a realistic business approach toward IT investments; IBM head Lou Gerstner helped to clarify this idea in his keynote speech delivered at Partner World 2001. Gerstner had much to explain about "his" e-business; IBM had launched the term in 1997, in an attempt to distinguish it from the e-commerce hype.[2] Soon afterward, e-business became a generic term referring to the organic integration of business, as championed by the advocates of BPR. Further investigation revealed that the notion was too easily conceived. Gerstner said:

> *In the early going, e-business was an idea. It was a vision wrapped in a marketing message.... Thankfully, I believe we can say with a high degree of certainty that we've passed through the roller coaster ride of e-business Phase 1. And what a ride it was—an intoxicating blend of zany exhilaration, wild experimentation, and a whole lot of very unrealistic expectations. In that phase, which is well documented by now, there were a lot of false starts, and a lot of zealots marched into a lot of blind alleys.[3]*

Instead of shoring up ideals, universal concepts and frameworks will have to facilitate clearer, more dynamic and meaningful measurements and control loops that require standardized and tool-based metrics and measurement processes. Activity-Based Costing (ABC), which contributes enormously to the definition of a clearer link between business and IT, and Economic Value Added (EVA), which focuses on net value, are two key examples of such mature forms of IT measurement. For the young discipline of IT portfolio management, which considers risks and prioritization of paramount importance, ABC, EVA, and associated yardsticks fulfill a central role. The ship has now set sail but is only beginning to take wind; the narrow straits are, as in most cases, standardization and acceptance. In the context of the quest for a well-oiled system of IT management and the development of IT measurement, at the end of the chapter we will explain Microsoft's Rapid Economic Justification Framework and the Total Economic Impact of the Giga Group (now a subsidiary of Forrester Research). The operationalization of full-cycle IT governance by means of IT portfolio management will be discussed in Chapter 4. Chapter 5 will deal with ABC and EVA, along with other developments.

Before we turn our attention to a thorough examination of IT management, we will, in the next two sections, undertake a brief preliminary study, first into the strategic value of IT and then into both the impact and development of e-business.

IT IS INFRASTRUCTURE AND E-BUSINESS

Sometimes IT is placed on a par with other types of "infrastructural" renewal, like the steam engine, railway, telegraph, telephone, electric generator, and internal combustion engine. Nicholas Carr's article "IT Doesn't Matter" is a recent example of such views.[4] Because of its infrastructural character, so goes the argument, the strategically differentiating characteristic of IT is steadily decreasing, and the subsequent conclusion is that ultimately IT no longer matters. In the simple form of (1) major premise, (2) minor premise, and (3) conclusion, the propositions of a syllogism, this reasoning appears as follows:

1. Infrastructures do not possess any capacity to act as strategic differentiators.
2. IT is becoming increasingly more an element of the infrastructure.

3. In a strategic sense, IT has therefore less and less to contribute and (according to forecasts) will soon no longer play a significant role.

This all sounds logical. However, if we examine the infrastructure examples that Carr provides, we then see what the issue is:

IT is best seen as the latest in a series of broadly adopted technologies that have reshaped industry over the past two centuries—from the steam engine and the railroad to the telegraph and the telephone to the electric generator and the internal combustion engine. For a brief period, as they were being built into the infrastructure of commerce, all these technologies opened opportunities for forward-looking companies to gain real advantages.

Carr compares IT with three forms of power generation (the steam engine, the electric generator, and the internal combustion engine), one providing a means of transportation (the train) and two providing communication (the telegraph and telephone), of which one, the telegraph, is coded. Are these good comparisons with IT's abilities? The answer is no, as it is patently obvious that the nature of IT is mistaken and the ability of IT to be productive is underestimated. Someone like Carr, with limited IT experience, cannot do justice to the developments and application possibilities that are already on the horizon.

How then should we be looking at IT? First, as the incarnation of what is called Moore's law. In this light, IT is the cyclical miniaturization and acceleration of all digital electronics. Despite the physical limit that is frequently forecast and that by definition we must ultimately run into, we manage time and again to push back the boundary. How far can we go? At least far enough to have affordable computers with the processing power of the human brain and with unimaginable amounts of memory. At this time, we are rapidly on our way to double-exponential growth. When we combine science with rapid developments in the area of fixed and wireless broadband networks (think of the speed records that CERN and CalTech established in October 2000, 20,000 times faster than what we now know as broadband), it then becomes impossible to predict what IT has in store for us within the foreseeable future. We have had to wait 200 years for the technology, but now the technology is waiting for us.

MOORE'S LAW MEANS UNIMAGINABLE GROWTH

"A processor in 2002 is 10,000 times faster than a processor in 1982 was. This trend has been in place for decades, and there is nothing to indicate that it will slow down any time soon. Scientists and engineers always get around the limitations that threaten Moore's law by developing new technologies.

A CPU in the 2040 time frame could have the processing power of a human brain, and it will cost $1,000. It will have a PETAbyte (one quadrillion bytes) of RAM. It will have one EXAbyte of storage space. An exabyte is 1,000 quadrillion bytes."

Source: M. Brain, 2003. *marshallbrain.com/robotic-nation.htm*

Even if we *only* regard IT as infrastructure, we must still admit that IT has a special place as "the infrastructure of the infrastructures." Its development speed and diffusion are unique in history. If we look at this in the light of what is to be expected from the quickly growing convergence of nanotechnology, biology, medicine, the information sciences, and the cognitive sciences (NBIC), we see that each comparison falls short, in particular the forecast that IT, as an infrastructural element, will lose its strategically differentiating capacity. When related to IT, *infrastructure* is a term that has no relation to the way we have regarded infrastructure in the past.

Another question can be posed to reveal the extent to which a comparison can be reductive: What do we actually understand to be a telephone? Is this an apparatus or, for example, the telephone network? In the digital age, the telephone (the sound that comes and goes far) is at most one functionality among many—and the telephone net is absorbed by other broadband, fixed, and wireless networks that actually only consist of frequencies and communication protocols. This happens because of IT, which makes it possible to treat old functionalities, which have always been bound to physical carriers and equipment, as mere instantiations of the same thing.

This "same thing" boils down to standardized function sets, comprised of coding, processing, storage, and transport elements. This combination constitutes what we know as IT, currently in the form of digital electronics, software, and associated frequencies. Viewed in this way, IT erases the distinction between infrastructure and application. Instead, we are dealing with a rich and dynamic foundation for prismatic versatility, which we need "only" link, in a meaningful way, to usable functionality. In terms of *infrastructure* and statements made about IT infrastructure, this insight is of fundamental importance.

If we now consider the concrete impact of IT and therefore its functionality, IT can be seen as the heart beating at the center of our business processes (and of our economy as well). Because of its complex integration, in combination with the notion of a broad, dynamic foundation, IT remains completely unique and, also at this level, a potentially strong differentiator. In particular, what matters is how IT is incorporated in organizations and how it is used at the interorganizational level. Working against this differentiating capacity is, of course, the fact that each serious business integration of IT must be based on general standards—a necessary condition for the success of the interaction.

All in all, this means that differentiating elements, in principle, offer advantages for only a relatively short period of time. This explains the growing interest in legal protection covering the entire IT domain. Spreading out standards and functionalities is the way to go, until a stable harvest season is reached. This latter period must then be prolonged by organizations as far as possible.

IT therefore forces the economic race to a conclusion. No wonder many business operators want to find a relatively calm harbor somewhere. The fact that IT no longer exists for its own sake but must be dynamically integrated into a business establishes new requirements based on competitiveness and performance. More often than is the case with infrastructure, we are therefore now equating IT with business applications, which is justified because the difference between infrastructure and business application has begun to blur and because IT has become the heartbeat of business.

The dynamic interpenetration of business by IT has transformed the breadth and depth of our dealings with IT, with consequences related to new technology, revised content, altered structures, organization-related changes, and financial-economic factors. We are confronted with the need to manage all IT assets, all IT innovations, and all encompassing processes as integrated business components and to account for these elements at this level.

The manner in which we regard the existing intense integration of IT and its new interconnection with business-related and other contextual factors determines the value that we allow IT to produce. Compare IT with the color changes that occur when a crystal ball is slowly turned in front of a light. Although IT has undeniably important infrastructural characteristics, a crucial part of its business value lies in the prismatic versatility that characterizes its nature (as has already been noted).

The ease with which new successful business functionalities can be added shows how adequately this prismatic versatility of IT has received concrete form in what we term the *infrastructure*. Since 1997, the start of the first e-business phase, we have been busy bringing about this fusion. The following quote illustrates how infrastructure and business applications merge. The head IT architect must ensure that the infrastructure stimulates the development of business applications. Thus the infrastructure must itself already possess certain basic business functionalities.

OUR INFRASTRUCTURE MUST GIVE WINGS TO OUR BUSINESS

"The primary work of the chief architect is to design and evolve the IT infrastructure so that it will expand the range of future possibilities for the business, not define specific business outcomes. The infrastructure should provide not just today's technical services, such as networking, databases and desktop operating systems, but an increasing range of business-level services, such as workflow, portfolio management, scheduling, and specific business components or objects."

Source: "Foundation Report 109. New IS Leaders," CSC, 1997. *www.cscresearchservices.com/foundation/library/109/RP03.asp*

Making full use of strategic e-business opportunities is undoubtedly an important way to increase the value of IT. We can employ our inventiveness, our organizational structure, and the design of our infrastructure to steer ourselves in that direction. However, this remains entirely in line with the "old school" as long as we are not deliberately following this course by evaluating the business process-related economic performance of IT and keeping a lookout for all the risks along the way.

WHERE ARE WE IN TERMS OF THE MICRO- AND MACRO-ECONOMICS OF E-BUSINESS?

Now that we have explored e-business, if only at the conceptual level, the next question to be addressed concerns the extent to which we are making headway in a micro- and macro-economic sense, which is a meaningful question in the context of IT governance. The following five observations provide a brief impression of the development of e-business:

1. Cisco and Dell take the lead and, according to them, are miles ahead of all other organizations.
2. Thanks to e-business, the U.S. standard of living will enjoy spectacular increases in coming years.
3. Europe does not have its economic house in proper order.
4. In addition to the productivity of IT, difficult issues involve profitability, individual performance assisted by information systems, project difficulties, and complexity.
5. Europe cannot come close to sharing in the e-business success of the United States; the ground to be made up here is very large.

Dell and Cisco Take the Cake

In answer to questions about the maturity of e-business, Kevin Rollins and John Chambers from Dell and Cisco, respectively, issued the following statements in May 2003:

> *Dell President Kevin B. Rollins calculates that his company, the leader in Web-powered business, is merely halfway to using the*

Net's potential. And the rest of the pack? Rollins estimates that they're barely a fifth of the way.

Cisco Systems CEO John T. Chambers says that productivity payoffs accelerate fully four to six years after installing new systems.... "We're one of the few companies that is beyond year three of the process."[...] As the U.S. progresses toward e-business, productivity will rise from the current 1 percent to 3 percent annually, to as high as 5 percent—potentially doubling the U.S. standard of living within 14 years.[5]

U.S. Standard of Living Is Going Up

Dell, like Cisco, is roughly halfway to making full use of the Internet, whereas the pack of other businesses is, at most, 20 percent of the way there. The result of the influence of e-business on U.S. productivity will be a growth rate of 5 percent a year (up from 1 to 3 percent, the norm at present). The living standard in the United States will double within 14 years.[6]

Europe Does Not Have Its Statistical House in Order

Top European business operators express themselves much less frequently in the way John Chambers did; Europe is far behind in measuring productivity. The attention to macro- and micro-statistics in the area of IT comes, not surprisingly, from the United States, where IT is presently best developed. Eric Bartelsman, director of the Economic and Social Institute at the Free University in Amsterdam, expressed his admiration in *Het Financieele Dagblad*:

> *It is astonishing what is done [in the United States] in terms of productivity research. I think that the Fed is, in any case, better at signaling how things actually stand with the economy. Production processes, labor markets, goods and transportation streams, price developments—at the Fed, there is knowledge of such things, right down to the smallest details. Both statistically and analytically, they have a grip on the growth potential of the economy. In contrast, I have the impression that the European Central Bank, insofar as applications are concerned, is still using theories from 10 or 20 years ago.*[7]

The Information Paradox: The Troublemakers

The remarks by Cisco's John Chambers discussed in the previous section about the growth of the U.S. standard of living as a result of e-business are directly related to the macro-economic productivity of IT. Nobel Prize winner Robert Solow had already raised this issue in 1987 when he observed that we encounter computers everywhere today except in productivity statistics. This "productivity paradox," which severely tarnished the image of IT, has occupied the minds of many thinkers over the past 15 years.

The productivity paradox is, however, only one of the controversial issues that arise when we consider IT. There are (at least) four others worth mentioning, and they are all directly relevant to the value that IT generates for businesses: profitability, individual performance, the problems created by expensive, time-driven IT projects, and the complexity that the integration of IT brings along with it. John Thorp, head of the Center for Strategic Leadership at Fujitsu Consulting, dedicates five chapters in his book *The Information Paradox: Realizing the Business Benefits of Information Technology*[8] to these concerns:

1. The impact of IT on the economy: the productivity issue
2. The impact of IT on the business: the profitability issue
3. The impact of IT on knowledge workers: the individual performance issue
4. IT projects: the delivery issue
5. Management blind spots: four critical dimensions of complexity (linkage, reach, people, time)

The managerial blind spots mentioned in the last point are, according to Thorp, directly related to the complexity that revolves around cohesion (linkage), significance (reach), personnel (the people who ultimately must deal with all this), and time (which does not always work in our favor). This combination of factors constitutes the core of the challenges confronting managers.

Recent years have brought many developments directly in line with Thorp's list of problems, providing more than sufficient inducement to be mistrustful and defeatist about the role of IT. Consider the

BLIND SPOTS CAUSED BY "COMPLEXITY"

The notion of complexity used by Thorp in this study conforms well with the views of such writers as John L. Casti, professor at the Santa Fe Institute. In his book *Complexification: Explaining a Paradoxical World through the Science of Surprise,*[9] Casti studies complex systems and the manner in which they induce surprising behavior. According to him, complex systems do not have any central management; they just consist of a large number of components that communicate with each other. Moreover, a complex system possesses many feedback loops. The most important point, however, is that a complex system is more than the sum of its parts. Thus all types of unexpected events occur, and the system is therefore unpredictable. We are then not surprised that John Thorp in *The Information Paradox* thoroughly explores the "blind spots" of management: cohesion, scope, people, and time. An excellent, readable introduction to the subject of complexity is provided by Flückinger and Rauterberg in "Komplexität und Messung von Komplexität."[a]

[a] M. Flückiger and M. Rauterberg, "Komplexität und Messung von Komplexität," 1995, *www.ipo.tue.nl/homepages/m rauterb/ publications/COMPLEXITY95paper.pdf.* This document can be accessed through Professor Mathias Rauterberg's pages on the website of the Technical University of Eindhoven.

CHAOS reports of the Standish Group, the return on investment calculations of Paul Strassmann, the deflation of the Internet bubble after March 2000, the related IT and telecom dips, and the scandalous bankruptcies of such companies as the e-business giant Enron and the Internet backbone company WorldCom (currently MCI).

IT Pushes Production Up but Europe Lags Far Behind

When we say that IT increases production and Europe lags behind, we are talking in terms of various micro and macro e-business factors If we focus on the macro factors, we see that we need to release our skepticism about the total factor productivity of IT, i.e., the productivity paradox, even if Europe remains something of a problem child. (Note: This macro indicator is not production divided by employment—in other words, labor productivity—but production divided by all inputs and therefore including machines and computers.) In April 2003, *Het Financieele Dagblad* published an article that managed to cut through this IT-versus-productivity knot. Four internationally renowned Dutch economists (Bart van Ark of the University of Groningen, Eric Bartelsman of the Free University of Amsterdam, Arnoud Boot of the University of Amsterdam, and Lans Bovenberg of the University of Tilburg) unanimously agreed that, according to recent statistics, IT is now beginning to produce real effects, at least in the United States if not yet in Europe. Van Ark says that "The productivity effect of IT in the United States can no longer be denied. Europe has fallen behind in terms of intensity, and this distance cannot be made up just like that. The United States has a larger IT sector and a higher investment level."

Bartelsman adds to that: "There are analyses showing that everything runs more efficiently: providing personnel, leasing office space and hotel rooms, using means of transport, in short, everything in which capacity utilization is important. This all leads to increased growth in productivity. And these applications are still in their infancy on this continent [Europe]."[10]

E-BUSINESS AND THE SHIFT FROM DECREE TO DIALOGUE

After we faced the threat that IT was uncontrollable, we concluded that a need exists for constant dialogue between business and IT. In reality, this threat did not involve e-business as we now know it, but rather the e-commerce hype to which IBM responded in 1997 with the term *e-business*. This phrase quickly became common currency. The e-commerce hype has quieted down, which is not to deny that sales of items over the Internet are growing steadily. In the United States, these sales already represent a few percent of total retail spending.

As previously mentioned, the first e-business applications were preceded and inspired by the vision of Business Process Reengineering (BPR). In contrast to Nicholas Carr's observations (discussed previously in the IT Is Infrastructure and E-Business section), the BPR movement saw IT as the catalyzer in the process of gaining competitive advantage. All business processes had therefore to be revised. In *Reengineering the Corporation: A Manifesto for Business Revolution*, Michael Hammer and James Champy brandished the following slogan: "Forget what you know about how business should work... most of it is wrong."[11]

However, along with all the good intentions to produce an enormous effect on businesses by revising business processes and introducing IT, the BPR movement has demonstrated its neglect of the human dimension. In daily practice, a life-size gap opens up between the simple BPR philosophy and its application and consequences in concrete organizational environments. Time and again, we have experienced changes that, although well focused, phased in, prepared, supported, communicated, and lived through, are simply too much for the employees, who ultimately must do the work. Without good dialogue and a common understanding of what needs to be done, we get nowhere.

NO MORE IT THAT SOWS SEEDS OF CONFUSION

"Corporations learned in the early days of e-business that costly new systems by themselves accomplish little. They can sow confusion and resentment among employees who figure they did just fine the old way."

Source: T.J. Mullanney, et al., "The E-biz Surprise," *Business Week*, 2003.

MANAGEMENT PLATITUDES
ARE INEFFECTIVE

"So often nothing fundamental changes as executives mouth platitudes and make big announcements while everyone else lets them have their fun and carries on exactly as before."

Source: S. Overell, "The Change Monster: Managers Need Superhuman Determination to Make Change Programmes Succeed," *Financial Times*, 2001. *www.bcg.com/change_monster/ change_reviews_ft.asp*

In addition to the immense issues involving IT-related programs for change, it was becoming clear in 1997 that e-business was stirring up the sense of freedom that PC usage had originally aroused. Business would decide and IT provide; we would finally be free of tech-heads. Of course, we had not progressed so far.

In *CIO*, Waverly Deutsch of Forrester Research was already sounding the alarm, based on a new research report: "The Technology Democracy."[12] She laid the foundation for the dialogue principle that Forrester still preaches, albeit in a more refined form; Forrester now identifies the willingness to dialogue as the fundamental attitude for successful implementation of IT.

THE IT DEMOCRACY

Around 1997, business began to take possession of IT. This brought a straightforward competence and management crisis to a head. Deutsch tells the tale of a director who had a website built for online banking, thus engaging in e-commerce, a hip activity at the time. However, the amazing interface and functionality were not the reasons this bank made headlines, which was because client data were stolen. The outraged CEO called in his CIO and fired him on the spot. This CIO had not even known about the website! CIOs had lost control of information and IT around 1997. In the second half of the

1990s, IT began to be a part of every product and service, and by means of the Internet and Intranet, employees, clients, and business partners began to interact directly with business processes. All at once, IT was much more than the automation of back-office processes or a collection of databases.

Thus the time had come to put our IT house in order, specifically in the form of an IT democracy. This was a way of bringing IT innovation and business risks into balance. In an IT democracy, the IT ministry would offer IT to citizens so that new opportunities could be readily grasped and business problems resolved as well. Additionally, the governance role was to shift from one involving management and the exercise of power to one concerned with facilitation. Of course the CIO and his or her employees could not change a totalitarian IT regime to an IT democracy on their own; the business had to be ready to bear risks, and everyone was required to deepen their IT skills. An effort to professionalize would be inextricably involved.

The CEO and the CIO were supposed to be partners in the new governance model. Together, they would issue laws, watch over the national, overarching interests, and undertake "public works" (infrastructure and services) to improve the general welfare. In brief, a mini-business/IT government would be put into place that was concerned with such preconditions as infrastructure, security, responsibilities, and protection of interests. Otherwise the business citizens would be left to their own devices. Hence a sort of "withdrawing government" was constituted.

In the new order, a central role was also set aside for the IT community college. Deutsch advised us to quickly ensure a few spectacular successes, as the new model had to prove itself as quickly as possible. Once this happened, managers would be breaking down the door with requests and deep pockets full of funding from their own internal budgets.

The IT democracy needed to rescue the CIO and his or her people; they had been running to catch up with the accomplished IT facts with which business divisions were increasingly confronting them and for which they would be held responsible. The IT democracy was also going to pull down the pedestal on which ITers had stood; balanced dialogue was supposed to replace the decree as the mode of communication. Enlightened IT despots would become collaborating service providers, taking, in effect, a full step backward. If the democratic CIO and his or her people could handle things properly, they would be justly celebrated in the new order as true heroes.

If we evaluate this concept on the basis of what we now know, we cannot help but admit it was far too simplistic. Like the BPR movement, the vision that each business division would advance by leaps and bounds thanks to IT was extremely persuasive. Evidently the thought was that the common understanding that IT would lead to better business performance would reinforce the relationship between business and IT. In such an enthusiastic environment, the value that IT has for business processes is naturally taken for granted. With further insight, however, the path to dialogue and business success based on IT proved to be much more difficult. However, the first important step along the way to a well-oiled system of IT management—the awareness that a constructive dialogue between business was necessary—had been taken.

NOT DIALOGUE BUT BABBLE

In 1997, it was already clear that the role of the CIO would change from the undisputed king of information and IT to the person responsible for infrastructure and service provision, not because IT had become subordinate to business but because of the integration of the two. The traditional leading role of the CIO was transformed into one of sounding board, facilitator, inspirer, and empowerer, even though the CIO would not have any real power. This image fits the manner in which Peter Slator, CIO of Unilever, describes his work:

> *My job involves three principal tasks. The first is infrastructure management, ensuring that all hardware is working. Computers, data communication networks. That sort of thing. 50 to 60 percent of the total ICT budget, approximately 1 percent of sales [totaling $49 billion in 2002], goes into this. The second task is application management, managing the software that provides business information. The third is the administration of the information itself.[13]*

The responsibility became shared, and business interests became dominant, a state of affairs that Forrester labels "business ownership." In 2003, this was also splendidly demonstrated by Peter Slator, when he was asked about strategy: "We do not have a separate ICT strategy. There is only one strategy and that is the way to growth [fewer brands, higher margins]. Every ICT project must support the primary process and is tested against the business strategy."[14]

From 1997 onward, the business undoubtedly became the leading factor in relationship to IT, but initially without knowing where it had to lead to, and how. Viewed in hindsight, a heap of good intentions was around in 1997, but many of them were only sketchy ideas. By proclaiming IT democracy, the CIO instantly became the herder of a flock of enthusiastic e-business sheep running in all directions. The position of CIO had perhaps become more challenging but was actually hopeless. CIO = "Career Is Over" was the painful joke made at that time. The CIO, along with his or her staff, had to function in a business environment in transition.

At a minimum, there was a perception that business was undergoing change, and this perception resulted in the inevitable jitters. Clearer goals or altered processes were lacking. In effect, businesses were in a state of complete tactical and strategic disorder. In mid-1999, Lou Gerstner, Jr., the former CEO at IBM, compared the prevailing notion that large companies were about to be overtaken by e-business start-ups and spin-offs with "the fireflies coming before a storm."[15]

Because the upheaval was due to promises based on IT, all eyes were fixed on IT professionals. They could, of course, only really be helpful in perfect dialogue with the business, but no evidence of such a dialogue had yet been seen. Greater mutual communication had occurred in the last years of the past century, but this was mostly accompanied by greatermisunderstanding. Thus almost nothing changed in practice: Business remained business and IT remained IT. Excessive amounts of money were certainly invested in new IT solutions, which were constantly being revised. This investment was mostly made only to remain ahead of the competition, which appeared to be lying in ambush everywhere. However, the blessings of IT failed to materialize, or did so only in forms hopelessly short of predictions.Only when the dust of the dotcom hype and the New Economy had somewhat settled did it become clear that a limited number of conceptual e-business elements had been affected—those in the areas of standardization and integration, as well as the domains of customer, market, and supplier orientation. On the basis of this understanding, we entered a second phase of e-business at the end of 2000.

LIMITS TO THE BABBLE, BUT ALMOST ANY GOVERNANCE STRUCTURE WILL DO

Democracy in the old city state of Athens may have been clear and transparent, but today democracy is no longer simple, in either the political or the corporate world. This is particularly the consequence of polymorphous complexity (the final item in Thorp's list of problems explored previously in the "Where Are We in Terms of the Micro- and Macro-Economy of E-Business?" section of this chapter), in response to which institutions and processes have been established. We try to direct the democratic freedoms into the appropriate channels, and we also try to weigh and reinforce particular interests as effectively and efficiently as possible. In other words, in the context of dialogue, limits that need to be placed on the babble produced in a poorly governed democracy; institutions and processes are employed to do this.

How this actually occurs in any practice involving IT–an interesting question in the context of the quest for a well-oiled IT management mechanism—is the subject of a research project that MIT Professor Peter Weill has been conducting over the past few years in collaboration with Marianne Broadbent, who heads Gartner's Executive Program, in which many CIOs worldwide participate. The latest consolidated research results were presented by Weill in April 2003.[16] Using the slogan "Don't just lead, govern!", which Weill also used to title an article published in *Sloan Management Review*, Weill and Broadbent have found that solitary leadership is insufficient for the management of IT. (The subject of leadership will be discussed in Chapter 7.)

The new markers "B (business) + IT", "B" and "IT" alone, together with the percentage scores, and the gray patterns (see Exhibit 3.2) which attracted the notice of Weill and Broadbent, clearly show that—taking account of the combination of input and decision—a well-integrated dialogue between business and IT dominates on all fronts. Of course, in the case of IT architecture and infrastructure, the burden of the decisions lies with the IT organization; even so, good listening occurs ahead of time, as is revealed by the scores. The BU or process people (feudal) have primacy only once: concerning the requirements decision for the business applications. This is conceivable in some cases, and the score then only amounts to a meager 18 percent.

Weill and Broadbent also present a best practice of governance mechanisms within State Street Corporation. State Street is a world leader in financial services providing investment management, investment services, trading and research to investment managers, corporations, pension funds, mutual funds, and individuals. Looking at the best-practice "governance mechanisms" of State Street Corporation (see Exhibit 3.3), we arrive at the conclusion that at most, Weill and Broadbent's project emphasizes that dialogue linked to efficient decision making is the coming trend. When one focuses more deeply on the agencies involved with the governance mechanisms, their places on the score card, and the notions we have expressed about the regime types in Exhibit 3.4, the conclusion that it is all about organizing the dialogue is inevitable. Dialogue and efficient decision making can be organized in many ways. Because of IT's claim to value, a methodical, economy-based focus appears to be more fruitful than an attempt to zoom in on the alleged archetypes of IT governance (see Exhibit 3.5).

Together with Bobby Cameron, principal analyst at Forrester Research, we cannot avoid the impression that "almost any governance structure will do."[17] The "political" governance archetypes of Weill and

EXHIBIT 3.2 Scores for the Total Population

	IT Principles		IT Infrastructural Strategies		IT Architecture		Business Application Needs		IT Investments	
	Input	Decision	Input	Decision	Input	Decision	Input	Decision	Input	Decision
Business Monarchy B+IT		27					12			30
IT Monarchy IT		18		59	20	73				
Feudal B								18		
Federal B+IT	83	14	59		46		81	30	93	27
Diopoly B+IT	15	36	30	23	34	15	17	27		30

Source: Peter Weill and Richard Woodham, "Don't Just Lead, Govern: Implementing Effective IT Governance," April 2002, MIT Sloan Working Paper no. 4237-020. *http://ssrn.com/abstract=317319*

	IT Principles		IT Infrastructural Strategies		IT Architecture		Business Application Needs		IT Investments	
	Input	Decision	Input	Decision	Input	Decision	Input	Decision	Input	Decision
Business Monarchy		ITEC								ITEC CIO
IT Monarchy				CIO IT Leaders	IT Leaders Arch. Office	CIO IT Leaders				
Feudal										
Federal	ITEC CIO IT Leaders IT Org.		IT Leaders IT Org. Arch. Office						CIO Budgets SLA Act. Tracking	
Diopoly							ITEC Budgets	Business Leaders Vertical IT Units IT Leaders		

Governance Mechanisms at the State Corporation:

ITEC	*IT Executive Committee*	SLA	*Service Delivery Agreements & Chargeback*
Arch. Office	*Office of Architecture*	IT Org.	*Federated Organization (vertical & horizontal IT units)*
CIO	*CIO Staff*	Act. Tracking	*Activity Tracking System*
IT Leaders	*IT Leadership Group*	Budgets	*Enterprise-wide IT Budget Management*

EXHIBIT 3.3 Weill and Broadbent's IT Governance Scorecard as Completed by the State Street Corporation
Source: Peter Weill and Richard Woodham, "Don't Just Lead, Govern: Implementing Effective IT Governance," April 2002, MIT Sloan Working Paper no. 4237-020. *http://ssrn.com/abstract=317319*

Broadbent are not only unsatisfactorily described and applied, they are also now superseded categories that perhaps had a function when IT was still under despotic rule. However, development in the direction of full-cycle governance is dominant. The characteristics of this are a meaningful dialogue between business and IT, as well as an efficient decision-making process. On closer inspection, this is also precisely what the research of Weill and Broadbent actually reveals.

EXHIBIT 3.4   Governance Mechanisms Analyzed

	Membership	Role	Pros	Cons
IT Executive Committee	Senior Managers and Directors	To identify key business processes and strategies to be supported by IT; perform risk/investment analysis of proposed large IT projects; measure IT value; review IT sourcing, security and architecture policies	CIOs don't have to guess what the CEO wants from IT	Other C-level execs can be bored to death by technology details
IT Council	IT and/or Business Unit Executives	To monitor and evaluate ongoing IT projects for risk/value/cost; identify shared service opportunities across business units and IT; evaluate and approve IT architecture	Enables the enterprise to share best practices and avoid duplication of effort	May suffer from a lack of strategic direction
Architecture Committee	CIO and Direct Reports	To create and enforce standards for IT across the enterprise and to assess exceptions to the rule	Saves money	Too much standardization may quash innovation
Business Process Teams	Business People and IT	To improve process speed and quality and reduce cost	Focuses IT directly on business unit needs	May lack enterprise focus; difficult to coordinate efforts enterprise wide

Source: "Governance Mechanisms: What's Right for Your Needs," *CIO,* 2002.
64.28.79.79/archieve/091502/powers_sidebar_2_content.html

Pros and Cons of Governance Mechanisms

Instead of archetypes, it would be better if we concentrated on concrete issues, for example, the pros and cons of the governance mechanisms. We may do this if we can at least first assume that, for various situations, an appropriate procedure underlies government practice. In the autumn of 2002, *CIO* presented a concise outline, based on information derived from Peter Weill's CISR (Center for Information Systems Research, MIT Sloan School of Management), the IT Governance Institute, and its own articles (see Exhibit 3.4).

EXHIBIT 3.5   Weill and Broadbent's "Governance Archetypes"

Governance	Description	The Dialogue: B and/or IT
Business Monarchy	*A group of or individual business executives (e.g., CxOs) Includes committees consisting of senior business managers(may include the CIO) Excludes IT executives acting independently*	B + IT
IT Monarchy	*Individuals or groups of IT executives*	IT
Feudal	*Business unit leaders, key process owners or their delegates*	B
Federal	*Central government and "satellites" work together: executives at the main level and at least one business group (e.g., CxOs and BU managers)[a]*	B + IT
Duopoly	*IT executives and one other group (e.g., CxOs or BU managers)*	B + IT

[a] It appears from this description that IT is not represented, which of course cannot be the case when the central government and the "satellites" work together around IT. The example of State Street (Exhibit 3.3) illustrates this point. There we clearly find a business-IT dialogue on the federal level. In the decision domains of IT principles and IT infrastructural strategies, the federal input even appears to be predominantly an IT affair.

Source: Peter Weill and Richard Woodham, "Don't Just Lead, Govern: Implementing Effective IT Governance," April 2002, MIT Sloan Working Paper no. 4237-020. *http://ssrn.com/abstract=317319*

Governance of IT Projects

Interesting research data regarding the management of IT projects comes from a CIO 100 study.[18] Among the factors investigated were decision making, monetary source, and responsibility. For decision making, a distinction is made between the Executive Council (EC) and the IT Steering Committee (ISC). Sitting on the EC are board members from the organization, the CIO, and business unit managers. On the ISC are managers from the IT domain and business units. The research shows that the responsibility for IT projects is a joint effort of business and IT, with the money provided by the business in most cases. The results can be summarized as follows:

- **Decision making.** In half of the cases concerning both architecture and infrastructure (respectively 55 and 47 percent), it is the

ISC that makes the decisions. In a third of the cases, decisions are made by the EC. In a limited number of instances, decisions are made by an ad hoc group. For new projects, the situation is reversed. Half of the decisions involve the EC, and 40 percent involve the ISC. The remaining 10 percent of new cases are decided by an ad hoc group.

- **Money.** The money for projects comes from business in two-thirds of cases and from IT in the other third.
- **Responsibility.** In three-fourths of the cases, business and IT are jointly responsible for the projects. The responsibility for the remaining quarter is shared equally.

EXT: DEATH OF IT

In 1997, "The Technology Democracy" still tacitly assumed that the application of IT based on right-mindedness, good will, and belief in progress would yield great profits for business; at the beginning of 2000, Forrester Research announced through its spokesperson Bobby Cameron the death of IT. Of course this was done to grab headlines—but also to give warning that many businesses were changing too late and too slowly.

In Forrester's vision, vertically integrated businesses would fall apart at an accelerated rate thanks to the e-business possibilities that IT offers. The era of collaborative commerce in value-chain-spanning network organizations was upon us. Although a new age was theoretically emerging, IT and business continued to interact in the traditional entrenched manner, or so it seemed to Forrester. Interactions were being carried on traditionally, even though flexibility, inspiring dialogue, and renewal were required.

In "The Death of IT," Cameron proposed a rigorous outsourcing of as much IT as possible, in brief, converting to "exT."[19] Throughout 1999, this final step was on the verge of being taken. Such was the state of affairs revealed by the relevant Forrester reports included in "The Death of IT":

- The exSourcing Imperative (December 1999)
- Global eBusiness Requires eT (December 1999)
- Outsourcing's Future (April 1999)
- Driving IT's Externalization (January1999)

Dismantling a company's IT and involving third parties is, of course, a significant decompositional step for vertically integrated businesses. At the beginning of 2000, it was felt that in the e-business era, we must sooner or later agree to such disassembly, at least if we do not wish to become the last surviving dinosaur in the new world of agile enterprises focused on their key competences. All other functions are farmed out.

This would apply especially to IT, because internal IT organizations cannot deal with the new dynamic e-business needs. In other words, e-business is "the nail in IT's coffin." The additional need exists to determine precisely which IT services we are getting rid of through outsourcing. The entire exT movement should take place around business processes. Exhibit 3.6 shows the role that the process teams inside the business should, according to Forrester, play in relation to the exT service providers, whose systems provide vital e-business-oriented IT services.

In January 2000, in the midst of the New Economy, Forrester ventured to make the following forecast for the sector (see Exhibit 3.7). In a variant of the well-known high-low matrix, Forrester plotted the types of businesses on the sales side and on the purchasing side that

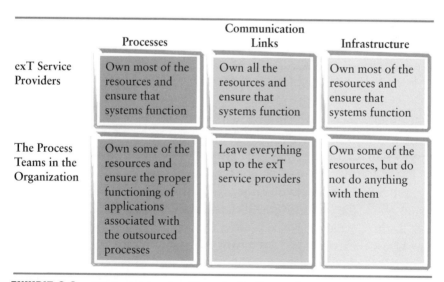

	Processes	Communication Links	Infrastructure
exT Service Providers	Own most of the resources and ensure that systems function	Own all the resources and ensure that systems function	Own most of the resources and ensure that systems function
The Process Teams in the Organization	Own some of the resources and ensure the proper functioning of applications associated with the outsourced processes	Leave everything up to the exT service providers	Own some of the resources, but do not do anything with them

EXHIBIT 3.6   IT Activities that Remain for Internal Process Teams When Service Providers Are Involved
Source: Adapted from B. Cameron, R. Shevlin, and A. Hardisty, "The Death of IT," The Forrester Report 2000. *www.matrixres.com/matrix/website.nsf/Files/CRCMarket_1/$File/Death_IT_2000.pdf?Open*

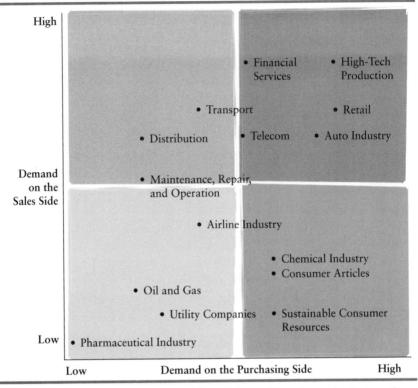

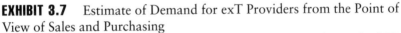

EXHIBIT 3.7   Estimate of Demand for exT Providers from the Point of View of Sales and Purchasing
Source: Adapted from B. Cameron, R. Shevlin, and A. Hardisty, "The Death of IT," The Forrester Report 2000. *www.matrixres.com/matrix/website.nsf/Files/CRCMarket_1/ $File/Death_IT_2000.pdf?Open*

will rapidly involve themselves with exT providers, along with those who will not. In this way, the demand for and supply of e-market-places will also increase. Large corporations will, after all, organize exT in a sector- and market- oriented manner.

Obviously, the extent of the effort organizations had to make to bring about the exT movement was an issue. For a start, as Cameron states, the CIO is supposed to devise a concrete "exT" plan for all of the IT in the company. By means of outsourcing, the value of IT immediately becomes measurable, and we can thus vary the dynamic of new management and supply structures. The CEO and the CIO are then meant to propagate and monitor the exT program jointly. Activity-Based Costing—the concrete calculation of both the direct and indirect costs of business activities—will fulfill a central function in the new situation.

In "The Death of IT," Cameron expresses the consequences for the organizational structure in a noteworthy and provoking manner. The entire exT exercise will make the role of the CIO superfluous. CIOs can pass the rest of their days as business managers, or perhaps as either CEOs or COOs. The most important opposition to exT, Cameron suggests, will thus probably come from the CIO party. Three years later, in April 2003, Cameron qualified his views: "it will still take a number of years before things actually get so far." For that matter, Paul Strassmann, ex-CIO of Xerox, Kraft Foods, and NASA, argues that the CIO position will not, in fact, disappear and even argues for an upgrading of the function (see later section on "The Strategic Role of the CIO" and Exhibit 3.8).

Forrester adds that, given the trend toward outsourcing and the emphasis on business processes, the CIO can probably also provide

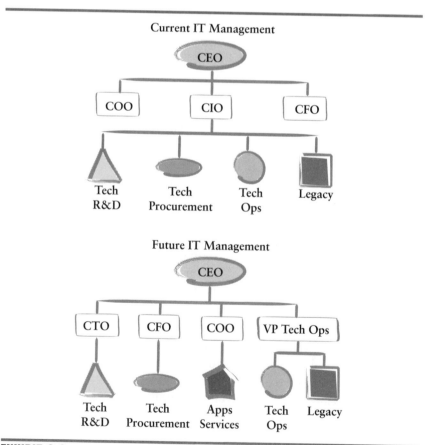

EXHIBIT 3.8   Disappearance of the CIO

good service in a new function involving these factors. The idea was not as crazy as it may have seemed at first: practices were already being transformed. Two years after "The Death of IT," the trendsetting German newspaper *Wirtschaftswoche* published a report that referred to the process-based function of the CIO (which is in complete harmony with the view sketched in Exhibit 3.6):

> *The main focus of the CIO's duties and responsibilities shifts in the direction of operations and processes. The individuals responsible for IT will identify and manage future, company-wide business procedures.... Perhaps the Chief Information Officer will even undergo a change of title to Chief Process Officer.*[20]

KEEP IT SIMPLE, STUPID!

The subject of IT governance demands solutions, in the form of practical tips and hints, especially at times like now when spending money without a business reason is sinful. Forrester Research understands this point very well. Consequently, the findings of this research and consulting organization have a refreshing usefulness. As mentioned, Forrester has absolutely no further concern about governance structures: monetary-based measurement and control loops are simply applied. Economic valuation is the lingua franca of all of humanity, and business and IT should just use this same language.

Forrester takes the position that nearly every governance structure is sufficient, provided that business decisions are actually made and business people implicated. Given the current lack of maturity in most businesses, Forrester makes the case for starting with good cost accounting by means of Activity-Based Costing. After having named the activities, Forrester then brings up the issue of the value that IT has for business processes. This question—"What will that yield?"—effectively puts the ball in the business's court and therefore compels a dialogue to begin. This is perhaps still the greatest gain. Isolated IT is, after all, a malevolent presence in our current e-business environment. Early on, it was already apparent on various fronts that the new ITers must never be allowed to operate on their own. The "New IS Leaders" report by the Computer Science Corporation (CSC), one of the largest

IT service companies, said so at the time: "Chief architects may have to spend much of their time with business executives, deriving the elements of persistent value to the business from discussions about future directions and strategies."[21]

Professionalism and Simplicity

When we list the analyses and recommendations made since January 2000 by Forrester Research concerning IT governance and tie up a few loose ends, we then see a consistent picture that has been built up in recent years, one that remains consistent with "The Technology Democracy" from 1997—only put in a more concrete form.

The first thing that strikes us is the central importance of three requirements: an unceasing strategic organizational focus, money, and dialogue based on trust. These three constitute the lubricant, as it were, of each organizational transaction.

Money is important as the objective basis of value that clarifies the responsibility for the financial result, as well as its accountability. Of course, financial value cannot stand alone. Such value demands trust in the demonstrable expertise and integrity of the financial personnel and of the business and IT staff in particular. In this way, the combination of money and trust presupposes and stimulates an optimal complementary understanding: a good dialogue. In the end, this plan-do-check-act dynamic is synonymous with professionalism (see Exhibit 3.9). This is what Forrester would like to express. Consequently, the governance of information and IT boils down to human interaction and subject matter geared to the performances of the business processes and tested on their bases. Ideally, this is further based on precise cost accounting (by means of Activity-Based Costing) and the determination of exact net value (through Economic Value Added). Chapter 5 will discuss this point further.

The consequence for IT is that it ultimately proves to be too expensive and complex to keep all IT in the organization, as had previously been done. Moreover, this impedes the value-chain innovation represented by e-business. Vertically integrated organizations and their IT must therefore be broken up. In terms of both organization and IT, each enterprise must be structured in the clearest and simplest

EXHIBIT 3.9   Continuous Dialogue between Business and IT Takes Place on the Basis of Trust in Expertise and Integrity and Has Optimal Business Processes as Its Goals

Do/Act	Organizational Activities	Concrete Business Operations
Check	Responsibility for financial results and the accountability of them	By means of accurate cost accounting and determination of actual net value
Plan	Strategic organizational focus	Competences of value chains → business processes involved in value chains → (out)sourcing of business processes and IT (exT)

manner possible. Because we need to understand businesses as activities within interorganizational value chains, we must latch onto business processes that, in their turn, must maintain a logical association with our key competences. Illustrative of this is the answer given by Unilever CIO Peter Slator to the question of how Unilever's IT strategy could actually be viewed in the light of its explicit efforts to strive for simplification. Slator answered that Unilever did not have a separate IT strategy and that each project provides support for the primary process and is tested on the basis of the business strategy (see "Not Dialogue but Babble" earlier in this chapter).

E-business-oriented IT has the potential of allowing all (inter)organizational transactions to occur in the most efficient and effective manner possible while keeping things simple. Then we must of course employ IT in the clearest and simplest way possible as well. First, the business must be responsible for the results of all IT investments; after all, we are dealing with private enterprise. About half of all businesses, according to Forrester and others, express IT success in terms of such tactical categories as accessibility and response time. Consequently, far too little added business value is recorded. Second, we must make sure that IT contracts provide good material, financial, and time-related benefits.

Because internal IT organizations are not, in Forrester's view, capable of continuously remaining up to date with the changing needs the development of e-business requires, it would therefore be best if we located IT outside the process organization (Exhibit 3.6). This immediately produces the necessary responsibility for the financial results, along with their accountability.

In sum, the following realistic view of the governance of information and IT may be termed the top five:

1. Optimum business performance is always the first priority.
2. For this purpose, business processes must be adorned and performed clearly and simply.
3. With e-business-oriented IT, we build efficient and effective value chains consisting of interorganizational business processes.
4. The business must be responsible for the results of all IT investments.
5. Money makes the world go round.

In addition to a good dialogue between business and IT personnel, trust in each other's expertise and integrity, as well as a persistent strategic and organizational focus, are necessary to establish an objective basis of value for IT. We can use Activity-Based Costing for this purpose, as it records the direct and indirect costs of business processes (see Chapter 5). The investment calculations that we then can make based on the five points just listed will reflect responsibility for the results. This complies with the requirements of professionalism and simplicity. In the final analysis, everything in business revolves around money. A financial sounding board, provided it involves focus, dialogue, and trust, makes unambiguous intervention possible. In this way, IT governance can be intricately interwoven into financial governance and budgetary rounds.

Existing governance structures and processes have the objective of facilitating dialogue and trust. Because they can vary enormously from organization to organization, it is advisable to grow into these practices in an effective way; just taking a shot at it can have a devastating effect on an organization. For this reason, Forrester takes the position that almost any governance structure will suffice. The trend, as we have seen in Peter Weill and Marianne Broadbent's research, is clearly toward maintaining a dialogue between business and IT, one that is furthermore linked to efficient decision making (see "Limits to the Babble, but Almost Any Governance Structure Will Do" earlier in this chapter). Comparisons with poorly defined types of political regimes disguise more than they reveal.

Instead of linking financial, substantive and organizational policy more transparently with collectively established responsibilities for results, fundamental, shared and strategic activities are too often left out of the business economy. In an environment concerned with profitability, this is unprofessional. No matter how difficult it may be to allocate certain "general costs," an effort to do so must be undertaken. A private company is, after all, not a playground for public works.

MONEY MAKES THE WORLD GO ROUND: RAPID ECONOMIC JUSTIFICATION AND TOTAL ECONOMIC IMPACT

The insights from Forrester Research and others are therefore a direct extension of the simple truth that everything revolves around money. However, this view must be acted meaningfully, keeping the goal of a collective, business process-oriented, economic valuation of IT in mind. Private entrepreneurs must not, in this respect, concern themselves with the technical content of IT. They must focus on the formulation of business opportunities and, at most, on the question of how IT can be exploited in a conceptual sense.

Business people and those responsible for IT must engage in an intensive dialogue that links IT and business in terms of measurable costs and benefits. As stated before, the question "what will that yield?" puts the ball in business's court—forcing it into a dialogue—and this question places the central concern on the value that IT actually generates for the various business processes. Too many businesses still list IT investments only as general cost items without indicating the actual yield.

Financial accountability must therefore be firmly related to business performance and must stimulate intensive contact between business and IT. Activity-Based Costing is therefore an excellent approach; this is what Forrester Research understands as "business-owned IT," an application of IT that is accountable from a business perspective. The combination of processes, costs, and benefits promotes meaningful dialogue between business and IT. Risks and prioritization complete the picture. By the addition of these last two considerations, we finally arrive at what we would call portfolio management, which is the subject of Chapter 4.

Two related methods of measuring IT value are the Rapid Economic Justification (REJ) framework from Microsoft and Total Economic Impact (TEI) from Giga Information Group (now a subsidiary of Forrester Research). A salient point is that Microsoft's REJ services are audited by Gartner or Giga.

On the cost side, Gartner is above all known for Total Cost of Ownership (TCO). This research and consulting agency currently supplements this perspective with Total Value of Opportunity (TVO). In addition to the costs of IT, its value and revenue have now become collective focal points in tools and frameworks, together with risk and appropriate financial metrics (ABC, EVA, and others). We encounter the same thing in REJ and TEI. The prioritization of investments is a logical consequence of this. This prioritization, together with such Balanced Scorecard categories as Critical Success Factors (CSFs) and Key Performance Indicators (KPIs), provides a good basis for IT portfolio management, the subject of Chapter 4.

Exhibit 3.10 presents a concrete comparison of REJ and TEI. Common to REJ and TEI are the categories of costs, benefits, and risks. TEI adds the element of flexibility. In both cases, the result is business value (or Total Economic Impact). REJ is clearly a step-by-step procedure, whereas the steps to follow in the TEI model remain implicit. TEI focuses on the meaning of the four elements that determine value: costs, benefits, risk, and flexibility. This means that both models complement each other well. The role of the Giga Information Group as the REJ auditor underlines this fact.

TEI adds the extra category of flexibility. Additionally, attention is paid to the possibility that IT solutions perhaps have latent advantages that could be of value at a later stage, such as the groupware facilities of a text-processing package. It is advisable to exclude any possible later advantages, in compliance with the well-known principles of prudent accounting, or to make separate scenarios for them. A certain form of flexibility that we call scalability would be easy to incorporate.

Chip Gliedman, who developed TEI at Giga Information Group, uses the following simple standard sentence to indicate all that is involved: "We are doing X to make Y better, as measured by Z,

	REJ (Microsoft) Rapid Economic Justification	TEI (Giga Information Group) Total Economic Impact
1 Business to Be Done	Select interested parties, their critical success factors, their strategy for realizing this and their performance indicators.	
2 Solutions	Come with solutions based on comparison of business processes with their desired results.	
3 Costs	Use modeling tools to optimize results.	The technology costs (TCO). The IT organization is responsible.
4 Benefits	Quantify the costs and benefits for the business.	We understand that "benefits" mean the concrete outcomes that the investments produce for the business. The business is responsible.
5 Flexibility		The unused options, financially valued.
6 Risk	Name the risks and quantify them; make sensitivity analyses to optimize the economic effect of the investment.	Uncertainty, such as that caused by assumptions. Strengthen the business case.
7 Financial Metrics	Record the effect of IT investment in financial terms such as marginal EPS (Earning Per Share) and EVA (Economic Value Added).	
8 Business Value	Objectified and determined in dialog between business and IT.	Objectified and determined in dialog between business and IT. The claim is that the resulting business value reflects the total economic impact (TEI).
Cases	www.microsoft.com/value	www.gigaweb.com/mktg/tei/default.asp

EXHIBIT 3.10   Concrete Comparison of REJ and TEI

which is worth $.”[22] You can use it as a memory aid. Also, keep the risk factors well in mind and, if necessary, be flexible.

The real work behind REJ, TEI, and comparable models consists of a divergent set of coherent measurement and control activities. At present, templates and software tools are being used more and more frequently to support these activities. (We will go further into this topic in Chapter 4, IT Portfolio Management). To sum up, all these exercises are meant to chart investments and their value for business

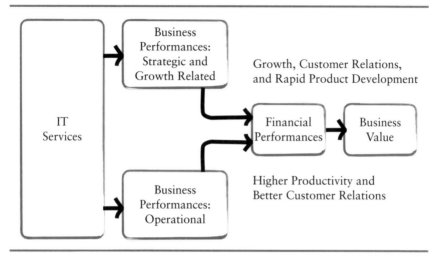

EXHIBIT 3.11   IT Generates Value for the Business along the Strategic and Operational Flank

processes and to follow their course on the basis of a constant dialogue among the stakeholders. The dialogue must be based on clear, collectively established performance indicators. Exhibit 3.11 illustrates how the business value of IT originates.

THE STRATEGIC ROLE OF THE CIO

In the previous sections, frequent mention has been made of the CIO, the official who has the most to do with information and IT. The CIO, as this individual is invariably titled in English-speaking countries and in many international corporations, plays a crucial role in IT management and frequently its structuring. This role is not always so simple. In the following discussion, we will examine the role of the CIO through the eyes of various leaders of thought in the field. Forrester argues, for example, that the function of the CIO should be completely eliminated, and Marianne Broadbent of Gartner has the same view. We begin with Paul Strassmann, who takes the opposite view.

Paul Strassmann and W. Brian Arthur

In today's economically unruly times, everything once again comes down to money. In March 2003 Paul Strassmann, a former CIO at Xerox, Kraft Foods, and NASA, member of the editorial board of *Information Economics Journal*, and author of *The Squandered Computer*,[23] among other works, made a case for giving the CIO more power, just as much as the CFO. This position contrasts sharply with the Forrester proposal (see the previous section, exT: The Death of IT) to eliminate the CIO. Strassmann additionally identifies a pre-eminent strategic task for American CIOs, who are the guardians of the United States' digital world supremacy.

Put the CIO on the Same Level as the CFO ...

Strassmann wants to see the next generation of CIOs elevated to the status of chief financial officers. "The primary job of a CIO is power politics," he said. "The game is not technology any more. From now on, it is a game about budget."

... This Is in Our National Interest

"The CIOs must start viewing themselves as general officers whose purpose is to maintain the overwhelming lead of the United States of America in the applications of [IT]," he concluded. "The legitimacy of the political power of strategic CIOs is therefore a matter of national importance, not exclusively a matter of personal career."

Source: M. Lisagor, "Paul Strassmann: Make CIO Equal to CFO," *Federal Computer Week*, 2003. *www.fcw.com/fcw/articles/2003/0317/web-cios-03-19-03.asp*

Such a remark may seem oddly nationalistic, but W. Brian Arthur, a professor at the Santa Fe Institute, supports Strassmann's opinion— probably unintentionally, which serves to strengthen this view:

> *This country's one and only economic driver for the next several decades rests solely in the hands of CIOs. That's the conclusion of economist W. Brian Arthur, Citibank professor at the Santa Fe Institute, who developed the modern theory of increasing returns....*
>
> *As industries "encounter" digital technologies, they are being fundamentally and organically transformed. Technology inexorably invades an industry's neurological process, connecting systems, processes and functions within and among companies. The technologies will carry on intelligent, ongoing conversations between themselves. The effect will be previously undreamed-of processes and functionality that will alter what companies do, fundamentally transforming their industries. Witness already the transformation of the pharmaceutical industry with the advent of genomics and combinatorial chemistry-breakthroughs that would have been impossible without IT.... "The transformation process I'm describing is inevitable—and it's well under way already in the military, banking, manufacturing and grocery retailing industries."[24]*

It remains to be seen whether this view will prevail or whether the function of the CIO will be eliminated in advance of or in the wake of persistent outsourcing, as a result of which the CIO may be transformed into a Chief Process Officer. The fact is that, at this time, the authority of the CIO, who is often "just" called the IT director in the Netherlands, appears to be determined regionally. Peter Slator, CIO of Unilever, had this to say in an interview for *Het Financieele Dagblad*:

> *The position of the CIO differs from region to region.... In the United States, the CIO is a high-profile manager who sits on the board of directors or reports to the financial person sitting on it. On the European continent, one finds the other end of the spectrum. The position of the CIO is there much less visibly powerful. At Unilever, the situation is a little in-between.[25]*

The CIO's position in the organization depends largely on the possibility of playing a strategic role. In the course of her practice, Marianne Broadbent of Gartner has formulated a clear opinion about the CIO's possible capacity to act in ways involving what she identifies as *strategic synchronization*. This notion is closely related to "alignment," a term that was resolutely discarded by Forrester at the end of 2001, and also with "agility," which is the ability to adapt to transitions in businesses.

Marianne Broadbent

Marianne Broadbent is the research director of Gartner's Executive Program. In this capacity, she regularly comes into contact with members of management teams. In the context of governance, she has paid special attention to strategy formulation and the role of the CIO.

Maintaining a neat strategic line is no longer necessary; rather, it is normal to be out of balance. We must continuously keep our feelers out and react quickly; we need to "sense and respond." Strategy has become an unceasing activity; every organization must continuously adjust to circumstances in order to coordinate its ambition with any situation that might arise. The business world is in constant motion, continuously undergoing technological, political, and social transformations. Whoever claims to be in step nowadays either sets the bar too low or invests too much in technology.

In each organization, there are only a few people who know how all the pieces of the puzzle fit together. They are the CEO, the COO, perhaps the CFO, and especially the CIO. Thus the CIO has a crucial role. For one thing, this official must ensure that the appropriate information is always present, to allow the subsequent wave of synchronization. In addition, he or she must ensure that the organization has cost-effective IT services available.

These IT services depend on the CIO's credibility. To realize them, each CIO must make the conditions that have to be met clear to his or her fellow board members before the rose-colored expectations of IT that they may possess can be fulfilled. The CIO therefore has a rather schizophrenic role to play, one involving a combination of guru and gas fitter, as it were. For this reason, many organizations now also have a CSO (Chief Strategy Officer) and a CTO (Chief Technical Officer). Of course, establishing these positions makes an extra demand on communication and coordination.

Some businesses, especially in the production field, have recently thrown the CIO function overboard, as Forrester Research has recommended, especially because they are only purchasers of IT. As a result, they have no one on the strategic level who is able to adjust the course of the business by contributing ideas on information provision in the broader sense; Marianne Broadbent feels that sooner or later they will come to regret this decision.[26]

Chris Verhoef

Broadbent's practical experience reveals the extent to which the position of CIO is a thankless one. We conclude this section by drawing attention to three ways by which the CIO will be better able to keep his or her position, but first we present an exhibit of Chris Verhoef, professor at the Free University of Amsterdam, one that succinctly demonstrates the awful nature of the CIO's job (see Exhibit 3.12) Instead of "Career Is Over," for Verhoef the acronym CIO means "Commander of Impossible Operations."

Three Critical Success Factors for IT Managers

The best ways to act in order to remove or reduce the practical problems that Broadbent and Verhoef identify are indicated in the report "Maximizing the Success of Chief Information Officers."[27] The

---

Imagine yourself responsible for:
- A multimillion dollar IT budget
- Millions of lines of code in production
- Hundreds of decisions on:
  - Proposals for new IT
  - Enhancements on existing IT
  - Implementing regulatory changes
- 75% of the IT effort not on your radar
- And you have no IT background

Then you must be the CIO—the Commander of Impossible Operations

---

EXHIBIT 3.12 Responsibilities of the CIO

report was written on the basis of a literature study, as well as insights provided by the CIOs of prominent organizations in the private sector and government.[28] The three critical success factors given in the report are as follows:

1. **Create the Conditions in which IT Managers Can Create Value.** The CIO and his or her people must be actively supported by the top level of the organization. If not, the impact of their efforts will be limited, despite the contribution they can provide to the realization of business goals. The upper level of the organization must promote a culture in which the CIO and his or her people can participate fully in each important decision, especially in terms of long-term planning. This is necessary to make maximum use of all IT goods, including the IT infrastructure. The infrastructure must put the business in a position to adopt new strategic directions. Furthermore, the entire organization must be convinced of the potential that IT has to create value. Commitment from top management is also essential for the concrete realization of this value. The importance of IT for the organization must be expressed at the highest level, as an example for the rest of management.

2. **IT Managers Have to Prove Themselves.** Of course, the CIO along with his or her people must, in turn, ensure that the active support from the top and the organization's trust in the value of IT is justified. They must adopt effective measures and solutions in order to bring critical projects to successful completion, to maintain good work relationships, and to appear as partners of both their customers and their subordinates. The performance criteria that apply to the CIO and his or her employees must be firmly linked to business goals. Because of the short history of this requirement, more attention must be paid to this link. This is crucial for the IT organization's ability to demonstrate its value.

3. **IT Managers Must Deliver.** The success of an IT organization depends on many variables, among them its structure, of course, as well as the manner in which the organization is managed and the manner in which work is done. IT personnel must always be employed in such a way that they are able to serve the interests of their customers in the best possible way. The IT organization can best be set up as a matrix, with the business lines following

the functional IT lines. Moreover, the skills in the IT organization must always be updated to the latest standards. For this purpose, external expertise must be continuously incorporated. Basic skills can best be fully obtained through the hiring of employees. The establishment and interpretation of the corresponding "human capital plans" are predominantly the task of the CIO. Furthermore, the CIO is responsible for all IT decisions. In most cases, investment proposals must be formulated by the business.

STRATEGIC FOCUS AND ALIGNMENT

Although Forrester Research is not alone in regarding the notion of alignment as an emotionally charged relic from the 1980s that is demonstrably inadequate, alignment is often employed in highly respectable circles. Note that in the following quote, taken from Metricnet (a subsidiary of META Group, which was recently acquired by Gartner), the "fanciful" notions of "fluidly aligned" and "new-age IT" are employed in the context of IT portfolio management, which has important financial and risk components. On the subject of IT portfolio management, a development that has quickly taken shape as the ultimate operationalization of IT governance, more will be said in Chapter 4.

> *As information technology is further integrated into business and in fact "becomes" the business, it is critical that an enterprise's IT assets be fully "fluidly" aligned with business needs and actively managed from an investment perspective (risk, yield, benefits, etc.), instead of solely from a cost-side perspective, as is widely practiced today. From this perspective, the financial services metaphors of "portfolio management" and perhaps "fund management" are applicable and essential to the management of new-age IT.*[29]

We need to realize that certain terms and remarks are not meant to sting us into action; in essence they are perhaps nothing more than previous, less pregnant statements of good intentions that have taken on clumsy forms. The concept of *alignment* belongs to the terminology of the Balanced Scorecard developed by Robert Kaplan and David Norton.[30] The Balanced Scorecard, a topic to which we will return in Chapter 5, was an early attempt to arrive at an integral economic-based determination of value, one that goes further than financial metrics alone.

David Norton, who currently heads up the Balanced Scorecard Collaborative, has, over the past 25 years, come to know the alignment theme like the back of his hand. It is and remains an unruly subject in terms of the continuous adequate mutual integration of IT and business strategy. Norton has examined the problem from all sides and thinks that a solution is in the offing.

In his opinion, because of the current speed of business, it is senseless to be preoccupied with alignment, a basic ingredient of governance structures and processes, when a continuous, collective focus on strategy is lacking. This is not too different from the concept of Peter Slator, who says that Unilever's only strategy is a focus on the business (see the previous section Not Dialogue but Babble). Norton's concept also links seamlessly with the notion of dialogue that Forrester propagates. For Norton and his followers, alignment is what greases the cogs of IT governance. Over time, financial parameters came to be applied mechanically. Then, in the first e-business period, we used alignment to wildly overemphasize the qualitative side of opportunities that we were not allowed to miss. Among others, Forrester has called for a new professionalism to put a halt to this practice.

The key problem, according to Norton, is the manner in which many organizations deal with strategy. Company management as often fallen into an abysmally poor state. In the separate areas for which the various directors are responsible, everyone has their own ideas, but nearly nothing is done in terms of any methodical aggregation.

This means that the alignment question is raised everywhere in the organization, not only in terms of IT. However, IT is the discipline that is most in the spotlight, because of the interest in its infrastructural services, because of the high costs, and because of the volatility on the supply side. In effect, we all more or less regard IT as strategic. However, suppliers blow up this notion out of proportion; they make tons of money and often frustrate the objective development of IT with innovations that are for the most part intended to increase the market share of IT companies.

IT cannot be viewed independently of other resources, such as business processes, people, and information. Only in combination are we able to achieve our strategic goals. To begin with, we have to break down our silos. How can you synchronize IT with strategy when all other activities are also not well coordinated? This is the responsibility of the relevant board members.

These are mostly specialists in their own fields. Unfortunately, you do not often find that they take the time to establish a clear and effective strategy. The average board of directors does still not spend an hour a month on this activity. Most governance processes are based on the monthly budget periods, the result being a strong focus on operations. In the industrial age, this approach might have been sufficient, but this era ended nearly 100 years ago. Nowadays, everything happens many times faster, and an integral and well articulated strategy is therefore more important than ever. Currently only 15 percent of the value of a Standard & Poor 500 firm is attributable to physical production resources.

The solution of the alignment problem is thus a part of the responsibility of the directors, and this goes for more than IT. Breaking down silos and establishing a collective process that keeps an eye on the quality and direction of the strategic focus is the only way out of the impasse. Otherwise, everyone is floundering around. The ITers must ensure that sufficient measurement data are continuously available to nurture integral strategy formation adequately on the basis of IT.[31, 32]

IT GOVERNANCE: FROM STRUCTURES TO MECHANISMS AND TECHNIQUES

In this chapter, we have developed ideas along various lines about a well-oiled system of IT management. We have discussed e-business and the various IT paradoxes, as well as political details of governance structures, concrete governance mechanisms, and the research into them. A full-cycle business governance of IT is modeled on the essential factors of dialogue between business and IT, combined with tangible economic-based accountability using ABC and EVA (see Chapter 5). Perhaps ABC and EVA have not come into their full potential, but in any case the business value of IT, with its risks and investments, are key considerations. This manner of measuring IT completes the well-known triplet of IT management, IT governance, and IT strategy.

Accountability based on economics is presently receiving a great deal of attention as a means of greasing the operational cogs involved in a smoothly running system of IT management. In addition, there are other issues that must not be overlooked, as emphasized by the Balanced Scorecard. Business value, risks, and investments, together with prioritization, currently form the key points of IT portfolio management (see Chapter 4). When we employ full-cycle IT management we are moving in this direction. Full cycle here means throughout the entire organization, present in all budget cycles over time and linked to quantified performance indicators.

IT governance is increasingly becoming more an affair of highly-effective "mechanisms" and transparent techniques, while we maintain full awareness that we are dealing with human work and that overemphasizing either the techniques or the human factor has unfortunate consequences. Such a view reflects the strategic importance of information and IT in organizations.

ENDNOTES

1. S.L. Botwinik, et al., "Reinventing Technology Management," Forrester Research, 2001.
2. IBM, "History of IBM," 1997. *www.ibm.com/ibm/history/history/year_1997.html*
3. Lou Gerstner (speeches), "Partnerworld 2001," IBM, 2001. *www.ibm.com/lvg/0227.phtml*
4. N. Carr, "IT Doesn't Matter," 2003. *www.nicholasgcarr.com/articles/matter.html*
5. T.J. Mullaney, et al., "The E-biz Surprise," BusinessWeek, May 12, 2003. *http://www.businessweek.com/magazine/content/03_19/b3832601.htm*
6. Ibid.
7. H. Jessayan, "Productiviteitswonder VS breekt nu écht door. Nederlandse economen waarschuwen voor structurele achterstand van Europa," *Het Financieele Dagblad*, April 22, 2003.

http://www.accf.nl/pages/members/22%20april%20artikel%20 2%20boot%20et%20al.%20pdf.pdf

8. J. Thorp, *The Information Paradox: Realizing the Business Benefits of Information Technology,* New York, McGraw-Hill, 1998. *http://www.fujitsu.com/us/news/publications/books/ip.html*

9. J.L. Casti, *Complexification. Explaining a Paradoxical World through the Science of Surprise,* New York, HarperCollins, 1994.

10. See note 7.

11. M. Hammer and J. Champy, *Reengineering the Corporation: A Manifesto for Business Revolution,* New York, HarperCollins, 1993.

12. W. Deutsch, "The Technology Democracy," *CIO,* January 6, 1997. *www.cio.com/archive/060197/forrester_content.html*

13. Ibid.

14. L. Willems, "Men denkt dat ik veel met IT'ers praat." Interview with Chief Information Officer Peter Slator of Unilever, *Het Financieele Dagblad,* 2003.

15. C. Dembeck, "Big Blue Regains Lost Luster," *E-Commerce Times,* July 23, 1999. *www.ecommercetimes.com/perl/story/856.html*

16. Peter Weill and Richard Woodham, "Don't Just Lead, Govern: Implementing Effective IT Governance," April 2002, MIT Sloan Working Paper no. 4237-02. *ssrn.com/abstract=317319,* or *www.csbs.org/pr/presentations/2003/AMC2003_Weill_DontJust Lead-Govern.pdf*

17. B. Cameron, "Transforming IT Governance," Forrester Research, 2002.

18. A. Dragoon, "Deciding Factors," *CIO,* August 15, 2003. *www. cio.com/archive/081503/factors.html*

19. B. Cameron, et al., "The Death of IT," Forrester Research, 2000.

20. "Prozessabläufe Wichtiges Thema für Chief Information Officer," *Wirtschaftswoche,* September 28, 2001.

21. "Foundation Report 109. New IS Leaders," CSC, 1997. *www.cscresearchservices.com/foundation/library/109/RP03.asp*

22. Giga Information Group, "Total Economic Impact." *www.gigaweb.net/tei*

23. Paul Strassmann, *The Squandered Computer,* New Canaan, CT, Information Economic Press, 1997.

24. R. Pastore, "IT Reloaded. Interview with W. Brian Arthur," *CIO*, 15 July 2003. *www.cio.com/archive/071503/reloaded.html*

25. See note 14.

26. M. Broadbent, "How Successful Companies Synchronize Business IT," *CIO Insight*, January 7, 2002. *www.cioinsight.com/article2/0,3959,283998,00.asp*

27. General Accounting Office, "Maximizing the Success of Chief Informations Officers. Learning from Leading Organizations," GAO, 2001. *www.cio.gov/documents/d01376g.pdf*

28. For further information on the strategies to follow and sample case studies, we urge you to read the whole document, which is available on the Internet at the site given in the previous footnote.

29. Metricnet. *IT-portfoliomanagement   128.121.222.187/specials/it_portfolio_management.html*

30. R.S. Kaplan and D.P. Norton, "The Balanced Scorecard—Measures that Drive Performance," *Harvard Business Review*, 1993.

31. R.S. Kaplan and D.P Norton, *The Strategy—Focused Organization: How Balanced Scorecard Companies Thrive in the New Business Environment*, Boston, Harvard University Press, 2001.

32. D.P. Norton, "The Alignment Enigma," *CIO Insight*, July 1, 2002. *www.cioinsight.com/article2/0,3959,283925,00.asp*

CHAPTER 4

IT Portfolio Management

Portfolio: Costs, Benefits, Risks, and Choices

In the metaphorical sense, every portfolio is a coherent set of affairs and activities whose values can fluctuate. The presence of this flux immediately means that a portfolio only makes sense when we manage it actively. To do this, structural consideration must be given to the costs and benefits of the portfolio's content; thus choices must be with the risk factor consciously included.

Business Portfolios

In organizations, we are concerned with business portfolios containing cohesive collections of resources or activities with economic value. Then we can consider their contributions to the results of the enterprise and make better decisions. However, the value of business portfolios exceeds the purely financial character of stock portfolios, for example, meaning that the value of business portfolios must never be viewed independently of the business goals that these portfolios must achieve.

IT Portfolio Management as a Cornerstone

META Group (which was recently acquired by Gartner) regards the process of IT portfolio management as the cornerstone of the dynamic alignment of business and IT. By dealing with IT from an investment perspective—one in which we continuously focus on costs, benefits, risks, and priority setting—businesses are able to reduce their costs by 30 percent, while IT brings in two to three times as much.

Legislation for IT

IT portfolio management is the first widespread and widely supported operationalization of IT governance. In the United States, IT portfolio management has been given a legal foundation. Perhaps a general law for all government organizations needs to be enacted in reference to IT in Europe as well, as Chris Verhoef proposes.[1] By making portfolio management required by law, less IT capital will be destroyed in the public sector.

Integrate All the Various Portfolios

Portfolio management is the operationalization of performance measurement and weighting. After all, we are coming to regard the organization as a complex compilation of diverse portfolios. Portfolio management therefore involves the manner in which these portfolios and their contents contribute to business performance.

En Route to Consolidation and Standardization

Portfolio management is no magic cure; it is hard work to construct better performance measures step by step. We are always seeking greater coherence. Consolidation and standardization are, in this respect, extremely important for bringing about the proper value focus in IT portfolio management. In the United States, where IT portfolio management is presently the most widespread, it is perceived as both valuable and necessary but also as an enormous task.

WHAT IS INVOLVED IN A PORTFOLIO APPROACH?

In the business and financial world, *portfolio* is a well-known term. Everyone has heard of an order portfolio or a stock portfolio. What does portfolio actually mean in such cases? Properly viewed, nothing at all. In fact, we can almost abandon the word. Then we are only talking about our orders or our shares. Insiders view things differently, however. Anyone aware of modern portfolio theory also knows that Harry Markowitz, Merton Miller, and William Sharpe received the Nobel Prize for it in 1990. The optimization of financial portfolio performance is a central concept in their work; it is all about making money by clever investment, by being continuously alert to what does and does not yield a return—trying to have one's cake and eat it too by making rational choices. We then give such practices the elegant term of portfolio management.

Everything is measurable in terms of money. Naturally we do not make such measurements all the time, but it would be possible theoretically, if we could only achieve some agreement about the costs and benefits of what we want to value. In every collection of such things, we are automatically dealing with a portfolio, not a purely financial one, such as a stock portfolio, but one that is assessed on the basis of financial criteria, for example, the portfolio of all resources required to make a certain product or bring a given service to the market.

We undertake such valuation exercises on a permanent basis, or at least periodically, to examine whether we are doing well in a business-economic sense and whether we can remain ahead of the competition. Of course, no one can make this assessment on his or her own. A great deal of input, agreement, and feedback is necessary, because we relate our evaluation to certain sets of business goals, objectives that we can use as a vehicle to keep all divisional employees involved and to show how everyone can contribute to the results.

The optimization of each portfolio's performance is attained by making choices within the constraints of the available budget. In so doing, we deliberately involve ourselves with risks: we accept or avoid them in a calculated manner. This optimization of performance is a logical issue, as of course we do not make all this effort to detail the costs and benefits for no reason. In a share portfolio, we can only get rid of or replace performing parts. To provide an example, if today we sell Sony shares, replace them with Unilever, and tomorrow acquire some extra Ahold stock, this is money for money. Portfolio management involving the content of organizations is not so simple. Organizations possess a certain cohesion, and any intervention undertaken on a purely financial basis can greatly disrupt the business operation. On the financial side of the business portfolio, it is therefore easy to make calculations And Markowitz, Miller, and Sharpe have devised the means to do this. However, we must never neglect business matters in economic-based organization portfolios.

This also holds true for IT, which is integrated into the business and presently functions as if it were the engine driving all activity. However, handling IT as a collection of portfolios (hardware, software, projects, enterprise resource planning [ERP], and so on) whose contributions to the results of various business processes we would like to know is a difficult and labor-intensive matter. It is often extremely difficult to determine a fair charge for the use of IT products and services, not to mention determination of added value and the subsequent economic-based prioritization that characterizes the portfolio approach. Indeed, this is also the case for entities other than IT. The immaterial nature of IT, along with the shared use of such aspects as a network structure, e-mail, or ERP, constitutes a major difficulty in determining the IT costs and benefits for concrete business activities.

Nevertheless, we must engage in such determinations: the time is long gone when we could simply dole out money to IT while believing that profits would follow. This belief was partially dispelled by the state of the economy at the end of the 1990s to the point that people no longer believe any still unrealized profits will materialize. Budgets have been reined in and kept under control. We must demonstrate the value of IT, taking much more into consideration than the payback period alone. Ultimately, we would like to determine the net value, the money that belongs to the owners or stockholders of the organization. It is, after all, on this basis that they decide to continue or discontinue their participation. This is what we call Economic Value Added (EVA). Together with Activity-Based Costing, EVA is the main subject of Chapter 5. In theory, these two mechanisms constitute the basis of the portfolio approach in businesses. As will be shown, IT portfolio management is not easy—but the effort is worthwhile. Stockholder value (i.e., EVA), which is the ultimate yardstick for business performance, brings us back to the financial origin of portfolio management; stockholders are, after all, (often) purely concerned with money. Keep in mind that we:

- Have a finite amount of money
- Must focus on mission, strategic goals, performance, and outcomes
- Must make strategic decisions about investments
- Try to get the biggest bang for the buck
- Then deliver on our commitment.[2]

AN IT PORTFOLIO APPROACH IN PRACTICE

In the 1998 book *Leveraging the New Infrastructure*,[3] Marianne Broadbent and Peter Weill[4] present the following, now well known IT portfolio pyramid (see Exhibit 4.1). IT systems are classified into domains: two horizontal ones (infrastructure and transactions), to indicate that these are "load bearing," and two vertical ones (information and strategy) that elaborate on the foundation. These four areas have different sets of problems and merits in terms of risks and revenues; using them to examine the IT portfolio can be extremely fruitful.

Broadbent and Weill's subsequent work makes it clear that a more refined, concrete classification is possible and has indeed been used (see "Limits to the Babble, but Almost Any Governance Structure Will Do" in Chapter 3). It must be emphasized that in practice IT portfolio management has little to do with abstract divisions. An infrastructure compartmentalization in 10 clusters and 70 services can be found in the article "IT Infrastructure for Strategic Agility,"[5] but IT portfolio management involves more concrete IT entities and approaches, as the following system-portfolio view and Exhibits 4.2 and 4.3 demonstrate. We should not forget that IT portfolios, along with their aggregation and integration, presently are in its infancy. The IT Investment Management maturity model is enlightening in this respect (see the subsequent section "Maturity and IT Portfolio Management").

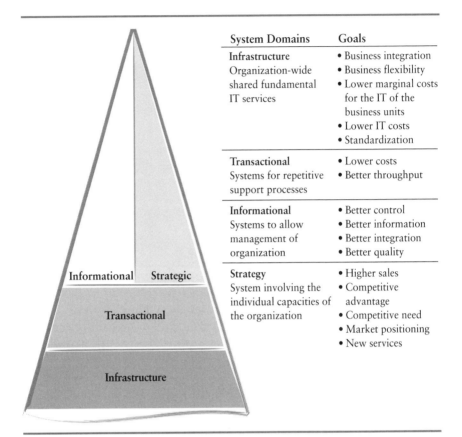

System Domains	Goals
Infrastructure Organization-wide shared fundamental IT services	• Business integration • Business flexibility • Lower marginal costs for the IT of the business units • Lower IT costs • Standardization
Transactional Systems for repetitive support processes	• Lower costs • Better throughput
Informational Systems to allow management of organization	• Better control • Better information • Better integration • Better quality
Strategy System involving the individual capacities of the organization	• Higher sales • Competitive advantage • Competitive need • Market positioning • New services

EXHIBIT 4.1   Broadbent and Weill's Portfolio Pyramid

Organizations currently make frequent use of special software for their IT portfolio management. The following two screen views from the PMOffice package are good examples.[6]

The first screen (Exhibit 4.3) gives a financial overview of four projects from a business's IT portfolio. The extreme left shows that the main portfolio file consists of four parts: projects with priority, ongoing projects, projects submitted for approval, and project proposals for the upcoming five years. Of the ongoing projects, the eCommerce Portal and the Enterprise Financial Interface have been selected, and the Upgrade to HR Systems and the New IT Server Strategy have been chosen from among the projects submitted for approval. These are all concrete and organization-specific IT issues. We see that the Enterprise Financial Interface project comprises a

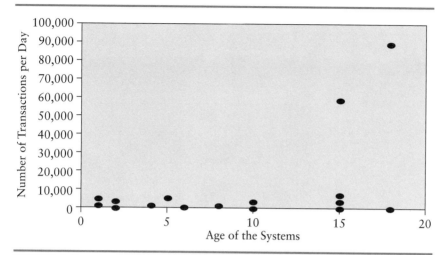

EXHIBIT 4.2   Graph of System Age in Relation to Daily Transaction Load: Portfolio View of the 16 IT Systems at a Mid-Size West European Bank
Source: H.P.M. Kersten and C. Verhoef, "IT Portfolio Management: A Banker's Perspective on IT," 2003. *www.cs.vu.nl/~hkersten/pdffinal_IT-portfoliomanagment_for_the_Journal_of_ITM_1.pdf*

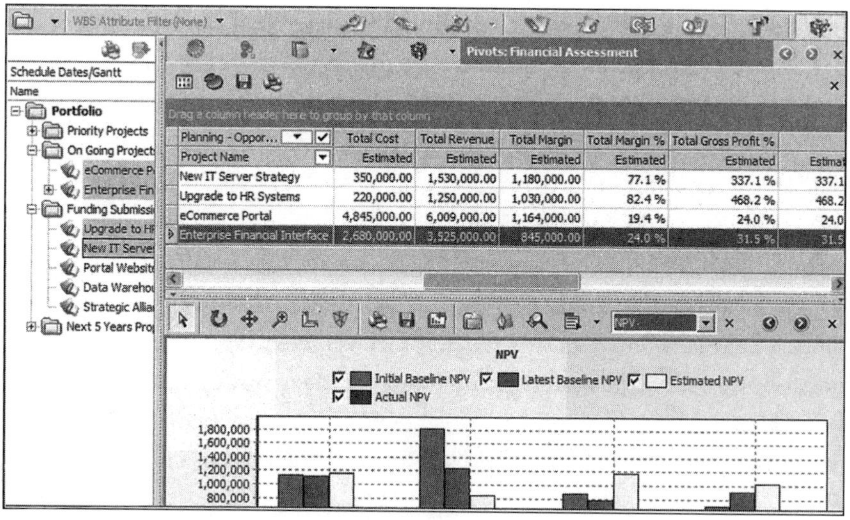

EXHIBIT 4.3   Financial Overview of Four Projects in the IT Portfolio
Source: PMOffice.

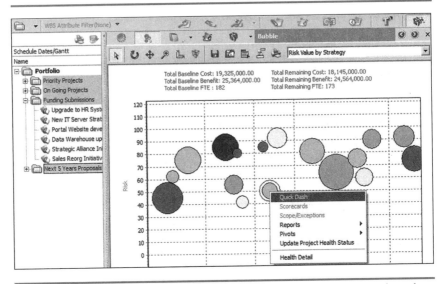

EXHIBIT 4.4   Bubble Chart of the Risks Involved in Each Approach and the Total Financial Consequences of All IT Projects Submitted for Approval
Source: PMOffice.

number of subprojects. The uppermost frame displays an estimate of the costs, benefits, and margin for all four projects in question. Beneath it, we can also see a Net Present Value (NPV) assessment for various times. NPV is a financial metric for cash flow.

The second screen (Exhibit 4.4) displays all the projects submitted for approval. It shows a bubble chart of the risks associated with a given approach (Risk Value by Strategy). Above the chart are estimates of total costs, benefits, and required staffing; on the right, there is an indication of a possible outcome for a given scenario. Additional information on each project and given level of risk can be examined in the bubble chart's menu. Scorecards and information about range and exceptions are not provided, but reports and data about the soundness of the project are available.

IT PORTFOLIO MANAGEMENT BEGINS WITH OUTLINES, ARCHITECTURE, AND CALCULATION

Given the enormous amount of catching up that most companies have to do, it is easy to harvest the quick wins that can be achieved with the very first steps. These involve savings, improved efficiency, better focus, and reduced complexity. For example, just by making a few short lists of projects, addressing redundancy issues, and prioritizing a little, organizations can almost immediately save thousands of dollars (see lesson 3 in the subsequent section "The Nine Initial Practical Lessons, Plus One"). This "low-hanging fruit" is abundant, so there is no excuse not to begin.

2001: $3 Million Saved in Year 1

By creating a single database of the IT projects under way at Schlumberger (a global oilfield service company), Portfolio Manager Jane Walton saved the company $3 million in the first year.[7]

2002: Better IT Performance for Less Money

From 2001 to 2002, Vodafone Nederland strongly improved its IT performance and lowered costs by 40 percent from $70 to $45 million. How? All IT departments were centralized, and the entire project portfolio was held up to the light. The 200 projects given top priority were reduced and reprioritized.[8]

This case is well known because of the cost savings realized, but IT is, for Vodafone, an enormously important asset that can make or break market success. The business value of IT is therefore essential to the business. It is accepted that savings are of secondary importance. At present, Vodafone is making a great effort to "get more value from IT."

2003: More than $13 Million in Redundant IT Projects Detected

One corporation studied by META Group senior research analyst Melinda-Carol Ballou eliminated redundant IT projects and saved $13.2 million.[9]

These are recent examples demonstrating the benefits of IT portfolio management. Businesses that do not immediately begin serious portfolio management along measured lines may come up short. Of course, redundancy must be examined with an understanding of the issues involved. Because all these factors are interdependent—with business but also with mutual systems—we need to know exactly what we are doing when we delete, reduce, or otherwise rearrange certain assets.

Moreover, beginning with the infrastructure (in terms of assets and projects) is important because more than half the IT budget is spent on it.[10]

Need for Good Enterprise Architecture

With good Enterprise Architecture (organization architecture), we can quickly detect dependencies. Enterprise Architecture gives specific insight into the coherence of organizational components on various levels having to do with processes, information, and IT. Not surprisingly, together with IT portfolio management, the presence of such an architecture is stipulated as legally mandatory for government organizations in the United States. On the base of an organization's mission, an Enterprise Architecture defines the information

ENTERPRISE ARCHITECTURE IS A STRATEGIC INFORMATION ASSET BASE, WHICH DEFINES:

- The business mission
- The information necessary to perform the mission
- The technologies necessary to perform the mission
- The transitional processes for implementing new technologies in response to the changing mission needs

Source: "Updating the Clinger-Cohen Competencies for Enterprise Architecture," CIO Council, 2003. *www.cio.gov/ documents/FINAL_White_Paper_on_EA_v62.doc; www.cio.gov/ documents/Clinger_Cohen_Competencies_June_2003.doc*

and technologies needed to achieve the mission as well as the changes needed to implement new technologies in response to altered needs.

Enterprise Architecture is expressed in at least the following four subsidiary architectures:

1. **Business Architecture.** Involves the business mission, strategy, business components, organizational structure, business-process models, business functions, and so on.
2. **Information Architecture (also called Data Architecture).** Reveals who requires what information to achieve their mission and how this information is made available.
3. **Application Architecture (also called Functional Architecture).** Involves the application of a portfolio that is necessary for the business mission and the information needs of the organization. It also gives insight into the business divisions and business services in which use can be made of applications.
4. **IT Architecture.** Shows which IT services are necessary for the application portfolio of business; also documents the software, hardware, and network products.

Exhibit 4.5 shows a starting organizational architecture and an end organizational architecture, along with three so-called intermediary architectures. They are linked to the desired portfolio state in 2004, 2005, and 2006, respectively. Based on the end architecture, we determine the progress we must record at this time to attain the results we have in mind. The portfolio approach implies that we keep an eye on the costs, benefits, and risks related to business goals and make the appropriate economic-motivated choices concerning our IT.

In the fall of 2003, the Enterprise Architecture extension of the key competencies prescribed by the Clinger-Cohen Act came into force.[11] This law, which was enacted in 1996 and effectively prescribed the employment of IT portfolio management, had already established the mandatory deployment of IT architecture. The Office of Management and Budget required that this IT architecture be aligned with the various federal and specific Enterprise Architectures by the end of the year 2000. This alignment is supported by various approaches, models, and definitions laid down in the Federal Enterprise Architecture Framework (FEAF), which promotes the government-wide development and application of processes and

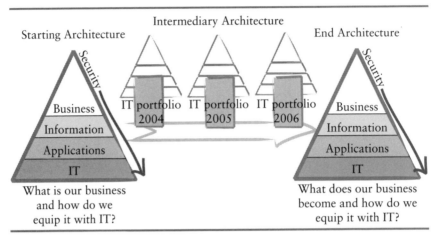

EXHIBIT 4.5   Using IT Portfolio Management to Arrive at a New Organizational Architecture
Source: Adapted from P. Pizzella and L. Callahan, "Citizens-Centered E-Government: The President's Management Agenda and Value Chain Management, 2003. *www. governmentperformance.org/gp/presentations/pizzella-callahan.pdf*

information. In this respect, the Federal Enterprise Architecture Program Management Office (FEAPMO) developed five reference models (see Exhibit 4.6), which were required to help attain the necessary standardization.

Quantitative IT Portfolio Management

Unfortunately, the development of IT portfolio management, still in its infancy, is not running smoothly. Chris Verhoef, professor at the Free University of Amsterdam, puts it more strongly, speaking of *terra incognita*,[12] in other words, unknown land. We must not sell ourselves short here, however—with a little consideration of certain IT components, we can quite easily put a finger on the most troublesome areas. These were and are the IT expenditures of many businesses; the most prominent examples involve the bottomless money pits deemed necessary for one reason or another. We should not despair, however. In October 2001, for example, an article appeared in *CIO* entitled "Do the Math," which advised as follows: Simply go over your IT with a fine-tooth comb, compile an inventory, and make

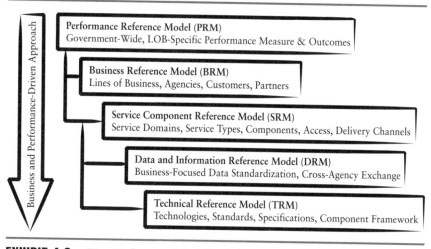

EXHIBIT 4.6 Five Reference Models of the Federal Enterprise Architecture Program Management Office

a systematic beginning in an effort to perform some calculations. This need not be so burdensome. In addition, given the shoddy portfolio discipline that most companies currently practice, any portfolio activity can produce a large gain.[13] The three examples at the beginning of this section speak for themselves: The sums involved are considerable.

Over the last decade, some have suggested that there is no sense in doing the IT numbers—but this is just not true. Strassmann's observations raise the suspicion that our IT spending is uncontrolled, with little or no consistency. Portfolio management—a good expression for something that is quite simple and sensible—can revamp our spending practices.

In an article of more than 96 pages entitled "Quantitative IT Portfolio Management,"[14] Verhoef enumerates step by step the formulas that apply to the situation of most organizations today : total lack of insight into the organization's own workings (what he calls CMM level 1). Nothing more is required than to roll up our sleeves, gather and assemble information, and gradually build up our knowledge. Fortunately, Capers Jones and his Software Productivity Research can function as a benchmark, as well as the International Software Benchmarking Standards Group (ISBSG).[15] Capers Jones' database currently contains detailed information on more than 10,000 different IT projects from recent decades. Verhoef shows in addition that function point analysis, a well elaborated measurement instrument, is a tool well worth implementing when we are establishing our IT portfolio views.

Given the fact that IT systems are always "in motion," we need to lump together all the activities in organizations that involve software systems, such as analysis, design, programming, testing, and even use. The Activity-Based Costing literature on IT teaches us that there are no more than 25 categories, all strongly interrelated. This helps considerably when we are establishing the formulas with which we intend to chart the IT portfolio. For the different kinds of work activities and software, Verhoef draws up a variety of formulas and parameterizing constants. Using these tools, you can, for example, arrive at a number of Total Cost of Ownership (TCO) calculations.

MATURITY AND IT PORTFOLIO MANAGEMENT

Metricnet, a subsidiary of META Group, regards IT portfolio management as a decisive step toward the mature handling of IT. IT organizations appear to undergo four evolutionary phases:

1. **IT as Service Performance.** In this phase, IT does not contribute directly to the business growth and in this sense is not a strategic element. Attention is predominantly paid to cost-efficient operation. Benchmarking is often implemented, as well as radical downsizing.
2. **IT as Business Enabler.** IT contributes somewhat more to growth and can produce new ways of increasing profitability. Substantial investment is often undertaken during this phase. Attention is directed toward costs and immaterial "effectiveness." More developed IT organizations use Balanced Scorecards to chart financing, along with the effects on customers and processes.
3. **IT as a Business within the Business.** Stricter cost and performance standards for the IT organization make it possible to compare IT with market parties. Scorecards also play a role here, with the emphasis placed on costs, quality of service provision, and contacts, as well as process efficiency and effectiveness.

4. **Full Integration of IT in the Business.** The IT organization acts as a business and is managed as such. This is the stage in which portfolio management comes into effect. The IT organization manages its activity portfolio—business support, replacement and development, along with its high-risk business/IT initiatives—as actively and adequately as possible. Portfolio management is necessary to grow further toward the goal of full integration.[16]

In practice, IT portfolio management involves constant control over both the performance of the investment portfolio and the process with which we adjust this portfolio by means of projects. If we want to gain a good view of performance, we need to know the costs, benefits, risks, and goals (all in business terms, for that is what it is ultimately all about—the business).

Because the performance of the portfolio is the focus, performance management is, in practice, the same as portfolio management. In phase 4, we are no longer involved with the performance of the organization but with the composition of portfolios. IT is more simply said than done; witness what Metricnet has to say about the concrete approach. First, an inventory must be made of existing assets. Then, all costs must be determined, along with the use of resources and the ranges for costs and quality. Systems of measurement must be implemented, especially for the following items: money, quality, performance, changes of speed, staffing and skills, risks (and perhaps audits), profiles, and effectiveness. Next, we need to decide whether anything should be updated, developed, replaced, or phased out.

These same steps should be followed for existing projects. Along with other criteria, process metrics must show whether a project remains on schedule or on budget, whether the scope is still appropriate, whether the added value for the present or future still conforms to expectation, what is happening at the risk level, what the trend-related developments are, how the portfolio is influencing the project and vice versa, and whether the project needs to be reevaluated.

The separate portfolio management systems for assets and projects must be engaged with each other in a meaningful way. Both firmer and looser connections will exist. Portfolio management builds a solid bridge between business and IT. Costs, benefits, risks, and priorities must all be considered within this framework, and contributions are required from all interested parties—programmers, project managers, business managers, and IT managers. In this way, IT portfolio management is a model for full-cycle governance. Moreover, IT investments by the company are also regarded as business opportunities.

Interdependence of Portfolios

As discussed, the number of portfolios and portfolio views to be made is enormous. In terms of IT, we can, for example, distinguish the hardware portfolio, the software portfolio, the IT services portfolio, and the project portfolio. The latter is the most undifferentiated because most IT activities are organized into projects. The CHAOS Study by the Standish Group, among others, shows how this view is put into practice (see "Eight Challenges Plus the Millennium Problem" in Chapter 2).[17]

Because of the involvement of IT in all types of business portfolios, Metricnet argues for the establishment of an overarching "fund management":

Fund Management: The Sack of Money to Be Doled Out

The concept of portfolio management itself may not be enough. From a total enterprise perspective, the enterprise is a collection of portfolios. For example, in financial services there may be a retail portfolio, a global portfolio, a wholesale portfolio, and so on. Although IT is integrated into each area and there may be cross-area dependencies, the enterprise itself must decide how to balance and manage its investments across these business portfolios along with their IT components. Therefore, at the enterprise level, a "fund management" model may be appropriate to model the movement and allocation of funds across diversified investments.[18]

When we look for concrete examples of integrative portfolio management, as advocated in this section by Metricnet, we discover that none exist. Such exercises, which give evidence of a fully mature treatment of portfolio thinking, have a direct effect on the capacity of a company to distinguish itself from its competitors. They are therefore strictly confidential. This means that portfolio management is comparable, for example, with architecture. In the area of architecture, we see how such organizations as ABN-AMRO and ING openly exchange ideas and give external presentations about their own approaches.

ITIM: IT Investment Management Maturation Model

In 2000, the U.S. General Accounting Office (GAO) published a framework meant to help improve IT investment processes. The five different stages and their critical processes provide a good picture of the minimum amount of work that an organization must do in order to concretely determine and manage which IT investments contribute to the business goals (see Exhibit 4.7).

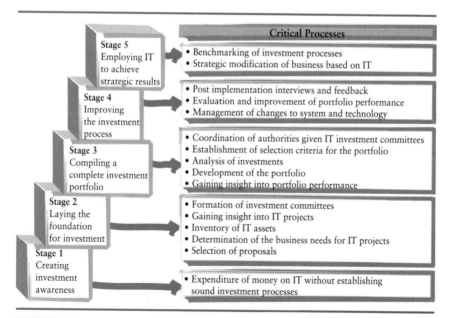

EXHIBIT 4.7 ITIM Model: Maturation of IT Investment from Project Level to Strategic and Organizational Level in Five Stages

GOVERNANCE, PROJECTS, PROGRAMS, AND PERFORMANCE

IT Governance

Governance in business, as we have already stated in Chapter 1 ("Governance in Corporations is All about Business Performance"), is the rational control required when risks, interrelations, and interests exceed the competences of the various lines and layers of management. Of course, we would like to institute an overarching authority to help realize the economic-related goals of the prognosticated business performance. Portfolio management is the first wide-ranging and widely supported operationalization of such control. Thus portfolio management is the operational framework for governance in business.

Given the interdependence of IT and business activities, as well as the high investment level, the governance of IT has been left hanging in the air for far too long. Portfolio management is meant to change that in several ways, including by means of the legal obligations that have been established in the United States. Against this background, foreign corporations with significant interests in the United States are also required to "introduce" portfolio management into the financial and strategic governance of their enterprises.

The sorely needed standardization of IT portfolio management derived from best practices, tools, and frameworks is just now beginning to get off the ground. We have already discussed this in the previous section and will explore more examples in the rest of this chapter. It is important for organizations to get involved quickly, by clarifying the IT projects that are already in the portfolio and then by introducing Activity-Based Costing—in other words, by initiating the concrete allocation of all IT costs to the various business processes. This is the first step on the way to gaining insight into the value of IT. Choices must then be made on the basis of this discerned value.

Portfolios, Programs, Projects, and Their Performance

Portfolio management is founded on a 50-year-old financial analogy of proven worth, one that overlaps with project management, program management, and performance management. In his book

Information Paradox, John Thorp connects these three and gives them the single label *proactive change management,* which he views as the operationalization of full-cycle governance.[19] Exhibit 4.8, which shows his concept, is thus connected to the exhibit that introduces each of the three parts of this book, which shows how our discussion is structured.

As will soon be made clear, this notion of "portfolio" connects to the fundamental insight that business investment decisions incur risk and must give a return—as is the case for a share portfolio. In terms of IT, this is a sensible observation. The risk level is considerably increased by the incorporation of IT in business, the interests that such incorporation represents, and the associated financial consequences in terms of costs and benefits; the result is a manifest insecurity, as shown by the longitudinal study conducted by the Standish Group (see "Eight Challenges Plus the Millennium Problem" in Chapter 2) as well as other studies. Because the value of IT for business is a central issue, it goes without saying that this principle question must be given consideration when one is weighing and measuring projects and other activities. In actuality, such consideration has not been given, or if it was, it was only on the cost side.

Portfolio management, as we have already said, is closely associated with performance management and is currently used as a synonym for this latter expression. We find performance measurement everywhere. Since the 1996 Clinger-Cohen Act (or IT Management Reform Act), IT performance measurement has been linked to portfolio management (see the subsequent section "The Portfolio Approach as an Aggregation of the Balanced Scorecard, Activity-Based Costing, and Economic Value Added"). In this regard, a noninclusive list of the leading U.S. initiatives, processes, and laws in which performance measurement plays a central role includes the: IT Management Reform Act, Investment Review Boards, Chief Financial Officers Act, Government Performance and Results Act, Federal Acquisition Streamlining Act, Federal Acquisition Reform Act, Budget Process, Capital Planning, Asset Management, Agency Strategic Plans, Office of Information Resources Plans, IT Modernization, Office of Management and Budget Guidance (Raines Rules), Business Case Strategies, Risk Management, Auditing, and Project Management.[20]

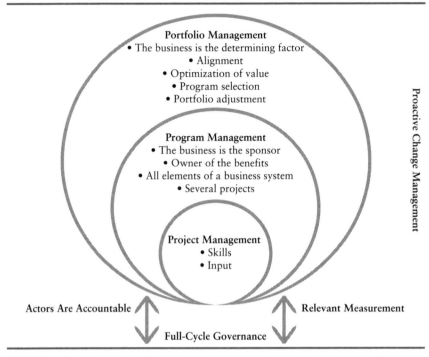

Portfolio Management
- • The business is the determining factor
- • Alignment
- • Optimization of value
- • Program selection
- • Portfolio adjustment

Program Management
- • The business is the sponsor
- • Owner of the benefits
- • All elements of a business system
- • Several projects

Project Management
- • Skills
- • Input

Proactive Change Management

Actors Are Accountable   Relevant Measurement

Full-Cycle Governance

EXHIBIT 4.8   Proactive Change Management According to John Thorp

In 2003, the Project Management Institute (PMI) released the first version of its Organizational Project Management Maturity Model (OPM3). OPM3 was developed to create a standard describing how organizations that manage by projects could increase their organizational capabilities. According to PMI, Organizational Project Management is "the systematic management of projects, programs, and portfolios in alignment with the achievement of strategic goals."[21] The intent is for organizations to increase their maturity within the project, program, and portfolio domains and ultimately be successful in achieving their organizational strategy. OPM3 provides the tools and best practices to implement portfolio management practices, successfully manage programs and projects, drive organizational improvement, and continually improve project, program, and portfolio management best practices. Within the concept of portfolio management performance, PMI, which provides the global standard for project management, established a means to assess and develop a roadmap for continuous improvement, with the aim of achieving an organization's strategy.

Although in many organizations project and program management was established earlier, they should adequately facilitate portfolio and performance management. Applied lower level metrics and performance indicators must, of course, maintain a clear link to the higher levels of aggregation.

THE PORTFOLIO APPROACH AS AN AGGREGATION OF BALANCED SCORECARD, ACTIVITY-BASED COSTING, AND ECONOMIC VALUE ADDED

We have seen that IT portfolio management has many ramifications and a strong history behind it. As a result, program management, project management, performance management, and governance can overlap. As we said earlier, the financial roots of the IT portfolio approach were laid down in the early 1950s. Here we will provide a short preview of the next chapter, which explores these issues in more detail.

IT portfolio management can be properly regarded as an elaboration on and aggregation of the following three items: the Balanced Scorecard, Activity-Based Costing (ABC), and Economic Value Added (EVA). Kaplan and Norton created the Balanced Scorecard to show that many factors must be taken into account, not just money. The goal of ABC is the allocation of indirect costs to activities, by means of which activities that add value are distinguished from activities that do not. EVA is the net added value remaining for the risk-takers, those for whom the organization exists. These are the stockholders, if there are any, or otherwise the owners.

It is common sense to use the portfolio approach, along with the Balanced Scorecard, ABC, and EVA. Making rational business choices while considering all the relevant factors is precisely what it is all about.

All activities that an organization undertakes to achieve good business-economic performances must be appropriately connected to the optimum result. Unfortunately, this connection, the changes involved in it, and its impact are often considered second, or even last, in the course of day-to-day operational concerns. When the issues involve IT, which is the business enabler par excellence and also the largest investment item, such unprofessional behavior is fundamentally misguided. Portfolio management is now beginning to bring about change in this respect.

In the era when IT was unthinkingly regarded as a strategic element and there was enough money to maintain the investment spiral, a clear determination of the costs and the values that IT had for the business was of secondary importance. Because of the problematic economic and managerial developments of recent years, we are beginning to change. The insights that lay the groundwork for such change have of course existed for quite a while.

In the United States, the lead has been given by legal prescription, mandatory reporting and guarantees, along with the best practices, tools, and frameworks that would allow IT projects to be made as sound as possible by means of portfolio management. In this way, portfolio management is placed at the top of the management agenda when the useful implementation of IT is concerned. Still, a lot of ground must be made up.

Originally, purely financial portfolio management boiled down to the following concrete elements: the continuous evaluation and prioritization of business activities by at least one systematic financial process, such as ABC. This activity needs to be linked to objectives and business interests by means of a Balanced Scorecard (see Exhibit 4.9) and to the actual net (stockholder) value through EVA. This is the same proposal as the one made by Stern Stewart (see Exhibit 4.10).

It is important to understand that Exhibits 4.9 and 4.10 present two complementary views, one more abstract and wide ranging (Balanced Scorecard) and the other more concrete and focused (the EVA system from Stern Stewart). In the context of IT portfolio management, both form the desired background against which risk and prioritization—two distinct characteristics of the portfolio approach—must be treated. However, despite the relatively long history of the Balanced Scorecard, ABC, EVA, and their combinations, their application is still in the pipeline and will probably

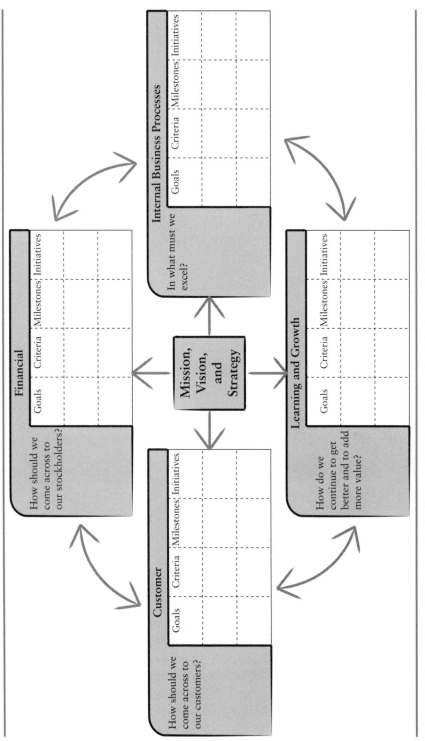

Financial

How should we come across to our stockholders?

Goals	Criteria	Milestones	Initiatives

Internal Business Processes

In what must we excel?

Goals	Criteria	Milestones	Initiatives

Mission, Vision, and Strategy

Customer

How should we come across to our customers?

Goals	Criteria	Milestones	Initiatives

Learning and Growth

How do we continue to get better and to add more value?

Goals	Criteria	Milestones	Initiatives

EXHIBIT 4.9 Balanced Scorecard: If All Items Are Appropriately in Balance with Each Other, the Objectives of the Organization Can Be Achieved

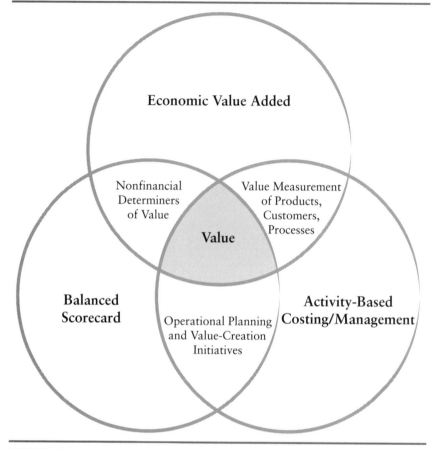

EXHIBIT 4.10 Stern Stewart Approach: Economic Value Added (Actual Net Value) in This Combination Is the Focal Point for Control of the Entire Organization (i.e., an Implementation of Full-Cycle Governance)

continue to stay there in most cases. The application of these concepts is not a sinecure (see Chapter 5).

An important added value of the portfolio approach using these three systems and their combinations is the intensive dialogue required for success among representatives of the different disciplines in the business. The goal is to continuously arrive at better business performances and results, with the most important challenges being avoidance of unnecessary delays and bureaucratization. Either of these is a deathblow to good intentions. Therefore, keep it simple, strive for clarity and good communication, and keep your eyes open for innovation possibilities. By focusing on historical data alone (using ABC, for example), we may give too little of our attention to renewal.

AFTER 50 YEARS OF PORTFOLIO THINKING, IT'S TURN HAS COME

We will now examine how portfolio management has developed in relation to IT. We begin in 2002 and then go back half a century, to 1952.

2002: First Experiences with IT Portfolio Management

The most important milestone marking the recent period was a report on the first official experiences with IT portfolio management, published by the American CIO Council in 2002 as "A Summary of First Practices and Lessons Learned in Information Technology Portfolio Management." We will explore this report in detail in the section "The Nine Initial Practical Lessons, Plus One."

1952: The Beginning: Modern Portfolio Theory

The theory of IT portfolio management first saw the light exactly 50 years before 2002, in the ground-breaking article "Portfolio Selection" by Harry Markowitz, which appeared in the *Journal of Finance*[22] and laid the basis for portfolio management. In 1990, Markowitz, together with Merton Miller and William Sharpe, received the Nobel Prize for what had come to be known as Modern Portfolio Theory (MPT).[23] MPT describes how, for a given level of risk, we can arrive at an investment mix that yields optimum returns. The concept of statistical variance was the key. In Markowitz's own words,

Risk and Return

Investors diversify because they are concerned with risk as well as return. Variance came to mind as a measure of risk. The fact that portfolio variance depended on security covariances added to the plausibility of the approach. Since there were two criteria, risk and return, it was natural to assume that investors selected from the set of Pareto optimal risk-return combinations.[24]

1981: Modern Portfolio Theory and IT

More than 20 years ago F. Warren McFarlan established the relationship between MPT and IT, which at that time was becoming increasingly more important for business success. In his article "Portfolio Approach to Information Systems," McFarlan argued that the risk factors must be given primary consideration in the selection and management of IT projects.[25] There was still no talk of a specifically quantitative approach at that time.

1990s: IT Portfolio Management under Pressure

In the 1990s, IT portfolio management was being developed in the face of opposition. Realistic IT portfolio management had to share the spotlight with, among other things, the enthusiasm for Business Process Reengineering, Business Process Improvement, the Balanced Scorecard, e-commerce, and e-business. The second half of the 1990s was the age of increasing faith in progress based on IT, along with the promise of telecom and the Internet. On this basis, a growing "irrational exuberance" developed that was expectantly christened the New Economy. First-mover advantage had suppressed cautious operation, as opportunities appeared to be endless.

The private sector, which only became concerned with legislation and regulation in the area of IT performance and IT portfolio management when the Sarbanes-Oxley Act was passed in 2002,[26] was consumed by the spectacular IT investment spiral and was operating under the conviction that the opportunities sprouting up all over had to be harvested as quickly as possible. In the final years before 2000, venture capital was readily available. Any development in the direction of quantitative IT portfolio management was consequently, outstripped. Such management was viewed as an intrusive brake on innovation and as a piece of unsportsmanlike conduct—in spite of all the biannual CHAOS reports from the Standish Group (see "Eight Challenges Plus the Millennium Problem" in Chapter 2).

1996 to the Present: Clinger-Cohen Act not Observed: It Is too Difficult!

Portfolio management guidelines for government agencies were established in the 1996 Clinger-Cohen Act (or IT Management Reform Act), as well as other mandates. These were meant to justify the commitment of public funds and are barely observed.[27] The Clinger-Cohen Act contained, for the first time, concrete mention of performance measurement related to IT portfolio management. Performance measurement had itself been a central subject of law and regulation for a longer time. However, many see difficulties in implementing these regulations in a sound and thorough manner.

> *With the new Information Technology Management Reform Act (Clinger-Cohen) measuring IT performance sounds good but when it comes down to actually measuring performance of IT and linking it to the mission of the organization or agency, that is a difficult matter.*[28]

Indeed, a report issued by Senator Fred Thompson on the observance of the Clinger-Cohen Act revealed that by and large few agencies were abiding by it, four years after its passage:

> *Agencies Aren't Complying with Capital Investment and Planning and Performance Measures.*[29]

Even the FBI Messes Things Up   The audit report on the FBI, which has doled out hundreds of millions of dollars on IT without having established a good selection process and good project control (see the ITIM process in "Maturity and IT Portfolio Management") is out and out humiliating. It is impossible for the FBI to determine whether IT projects will satisfy expectations:

The FBI is not effectively selecting, controlling, and evaluating its IT investments because it has not fully implemented any of the critical processes necessary for successful IT investment management. In the past, the FBI has not given sufficient attention to information technology investment management. As a result, the FBI continues to spend hundreds of millions of dollars on IT projects without having adequate selection and project management controls in place to ensure that IT projects will meet intended goals.[30]

It Is too Much and People Lack the Expertise   Seven years after its passage, the Clinger-Cohen Act still does not live up to its official name, which is the IT Management Reform Act. The intended reform of IT management has been insufficiently realized. In an article entitled "Overwhelmed? If Your Daily Work Leaves You No Time to Focus on OMB's Management Agenda, You're Not Alone," Paul Brubaker, a former deputy CIO at the U.S. Department of Defense, says:

There's a lot of going through the motions and pretending that we're CIOs, but folks don't have the knowledge to make these things reality.[31]

When we spoke to Paul Strassmann on this subject one week before Brubaker's outpouring appeared in *Federal Computer Week*, he responded by saying that in recent years those who had tried to give flesh and blood to the Clinger-Cohen initiatives had interrupted their efforts because of a lack of funds. The result has been a well intentioned checklist and enormous quantities of forms that everyone needs to complete. A usable structure and sufficient knowledge to allow fulfillment of the requirements are still lacking. People are fed up with it. In every organization, there is still a great deal of rummaging around in an effort to construct "IT portfolio management," as the entire exercise is so elegantly titled, from the ground up. However, it is imperative that such management be implemented, for it involves the most basic calculations we can make.

Budgeting Better   AT NASA, Strassmann was making an enormous effort to gain insight into the 3000 IT-related projects being run at that agency. This task could not simply be recorded on a spreadsheet.

The 50 MB of data and all the various views effectively required a separate operating environment. However, Strassmann was, in his own words, only concerned about "better budgeting."

1998: The Information Paradox

In 1998, the public at large was exposed to IT portfolio management by way of the book *The Information Paradox: Realizing the Business Benefits of Information Technology*[32] by John Thorp. Thorp shows how IT portfolio management can lead to spreading and reduction of risks in the IT and organizational areas, as well as to better performances. Thorp interrelates, among other factors, full-cycle governance, portfolio management, program management, productivity, and complexity (see the section "IT Portfolio Management in the Context of Governance, Projects, Programs, and Performance").

Government Managers, Pay Attention! Government efforts to promote IT portfolio management continued. At the beginning of 1998, the report "Executive Guide: Measuring Performance and Demonstrating Results of Information Technology Investments" was published by the American General Accounting Office.

Best Practice in Washington State In January 1998, the Information Services Board approved a set of rules of conduct, standards, and guidelines for portfolio management that it developed with the Customer Advisory Board of the Department of Information Services. This was the origin of the elaborate IT portfolio framework in Washington State. These "IT Portfolio Management Policy, Standards, and Guidelines," which are still being revised, include the following sections:[33]

- Executive Guide to Managing Information Technology Portfolios
- Information Technology Portfolio Management Standards
- IT Portfolio Management Policy
- IT Project Management Policy
- Project Management Guidelines
- IT Security Policy
- IT Security Standards

- IT Disaster Recovery and Business Resumption Planning Policy
- IT Disaster Recovery and Business Resumption Planning Standards
- Information Technology Investment Policy
- Information Technology Investment Standards
- Feasibility Study Guidelines

Together, this cohesive collection of guidelines and templates gives a good picture of what must be understood as IT portfolio management in U.S. government circles.

I-TIPS: The IT Investment Portfolio System   Although it is far from the case that all goes according to plan in practice, every effort is being made in the United States to get IT portfolio management off the ground. For this reason, the IT Investment Portfolio System (I-TIPS) and the associated federal IT capital planning process are accessible on the Internet. The I-TIPS templates enable public officials to initiate the proper dialogues, fill in the forms, and provide all the data as the legislators intended.[34] Undoubtedly, the use of this material must be based on good insight into and understanding of what is involved. The following list summarizes some of what I-TIPS has to offer:

- A way of understanding your IT strengths and weaknesses from the organizational, life cycle, business mission, business strategic, IT strategic, risk management, and service perspectives
- A single source for executive-level investment information
- Multiple ways of viewing and categorizing investments
- Agency-defined criteria for evaluating IT investments
- Consolidated information on risk and return
- Automatic generation of OMB Reports
- A structure compatible with GAO's IT Capital Planning Process
- The creation of a self-documenting business case for investments
- A central source of cost, risk, and mission support information
- Up-to-date information about individual IT capital planning initiatives
- Up-to-date information about the entire IT investment portfolio
- A means of assessing the impact on organizations of modifying the IT capital investment portfolio
- A focus for IT capital investments on critical missions, goals, and objectives

- Improvement of information dissemination and service delivery
- Minimization of IT infrastructure and operating costs
- Assessment of risk reduction for IT-associated investments

2001: Added Value of Project Portfolio Management

After the collapse of the New Economy, IT portfolio management was once again enthusiastically embraced. In his dissertation "The Added Value of Project Portfolio Management," Anthony R. van Tilburg gives a positive answer to the essential question about the surplus value of this approach.[35] Various individual elements must, of course, be adequately integrated, although this is—once again—more easily said than done!

2002: Business of IT Portfolio Management

The undesired economic and managerial developments of recent years resulted in a breakthrough for IT portfolio management. At the beginning of 2002, META Group issued a report entitled "The Business of IT Portfolio Management: Balancing Risk, Innovation, and ROI,"[36] which was discussed in the previous section "Maturity and IT Portfolio Management."

Homegrown Quantitative IT Portfolio Management　　Chris Verhoef, professor at the Free University of Amsterdam, published a substantial and groundbreaking article "Quantitative IT Portfolio Management" (QIPM). On the basis of his work for Deutsche Bank and ING, Verhoef shows how the QIPM process must unroll. It is his experience that data are collected without any idea of what to do with them. Teaching by illustration, Verhoef urges us to account for IT in a systematic way. Step by step, he proposes formulas for CMM level 1, the lowest level of maturity, the one at which most organizations are found (see the previous section "IT Portfolio Management Begins with Outlines, Architecture, and Calculation").

Initial Experiences with IT Portfolio Management　　The year 2002 ends with the report entitled "A Summary of First Practices and Lessons Learned in

Information Technology Portfolio Management," published by the CIO Council. We will explore this report in greater detail in the following section.

2003: Aligning Projects with Objectives in Unpredictable Times

In March 2003, Cathleen Benko and F. Warren McFarlan produced *Connecting the Dots*.[37] The subtitle of this book tells us the task with which we are confronted: *Aligning Projects with Objectives in Unpredictable Times*. This book provides a practical set of portfolio management tools.

Sarbanes-Oxley Act Takes Effect   In 2003, *ComputerWorld* published a number of articles on the impact of the 2002 Public Company Accounting Reform and Investor Protection Act (better known as Sarbanes-Oxley), which, as noted before, strengthened the reporting and accountability requirements for publicly traded companies. The CEO and CFO must personally sign for the accuracy of reports and are principally responsible. IT portfolio management is thus a must for every company listed on the stock exchange in the United States, as well as for organizations with a certain number of U.S. stockholders or with a large quantity of assets in that country. CIOs are assigned the duty of providing their CFO with more detailed data about IT projects:

> *CFOs Go to Their CIOs for More Data*
>
> *Many CFOs are demanding that CIOs provide them with more detailed information about ongoing IT projects, including spending and status reports, to help satisfy a provision of the Sarbanes-Oxley Act of 2002.*[38]

PortfolioStep: A Tool-Independent Framework   An addition to the various tools that have been available for some time went live in June of 2003—the PortfolioStep framework (*www.portfoliostep.com*). This framework is based on the PMBOK PortfolioStep and complies with the international standard of project management of the Project Management Institute. PortfolioStep provides methods and training for implementation of project management.

THOU SHALT PRACTICE IT PORTFOLIO MANAGEMENT

In the United States, portfolio management for IT received attention much earlier than in the rest of the world, not least because of legislation and regulations. In March 2002, the CIO Council issued its initial findings and recommendations on portfolio management.[39] This was an exceptionally important moment; for the first time since the first regulations in the direction of portfolio management were issued, an official document was made available that revealed how the regulations were being put into practice. This and the following section will focus on these initial recommendations. Exactly four years earlier, in March 1998, the GAO had put out guidelines for measuring the effectiveness of IT investment, for which the 1994 Federal Acquisition Act and the 1996 Clinger-Cohen Act had laid the foundations. Both sets of laws required performance- and results-oriented decision making for all large IT investments. Such decision making was also to be in accordance with the Government Performance and Results Act, a law implemented in 1993 stipulating that managers in public sector positions must define their missions, formulate their goals, measure their performances, and report on all of the above.

For years, an attempt had been made in the United States to make sure that the public money spent on IT was being managed properly, and for good reason. The total government IT budget, which was in 2000 a "mere" $38 billion, threatened in 2003 to reach $52 billion, a 37 percent increase.

The Clinger-Cohen Act contained for the first time concrete mention of performance measurement related to IT portfolio management:

1996: Toward Better Performance by Means of Portfolio Management

Reflect a portfolio management approach where decisions on whether to invest in IT are based on potential return, and decisions to terminate or make additional investments are based on performance much like an investment broker is measured based on managing risk and achieving results.

On page 5 of its first portfolio management report, the CIO Council again brings this fact to the attention of government officials: "portfolio management is the chosen, designated marching route, and the law says that we have to do portfolio management."[40]

However, the entire report makes it abundantly clear that portfolio management is by no means easy and a tendency may exist to give up or lose one's way (see "After 50 Years of Portfolio Thinking, IT's Turn Has Come" earlier in this chapter). Although it is possible to explain the core of the concept in five simple steps, such encapsulation also reveals the extent to which all of the steps depend on the manner of their execution. Consequently nine elaborate "lessons" especially dedicated to execution were contained in the report. Here we will consider both the five steps and the nine lessons.

Fine Recommendations, but What Is Their Source?

In establishing the first portfolio management recommendations, the CIO Council was careful to consult two "top teams," the first recruited from the private sector and the second from various government areas, including the following individuals:

- Director of Enterprise Governance at AXA/Equitable
- CSO/CIO advisors at Ingram Micro
- Senior VP for Information and Technology at Mitre
- Senior VP for the Public Sector at Oracle
- Executive VP of Operations at EDS
- VP of IT Operations and Planning at Ingram Micro
- CFO at GE Global eXchange Services
- CIO at GE Global eXchange Services
- CIO at Lockheed Martin
- CIO for the Wholesale Business Center at Verizon Telecommunications Group

- CIO at SRA International
- President of the Center for Project Management
- Director of IT Management at the General Accounting Office
- CIO/Director of Information Operations at the Defense Logistics Agency
- CIO of the Office of Personnel Management
- CIO of the U.S. Customs Service
- CTO of the Office of Management and Budget
- Associate Director of IT and E-Government at the Office of Management and Budget
- Deputy CIO of the Department of Labor
- Deputy CIO of the Department of Agriculture
- Deputy CIO of the Bureau of Land Management
- Deputy CIO of the Department of Housing and Urban Development

Take Heart: Portfolio Management Has Only Five Aspects

According to the CIO Council, portfolio management, in its simplest and most practical form, boils down to the following five activities. Note that a cautious approach to risk taking is a typical government practice. It must, after all, make sure that tax money is being spent in a responsible manner.

1. **Setting Goals.** Making the reasons why the portfolio was created perfectly clear.
2. **Examining Trade-offs, Accepting Them, and Making Them.** Determining the amount of money that must be committed to something in relation to other items.
3. **Discerning, Eliminating, Minimizing, and Diversifying Risks.** The investment mix may not imply any unnecessary risks; no limits of risk must be transgressed and risk must be properly spread across projects and initiatives so that the damage resulting from any problems can be limited as much as possible.
4. **Keeping Portfolio Performance in Mind.** Scrutinizing the progress that the portfolio makes in relation to its goals.

5. **Achieving a Desired Goal.** Trusting that the desired result will be achieved, given the amount of investment made.

The findings and recommendations have been laid down in nine necessary "lessons" for anyone who wants to engage seriously in IT portfolio management. Because lesson 9 contains a number of starting points, they are included in the following section as an extra lesson, designated lesson 0.

NINE INITIAL PRACTICAL LESSONS, PLUS ONE

The following lessons are adapted from "A Summary of First Practices and Lessons Learned in Information Technology Portfolio Management." The basic guidelines that concluded lesson 9 in the original document are explicitly included here as lesson 0.

Lesson 0: Basic Guidelines

Focus on standardization, efficiency, and communication in your project management approach:

- Ensure that there is a business case for all IT investments.
- Designate and substantiate the benefits and effects of IT projects.
- Remove unnecessary duplications from IT projects and initiatives.
- Consolidate IT activities whenever possible.
- Promote the use of the same information and auxiliary IT resources.

Lesson 1: Portfolio of Projects and Initiatives

Scrutinize the similarities and differences between portfolio and project management and act accordingly (see the section on "Governance, Projects, Programs, and Performance").

Project management is constantly alert to the way in which an initiative fulfils a requirement and remains satisfactory in terms of costs, time, technique, and performance. Portfolio management aims at a higher level of abstraction, involving the identification, selection, financing, monitoring, and preservation of the proper combination of projects and initiatives in order to achieve the objectives of the organization. Portfolio management specifically considers the total costs, risks, and revenues of all the projects in the portfolio, as well as the trade-offs that must be made.

Lesson 2: Leadership

Ensure that the (top) management in question remains motivated to make well-founded investment decisions concerning IT and that the observance of them is supervised.

Successful IT portfolio management demands strong leaders who, on the one hand, properly appreciate the value of IT for the organization and, on the other, recognize the advantages of portfolio management. The Clinger-Cohen Act expressly requires upper management to be involved in portfolio management insofar as this involves IT investment decisions. Such involvement requires a good examination of the business and the enterprise. In addition, IT investments must be made at project and portfolio levels. For this reason, higher management, portfolio managers, project managers, and other decision makers must always ask themselves two questions. At the project level: Do new or existing activities remain within budget and on time, and will they attain the desired technical and performance levels? At the portfolio level: Assuming a positive answer to the first question, is investment in a project (collection) desirable compared with other collections of projects? After answering the above, all managers involved must determine the size, significance, and composition of the IT investment portfolio. The conditions under which the portfolio can be adjusted must be well defined and communicated. Proposals in this direction must pass through a special committee (see lesson 8) and must be examined from an organizational perspective.

Lesson 3: Organizational Architecture

Make provision for an organizational architecture (Enterprise Architecture) that supports and substantiates investment decisions regarding IT (see the previous section IT Portfolio Management Begins with Outlines, Architecture, and Calculation).

Interviews revealed that the organizational architecture often functioned for management as a testing framework for IT initiatives within and between the various functional and commercial areas of the business. The organizational architecture is particularly valuable in formulating and focusing investment, activities that ought to improve the management and use of data and information. The same holds true for improvements to the development and implementation of applications, as well as to the use and maintenance of the IT infrastructure. Many organizations are still only just beginning to construct an organizational architecture, and a meaningful first step is to inventory systems and existing and planned IT projects.

Lesson 4: The "Holistic" Approach

Integrate IT portfolio management in the planning and financing processes and practices of the organization.

Leading organizations manage and maintain their IT portfolios by using various processes of strategic planning, budgeting, and purchasing, as well as IT capital planning and investment management. This nurtures the needed governance and encourages the structures required to guarantee that portfolio management permeates the entire organization (full-cycle governance). In this manner, the stages and steps in the formulation, management, and maintenance of the IT portfolio remain consistent and attainable.

Lesson 5: Define and Communicate

Define precisely the objectives that the IT portfolio must serve and make them known. The same holds true for the criteria and conditions governing portfolio selection.

This is necessary because the performance of an IT portfolio affects a large number of customers and other interested parties inside and outside the organization (see lesson 8). Also, the types of advantages that the organization is seeking and the extent to which it must be produced should be made perfectly clear. In addition, it is important to identify the risks that the portfolio performance can incur. Ensure that everyone involved knows what has to be done and what is available.

Lesson 6: Tools

Provide portfolio and project management, as well as methods and instruments for decision making and collaboration; use these tools.

The definition and management of the IT portfolio are extremely complex matters. Fortunately, a large number of many tools are on the market, including I-TIPS (IT Investment Portfolio System) from the federal government, as well as commercial products for investment management. All these tools vary enormously in functionality. The guide "Smart Practices in Capital Planning" goes into this material more deeply.[41]

Lesson 7: Dashboard with Lights and Meters

Continuously collect and analyze data and information that chart portfolio performance and make timely adjustments.

Improving the way you track and trace the results of IT investments can be done in several ways. Lessons learned shows that it helps to do the following:

- Periodically (quarterly, semiannually, or "whenever necessary"), inspect the IT portfolio and the individual projects. Above all, examine the commitment and the time spent by the sponsor, the critical path, the milestones, the deliverables, the current and prognosticated costs and resources, and the important issues that can make an impact on the business.
- Indicate clearly how much money is put to which use and what the return is. Good basic information is crucial here. The CIO is specifically responsible for communication throughout the organization, but business management is concerned with the IT

initiatives involving their own terrains. In practice, ownership, participation, and accountability are still often lacking.

■ As much as possible, extract the necessary information from existing sources, for example, from accounting and financial systems, as well as from project management systems. Of particular importance are:

- Return on investment, cost-benefit analysis, addition of value, increased profitability, cost saving, and payback time
- Strategic alignment, defined as support for the mission
- Impact on the customer, as defined in the performance metrics
- Technological impact in architectural terms
- The initial projects, the operations, and the plans
- The risks, along with avoidance and limitation of them
- General project management techniques and metrics.

The brochure entitled "Value Measuring Methodology" contains important rules of thumb in this area.[42]

■ Pay a great deal of attention to the strategic, tactical, and operational functions of an organization. At the strategic level, investment must conform to the organization's mission, its operational programs, and its set of objectives and priorities, as well as the articles of association, legislation, and regulation. At the tactical and operational levels, the portfolio projects and initiatives should progress in a proper manner (some of them in combination). Portfolio management goes hand in hand with IT capital planning and investment management. In this way, management can adjust the size, range, and composition of a portfolio, as well as the allocation of funds.

Lesson 8: Full-Cycle Governance: The Roles and Positions of All Interested Parties

In all respects, take internal and external customers for the IT portfolio into good account, as well as other interested parties.

For the most part, the IT portfolio directly serves the interests of the business divisions and, in so doing, the mission of the organization. Together, the business managers are the owners of the portfolio. They are effectively responsible for all portfolio decisions and investment results. However, this also means that, together, they must designate and utilize opportunities transcending any particular field. This is a substantial challenge, for which only a combination of informal and formal processes can furnish an outcome, because business unit interests, interests transcending any given domain, and organizational interests cannot, of course, just be "united." A good dialogue is vitally important to acquire understanding of each other's positions. The CIO has an intermediary task in this regard; he or she can use analysis instruments and score techniques to employ an entire range of objectives and criteria that have been created to guarantee objectivity and transparency. Obviously, all interested organizational divisions must be represented in the committee that ultimately makes the decisions. This entire system of "stakeholder buy-in" is absolutely essential for good portfolio management. It must guarantee that the organization's interest is served and that unbalanced growth of special interests is avoided.

Lesson 9: Interorganizational Collaboration

Pay close attention to the interorganizational feature of the IT portfolio.

Such collaboration is important not only for enabling better customer service but also for the standardization and simplification of functions, processes, and activities, including those involved in IT. The Federal Enterprise Architecture provides a good example of an overarching architecture, which the U.S. government uses to provide better service to the citizen by implementing more coordination and integration. There is much to gain here from IT portfolio management. However, more insight and understanding into the effects of IT investment outside the organizational limits naturally also entails correspondingly large challenges.

PORTFOLIO MANAGEMENT? BY ALL MEANS, BUT . . .

IT portfolio management is the definitive professionalization of the activities dealing with the integration of IT. It stimulates the dialogue between business and IT, as well as the mutual understanding between them. IT needs to be given a structured place around the subjects of costs, benefits, risks, and prioritization. What we contemplate is comparability. What is more, we are dealing with two sides of the same coin. The first side is the IT portfolio management internal to the organization and its meaningful integration. This is controlled by the operational needs and strategic goals of the organization. The other side is the portfolio approach as imposed by the legally enforced reporting prescriptions.

In U.S. government organizations, both sides are in line because transparency is essential (with the exception of secret projects). This is why we can find extensive examples on the Internet revealing, for instance, the exemplary manner in which the State of Washington deals with IT portfolio management, but also the extent to which the portfolio management of the FBI has been a failure in recent years. In business, portfolio management inside the organization is another question. Naturally not everyone should know how the various portfolios are regarded, nor is it desirable that the details of operational or strategic portfolio performance be known. Moreover, in the context of full-cycle business governance of IT and, correspondingly, of the professionalism with which we do business, no matter how "realistic" portfolio management may come to be, extensive concentration on portfolio management can never be a guarantee of the health and progress of the company. This depends, after all, more on such factors as fusions and unique product or service developments.

Furthermore, when businesses are confronted by large challenges, as many contemporary organizations are, it is less likely that they will pay attention to portfolio management and related issues. When the entire portfolio hangs in the balance or needs a major overhaul, the moment is right for making a fresh start. If good portfolio information had been available from the beginning, the problem situation might have been avoided, or at least the information could have contributed to a fast and appropriate resolution. However, professional management (and by this we do not mean the quick wins, however great) only bears fruit when a business environment has been stable for a long time. Portfolio management is a question of beginning and never giving up—which is the point made clear in this chapter.

Because of its financial underpinning, IT portfolio management will probably be implemented most extensively in the financial sector.

It is here that the most money is spent on IT and the integration of IT in the business processes is the greatest. No organization should overlook the general values of the portfolio approach: dialogue; knowledge of assets, projects, and innovations; a good allocation of costs; a focus on net value, awareness of risks, and prioritization; and the meaningful integration and aggregation of all these. In addition, the concept of *bounded rationality* devised by Nobel Prize winner Herbert Simon plays a major role: We use all sorts of rational constructs (including portfolio management) to set what are nearly superhuman goals. In other words, we humans are limited.

The most important key elements of portfolio management, which are Activity-Based Costing, Economic Value Added, Balanced Scorecard, and Applied Information Economics, will be discussed in Chapter 5.

ENDNOTES

1. P. van den Brand, "IT strategie voor managers," *CIO*, February 2003.
2. CIO Council Training presentation, 2001. *www.cio.gov/archive/a11_training_slides_updated_0717.ppt*; 'Companion Tool for Smart Practices in Capital Planning.' *www.cio.gov/documents/smpratc_tool_oct_2000.xls*
3. M. Broadbent and P. Weill, *Leveraging The New Infrastructure: How Market Leaders Capitalize on Information Technology* Cambridge, MA Harvard Business School Press, 1998.
4. Ibid.
5. P. Weill, et al. "IT Infrastructure for Strategic Agility," April 2002. *ssrn.com/abstract_id=317307*
6. PMOffice. *www.pmoffice.com*
7. S. Berinato, "Do the Math," *CIO*, October 1, 2001. *www.cio.com/archive/100101/math_content.html*
8. R. Zaal, "Beter blijkt ook nog eens fors goedkoper," *Automatisering Gids*, December 6, 2002. *www.markvanderpas.nl/beter.php*
9. P. Krass, "IT Projects: Get Smart", *CFO Magazine*, May 2003. *www.cfoasia.com/archives/200305-06.htm*

10. For an infrastructure partition into 10 clusters and 70 services that can be used in this regard, see P. Weill, et al., "IT Infrastructure for Strategic Agility," April 2002. *ssrn.com/ abstract_id=317307*

11. Clinger-Cohen/Enterprise Architecture, 2003, "Updating the Clinger-Cohen Competencies for Enterprise Architecture." *www.cio.gov/documents/FINAL_White_Paper_on_EA_v62.doc;* and I.L. Hobbs, "Competencies for the Enterprise Architect: The Solutions Architect in Government," 2003. *www.fedsources .com/elements/events/download/IraHobbs.pdf*

12. C. Verhoef, "Quantitative IT Portfolio Management," *Science of Computer Programming*, October 2002, Vol 45. *www.cs.vu.nl/~x/ ipm/ipm.pdf*

13. See note 7.

14. See note 12.

15. International Software Benchmarking Standards Group (ISBSG). *www.isbsg.org.au*

16. Metricnet. *IT-portfoliomanagement 128.121.222.187/specials/ it_portfolio_management.html*

17. Standish Group, "CHAOS Report," 2001. *www.xp2001.org/ xp2001/conference/papers/Chapter30-Johnson.pdf*

18. Ibid.

19. J. Thorp, *The Information Paradox: Realizing the Business Benefits of Information Technology*, New York, McGraw-Hill, 1999. *www.informationparadox.com* and *www.acs.org.au/nsw/ articles/1999062.htm*

20. M. DeVera, "Performance Measures Index," 2001. *wwwoirm .nih.gov/itmra/perform.html*

21. Project Management Institute OPM Presentation. *www.pmi .org/prod/groups/public/documents/info/1pp_opm3presentation .pdf*

22. H. Markowitz, "Portfolio Selection," *Journal of Finance 7*, 1952.

23. Modern Portfolio Theory. *www.riskglossary.com/articles/ portfolio_theory.htm*

24. Markowitz Autobiography, 1990. *www.nobel.se/economics/ laureates/1990/markowitz-autobio.html*

25. F. W. McFarlan, "Portfolio Approach to Information Systems," *Harvard Business Review*, September 1, 1981.

26. Sarbanes-Oxley Act, 2002. *www.sarbanes-oxley.com www .thecorporatelibrary.com/spotlight/regulatory/bush-corpres.html*
27. Clinger-Cohen Act and Related Documents, 1996, p. 4. *www .tricare.osd.mil/conferences/himss2003/Enterprise/Version_2/ DoD%20Clinger%20Cohen%20Act.pdf*
28. M. DeVera, "Performance Measures Index," 2001. *wwwoirm .nih.gov/itmra/perform.html*
29. "Investigative Report of Senator Fred Thompson on Federal Agency Compliance with the Clinger-Cohen Act," 2000. *www .senate.gov/~gov_affairs/101900_table.htm*
30. Office of the Inspector General, "Federal Bureau of Investigation's Management of Information Technology Investments," 2002. *www.usdoj.gov/oig/audit/0309/findings.htm*
31. D. Frank, "OVERWHELMED? If Your Daily Work Leaves You no Time to Focus on OMB's Management Agenda, You're not Alone," *Federal Computer Week*, October 6, 2003. *www.fcw .com/fcw/articles/2003/1006/cov-over-10-06-03.asp*
32. J. Thorp, *The Information Paradox: Realizing the Business Benefits of Information Technology*, New York, McGraw-Hill, 1998.
33. State of Washington, "IT Portfolio Management Policy, Standards, and Guidelines," 1998. *www.wa.gov/dis/portfolio/ index.htm*
34. IT Portfolio Investment System (I-TIPS). *www.itips.gov/cgi/ I-TIPS.cfm en www.usace.army.mil/itips*
35. A.R. van Tilburg, "The Added Value of Project Portfolio Management," 2001. *home.planet.nl/~avtnl*
36. META Group, "The Business of IT Portfolio Management: Balancing Risk, Innovation,and ROI," 2002. *www.verizonit .com/pdf/focus/portfolio.pdf*
37. C. Benko and F.W. McFarlan, *Connecting the Dots: Aligning Projects with Objectives in Unpredictable Times*, Boston, Harvard Business School Publishing, 2003.
38. T. Hoffman, "CFOs Demanding Detailed IT Project Info," *Computerworld*, April 2003. *www.computerworld.com/ managementtopics/roi/story/0,10801,80468,00.html*
39. CIO Council, "A Summary of First Practices and Lessons Learned in Information Technology Portfolio Management," 2002. *www.cio.gov/archive/BPC_portfolio_final.pdf*

40. Ibid.
41. CIO Council et al., "Smart Practices in Capital Planning," 2000. *cio.gov/documents/smart_practices_book.pdf*
42. "Value Measuring Methodology—How-To Guide," CIO Council, 2002. *www.cio.gov/documents/ValueMeasuring_Methodology_HowToGuide_Oct_2002.pdf*

CHAPTER 5

Activity-Based Costing, Economic Value Added, and Applied Information Economics

ABC and EVA: Pioneers of IT Portfolio Management

Portfolio management begins with a clear and structured insight into costs and benefits. We can then use prioritization (which is linked to risk assessment) to beef up the performance of an organization in terms of its objectives. We use both Activity-Based Costing (ABC) and Economic Value Added (EVA), for example, to determine benefits. There is no need to fear these instruments; their only aim is to delineate a fair and transparent cost structure as well as the net value that organizations ultimately earn.

Activity-Based Costing

Using ABC, we itemize all indirect costs—those comprising the overhead—and concretely attribute them to business activities instead of simply apportioning them. Simple apportionment—also called Traditional Cost Accounting (TCA)—is a source of problems because business divisions are almost always saddled with costs that are incurred by others. A good cost structure is necessary for several reasons, including the need to support price fixing for items such as IT services. ABC derives from the work of Robin Cooper and Robert Kaplan.

Economic Value Added

EVA reveals actual economic value by taking the costs of capital acquisition into consideration. This economic value—or shareholder value—is the basis on which every enterprise is ultimately evaluated. If there are no shareholders, we then speak of risk takers. The cash flow area with which EVA is concerned also involves Net Present Value (NPV). Because we would like to discuss the concept of net value here and not any of its specific variants (even if they are quite relevant in practice), we will not explore such metrics as NPV or IRR (Internal Return Rate) any further.[1]

EVA and Full-Cycle Governance

The use of ABC and EVA involves an enormous clean-up of financial reports. By means of the Balanced Scorecard (BSC) and ABC, we can use the actual economic value (EVA) as a leitmotiv for the entire organization in order to remunerate employees based on their positive EVA contributions. This ambitious total EVA approach warrants use of the term *EVAngelism*. The EVA package developed by Joel Stem and Bennett Stewart is, in fact, an implementation of full-cycle governance.

Applied Information Economics

We conclude this chapter with an examination of Applied Information Economics. This was an early attempt to consolidate economically based justification and standardization by combining the best of various fundamental subdisciplines, including Modern Portfolio Theory.

■ ■ ■

CHARTING COSTS

The internal governance of organizations means adequate economic-based control that stimulates behavior having a positive impact on performance. In its concrete form, this control amounts to the insightful prioritization of all sorts of special interests within the matrix structures of the organization (e.g., at the process or business levels). Internal governance of organizations takes place on the basis of small and large measurements and control loops. These permeate the entire organization; they are permanently active and continuously monitored. For this reason, we speak of *full-cycle governance*. These measurement and control loops should be as mutually self-correcting as possible, so that an insightful and organically functioning system exists within which everyone and everything finds its own way and its own usefulness, which are distinct from all the rest.

The insightful promotion and prioritization of all sorts of special interests to achieve optimal performance begins with the determination of costs. This immediately confronts us with a formidable challenge, as costs are often hidden, for example because business resources use the same processes, products, or services. The use of such common resources—often designated by the term *overhead*—must then be examined further and the costs concretely allocated to the processes, products, or services involved. A further step is often taken: toward the customers of these items. This approach has become known as Activity-Based Costing.

In establishing the ABC system, Kaplan and Cooper[2] distinguished the following four steps:

1. Determination of activities
2. Attribution of costs to activities
3. Determination of products, services and/or customers (cost objects)
4. Determination of the factors that set the costs (cost drivers): they link the costs of each activity to the products, services, and/or customers

The general ABC process model that conforms to these steps is presented in Exhibit 5.1. The direct personnel and material costs can easily be linked to the corresponding products, services, and/or customers. The cost determiners are divided into drivers relating to resources and costs relating to activities. We will see this reflected again in Exhibit 5.4, which further illuminates the implementation of an ABC system.

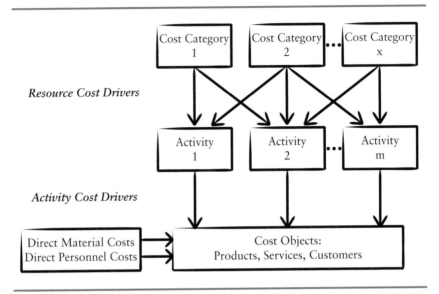

EXHIBIT 5.1   The ABC Process Model
Source: R.S. Kaplan and R. Cooper, *Cost & Effect: Using Integrated Cost Systems to Drive Profitability and Performance,* Cambridge, Harvard Business School Press, 1998.

Based on this allocation, strategic decisions can be taken that influence the efficiency and the effectiveness of processes. This is an important observation, for it means that ABC is something other than an operational examination of costs. ABC is concerned with aggregated costs, whereas operational costs are actual costs. The operational examination of costs is more meticulous but also more limited in its range.

If, as stated in Chapter 4, portfolio management is the first widespread and widely supported operationalization of governance inside organizations, then ABC is an important key element for this practice, in effect, the essential economically oriented component. The combination of prioritization and risk management—the characteristic heart of the portfolio approach—demands insight into benefits and therefore, as a point of departure, costs. However, like governance and portfolio management, ABC is both fundamental and conceptual at the same time. This means that, in practice, concrete application determines its utility.

It is not surprising that such a simple concept as ABC has a long history. As early as 1908, Alexander Hamilton Church, a well-known accountant, noted that indirect costs were increasing substantially, and in the 1920s and 1930s, many companies applied ABC-like methods because of the increasing costs of advertising, promotion, and distribution in a period of economic shortage. After World War II, the U.S. economy stabilized, as a result of which distribution costs became less of a concern. In addition, the high volumes and small product variation reduced the importance of ABC. This remained the case until the 1960s, when accountants at General Electric began to use the concept of "activity." In fact, the term had already appeared in the classic *Practice of Management* by Peter Drucker.[3] General Electric was handling thousands of products with only a limited quantity of direct costs and a large overhead, which needed to be distributed—but not to the products, as no production costs were involved. Consequently, a system was devised to allocate costs to activities. Only 15 years later, ABC would receive the form that it now has. In the 1970s and 1980s, the industrial prominence of the United States began to diminish, and it was necessary to be more careful about money. Such people and organizations as Robert Kaplan, Robin Cooper, and the Consortium of Advanced Manufacturing International (CAM-I) took the lead in this regard. In 1984, Kaplan made it clear that the existing accounting and management practices were recording production costs incorrectly.[4] Thus, when competition increased, good decisions could not be made about such issues as outsourcing, for example.

The need to divvy up investments and determine their impact accurately, which is the foundation of ABC, has grown in particular as a result of increasing pressure from competition as well as the increasingly expensive costs of IT, which was and is becoming more strongly integrated into business processes. In addition, our processes produce an increasingly greater variety of products. All in all, the cost structure has therefore been profoundly altered. Moreover, competition punishes mistaken decisions without mercy and makes frequent measurements of IT economical. We require accuracy and efficiency from the new costing system. Therefore we arrive at ABC. This is more or less the tale behind the diagram generated by Cooper and Kaplan, the fathers of Activity-Based Costing[5] (see Exhibit 5.2).

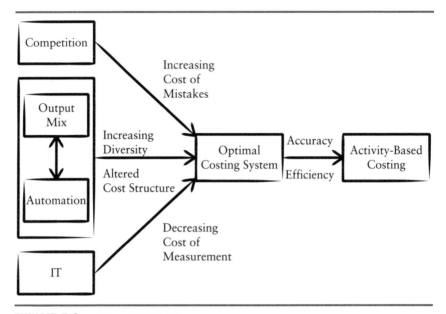

EXHIBIT 5.2   Why ABC Is Necessary

The following argument for ABC, which Raffish provided in the journal *Management Accounting*[6] and which concerns the production environment, is somewhat more concrete. Based on the situation in 1980 and the trend that was detected at the beginning of the 1990s, Raffish emphasizes the increase in overhead and the decrease in direct labor and material costs that U.S. business was then encountering. Only a very limited portion of the overhead is irreducible, and about half of it involves IT (see Exhibit 5.3).

In the mid-1980s, ABC began to undergo a successful development, along with its complement: Activity-Based Budgeting (ABB). The entire process is called Activity-Based Management (ABM). This development had an enduring influence on the manner in which financial information is collected and used.

It Is Possible to Underestimate the Value of ABC

ABC is one of the two or three most important management innovations in the 20th century and arguably the most written and talked about management accounting topic since 1985.[7]

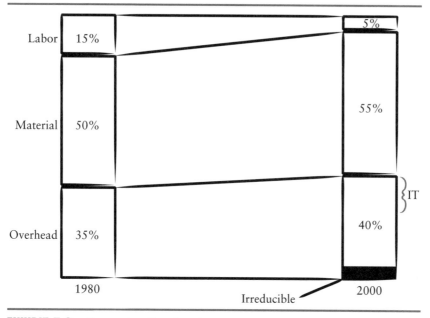

EXHIBIT 5.3   Increasing Overhead

Although ABC underwent what may be termed a successful development, in practice it ran into the inevitable objections. For this reason, many expensive advisors and system integrators were required to get the idea of ABC into people's heads and to begin its implementation, using the appropriate software.[8] Additionally, the criticism was made that ABC is historically oriented and therefore not really useful when we are interested in future costs (those involved in innovation, for example).[9]

Furthermore, the Japanese have never wanted to use ABC as a costing system for strategic decisions. In the eyes of the Japanese, it is more important to have a system of allocation that supports the long-term goals of the organization than it is to make any attempt to come to terms with production costs.[10]

HENCE ABC, BUT HOW?

Ernst & Young-ers Rafiq and Garg have described their work on the implementation of ABC in their article "Activity-Based Costing and

Financial Institutions: Old Wine in New Bottles or Corporate Panacea?"[11] They emphatically state that ABC must be properly implemented and configured and that it requires continuous maintenance. The appropriate information is, furthermore, of the greatest possible importance. This is discovered by means of interviews, accounting, monitoring systems, and IT systems. Once discerned, it is then inserted into a model incorporated in the ABC software system, which can then generate all types of business views. The ABC model in question must be properly adjusted to match any existing ABC system in order to avoid losing old data during integration. Exhibit 5.4 illustrates this point. The subsequent example (Exhibit 5.5), which Robert Kaplan uses in his lectures, is statistically related to the diagram.

In Exhibit 5.5, we can recognize steps 1 through 6 from Rafiq and Garg's model. We begin with a cost pool of €560,000. Scenarios A (Exhibit 5.5) and B (Exhibit 5.6) differ in the manner in which time is measured and the measurement of capacity that is possible as a

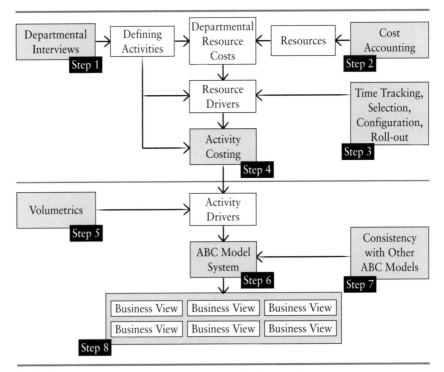

EXHIBIT 5.4   Implementation Framework for ABC

result. Scenario A involves a rough relative measure of time, whereas scenario B has a finer time scale. Kaplan also demonstrates in this fashion that it is worthwhile to use the same metrics when selecting specific factors out of the sea of data. Parameterization enhances an ABC system's maintainability.

ABC Scenario A: An Application That Is too Crude

Itemizable costs per quarter comprising the €560,000 include wages, supervision, computers, telephone, office space, support from other departments, and so on. The relative time requirement is, however, too crude in this case. In reality, we are only concerned about the amount attributed to each cost driver that is concretely derived from the number of productive work hours and the time that it costs to produce a single cost-driver unit, which is much more accurate.

ABC Scenario B: Refinement and Parameterization

Here we are using the example of 20 people who are paid for 500 hours in each quarter. If we consider that they spend one-fifth of their time on training, performing administrative activities, and drinking coffee, it then follows that, of their 10,000 hours, they effectively devote 8,000 hours to the activities we wish to analyze. In relation to the total quarterly costs of €560,000 that we must break down, the hourly rate is €70 (see Exhibit 5.6).

Subsequently, we subject the time that elapses in realizing a single cost driver to a thorough analysis. Let us say that we end up with

EXHIBIT 5.5   Scenario A: Too Much Guesswork

Activity	Relative Time Requirement (%)	Allotted Costs (€)	Realized Cost Drivers (€)	Amount per Individual Cost Driver (€)
Handling Orders	70	392,000	7,000	56/Order
Dealing with Complaints	10	56,000	200	280/Complaint
Checking Credit	20	112,000	350	320/Credit Check
Total	100	560,000		

EXHIBIT 5.6   Scenario B: Conclusion: Work Harder

Activity	Time Requirement per Single Cost	Hourly Rate (€)	Amount per Single Cost Driver (€)	Realized Cost Driver (€)	Allotted Costs (€)	Effective Number of Hours
Handling Orders	0.72	70	50.40/Order	7,000	352,800	5,040
Dealing with Complaints	3.60	70	252/Complaint	200	50,400	720
Checking Credit	4.11	70	288/Credit Check	350	100,800	1,440
Total					504,000	7,200

0.72, 3.60, and 4.11 hours. Multiplied by 70, the amounts for a single cost driver then come to €50, €40, €252, and €288, respectively. These are lower than the figures given above. Moreover, the calculation reveals that only 7,200 of the available 8,000 hours are effectively spent performing activities.

In this case, itemizable quarterly costs totaling €560,000 also include salary, supervision, computers, telephone, office space, support from other departments, and so on.

Keep It Simple, Stupid!

Tom Pryor led the renowned Cost Management System research project at CAM-I from 1986 to 1988. Thereafter, he launched the company known as Integrated Cost Management Systems. In addition to providing services, Pryor continuously publishes on ABC and related subjects. One of his concerns involves the complexity of ABC systems, which can quickly assume enormous dimensions. In smaller organizations, 50 activities can easily be distinguished and certainly 500 or more in larger groups.[12] Moreover, as many as 75 different allocation methods have been used, although experience has taught us, Pryor states, that no more than 10 should be used. He says that the best move we can make is to begin by implementing ABC for activities and processes involving the most money. We should not oversimplify; we should use our common sense and consider matters on the appropriate scale instead of getting lost in the details, a great danger that lies in wait. The slogan that Tom Pryor uses requires no further explanation: "An approximately relevant ABC system is much more valuable than one that is precisely useless."[13]

A further obstacle lying beneath the surface is the phenomenon represented by the "productivity rebel." This is a person who simply does not want to know anything about ABC, despite the demonstrable benefits to be gained from the resource when we implement it in an intelligent manner. Pryor gives an example of an ABC implementation that was cancelled at the last minute because the bonus systems in the organization were partially based on the variance in relation to standard costs.[14] Nobody had any idea how to do this under the new ABC regime.

Results Chains and IDEF0

In the mid-1990s, the U.S. Department of Defense published its "ABC Guidebook." For the first ABC step, the department advises readers to make use of "results chains" or "IDEF0" (pronounced "IDEF-nul").[15] Although such chains are intended as useful tools for attaining clear and structured insight into the most divergent types of costs, they can easily become goals in themselves. IDEF0 is a functional modeling tool for business and other system-analytical activities. It is based on the Structured Analysis and Design Technique (SADT) from the Softech Company and was later published as Integrated Computer-Aided Manufacturing (ICAM). IDEF0 belongs to the Ican DEFinition family. It uses graphic elements and detailed natural language descriptions to represent a system as a hierarchy of interlinked activities. This tool is in the public domain, has an American standard (FIPS 183), and can produce structured documentation for ISO 9000.

Results Chains

A results chain is a normalized flow chart that gives insight into the causal or logical links between the steps of a larger whole, leading to given objectives.

Results Chain

The causal or logical relationship between activities and outputs and the outcomes of a given program, policy, or initiative that they are intended to deliver. Usually displayed as a flow chart.[16]

Exhibit 5.7 is an example from the Treasury Board of Canada. It reveals how a results chain appears in the context of Results-Based Management and Accountability Frameworks. At the left of the shaded area we are within the organization itself, where the control of the chain remains in our own hands; efficiency is the central concern here. To the right of the shaded area, we are outside the organization, and the focus falls on influence and effectiveness.

Results chains are therefore an ingredient of the discipline known as Results-Based Management (RBM), a term that has only been used a few times. In the "RBM Handbook" for the Canadian International Development Agency,[17] results chains are regarded as processes leading from activities to impacts by way of short- and medium-term results. These categories can then be correlated with performance indicators, the source of data, the method of collecting data, the frequency of collection, and the desired staffing (see Exhibit 5.8).

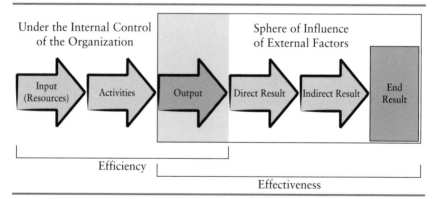

EXHIBIT 5.7   Results Chains in the Context of Results-Based Management and Accountability Frameworks

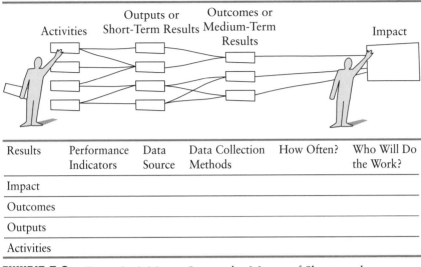

Results	Performance Indicators	Data Source	Data Collection Methods	How Often?	Who Will Do the Work?
Impact					
Outcomes					
Outputs					
Activities					

EXHIBIT 5.8   From Activities to Impact by Means of Short- and Middle-Term Results

Results chains also have a role to play in John Thorp's book, *The Information Paradox: Realizing the Business Benefits of Information Technology,*[18] which raises such issues as the need for portfolio management and full-cycle governance (see "IT Portfolio Management in the Context of Governance, Projects, Programs, and Performance" in Chapter 4). The results chains of an investment program, states Thorp, reveal precisely which areas must be measured. Such chains are not just pulled out of the air. They are the fall-out from discussions and should represent the consensus in management concerning the manner in which our business system program, labeled by Thorp Business-Technology-Organization-Process People (BTOPP), will yield results. A results chain therefore establishes our commitment. In the context of structured dialogue, one of the central themes of this book, this is a particularly important element with which we build the bridges in the organization that help us to realize the program. We are then specifically able to deal with important scope- and human-oriented questions. Exhibit 5.9 is a simple example of how Thorp views a results chain as containing four constituent elements.

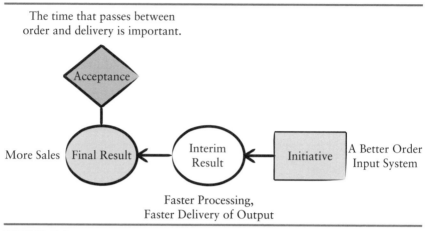

The time that passes between
order and delivery is important.

EXHIBIT 5.9   A Simple Results Chain

Source: Adapted from J. Thorp, *The Information Paradox: Realizing the Business Benefits of Information Technology,* New York, McGraw-Hill, 1998. *www .informationparadox.com* and *www.acs.org.au/nsw/articles/1999062.htm*

ABC: THE RIGHT PRICE AND IT

ABC relates output to the amount of activity that is necessary to produce it. If, for example, the total costs of business activities are collectively recorded (the costs incurred for all output altogether), nothing can be learned about any particular product or service. If these costs are simply apportioned, this naturally provides a distorted image of the individual products or services, or of groups of them. Prices that are too high or too low for certain services are the immediate consequences. By carefully analyzing and itemizing everything, it becomes clear which output uses up how much of a given activity: indirect costs become direct costs. The two examples from the banking world presented below illustrate these points.

ABC and IT

At present, IT represents the largest investment being made in many companies. IT is a fine-meshed, interwoven system that is indispensable in every business division. This value claim is key. However, of

EXAMPLE 1: ABC IN A LARGE REGIONAL BANK

"The use of ABC to efficiently allocate resources and to determine prices was the primary objective in the case of a large regional bank. Before ABC, the bank had no clear way to cost services or determine how resources were being consumed by different activities. In addition, since some of the customers were related parties, the bank wished to show that the charges being made to them were effort- and use-based (i.e., there was a direct correlation between the nature of service provided and the charge for this service). ABC analysis helped the bank to address both these issues—internal transfer pricing and strategic pricing."[19]

EXAMPLE 2: ABC IN A LARGE INVESTMENT BANK

"The drivers for implementing ABC in the global futures business of a major investment bank were both strategic decision making and internal transfer pricing. The bank had a clear need to determine which products and markets were profitable, and how it should correspondingly shape its business strategy. In this example ABC led to a fairly significant change in its internal transfer pricing and a dramatic improvement in its own internal performance measures. This is because ABC showed that the futures business had undercharged other business units in the bank for the provision of its services thereby reducing its own bottom line figures. ABC allowed more accurate and efficient charges to be made."[20]

course we must also know down to the last cent how the money is being spent, in order to allot the real price of the IT used to our profit centers and to determine, on the basis of these real costs, the value of our IT for these profit centers. Given the immense competitive pressure, this is a first requirement for adequate management. Otherwise, we are acting unprofessionally.

In most cases, IT costs are merely identified as indirect costs. When we simply apportion all the money, undoubtedly one department ends up paying for another. For this reason alone, we need to make IT costs into direct ones and keep them as such by means of ABC.

In 1995, Ness and Cucuzza wrote about the advantages of ABC at Chrysler and Safety-Kleen.[21] Five years later, in 2000, Cagwin and Bauwman demonstrated a relationship between ABC and financial performance in a study involving 205 businesses that measured three- and five-year returns on investment (ROIs).[22] There is no longer any room for doubt: ABC yields a great deal of fruit. However, how do the advantages of ABC for IT manifest on a concrete level? In terms of the application of IT, the following six advantages of ABC are dominant:

1. A clear definition of service, costs and activities
2. Information about areas that are susceptible to cost saving
3. A thorough pricing structure based on the use of resources
4. A view gained into the opportunities of outsourcing
5. Metrics for better cost management
6. Good basis for strategic planning and for the implementation of resources

What happens in practice? A terse sentence in the *Automatisering Gids* (*Automation Guide*) from mid-2003 leads us to suspect the worst: "The application of ABC to costs and revenues of information and communication technology (ICT) is still in its infancy."[23]

This is underlined in the thesis written by Henno van Maanen at the Technical University of Delft under the supervision of Maarten Looijen and Egon Berghoudt.[24]

By researching ten Dutch financial institutions, van Maanen showed that the internal costs of the IT organization were administered and budgeted in seven companies by means of cost centers. On this basis, there could be much too little control of IT costs. In three of these cases, there was a desire to use ABC. In two other cases, ABC was already in place. Even the remaining financial institutions were using an ABC-like approach based on the IT Infrastructure Library (ITIL). These last three "ABC organizations" were able to control their IT costs properly: it was possible to gain monthly insights into the costs of each activity or process, the costs of each product or service, and the activities devoted to the various products and services.

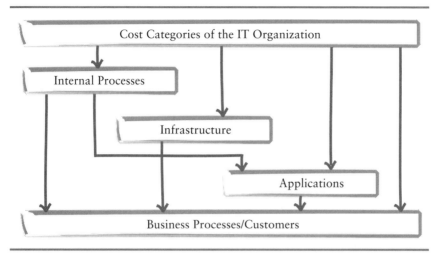

EXHIBIT 5.10 ABC Model for IT

In addition, these organizations considered linking to the Balanced Scorecard.

At the end of his thesis, van Maanen introduces the integrated ABC model for IT reproduced in Exhibit 5.10. In internal processes (i.e., maintenance), infrastructure, and applications, the Real-Cost-of-Ownership (RCO) approach of META Group can be used. For the sake of completeness, we introduce the objectives and the itemized cost categories of the various IT cost models in Exhibit 5.11, as published in the monthly journal *Informatie*.[25] van Maanen also differentiates four approaches, all of which are concerned with rough cost estimates and benchmarking.

REAL ECONOMIC VALUE AND THE ROI OF IT

An important question in the context of ABC concerns whether or not an activity actually adds value. Any activity that fails to do so should be eliminated in order to reduce the complexity of the production process; the remaining activities can then be optimized. However, it is not possible to simply eliminate everything that does not contribute direct value—for example, some endeavors may indeed help to estimate customer intimacy. We can distinguish three well-known and

EXHIBIT 5.11 Four Different IT Cost Models

	TCO Total Cost of Ownership (Gartner Group)	CNO Cost of Network Ownership (Index Group)	RCO Real Cost of Ownership (Meta Group)	WTR Cost of Worksites (Scientific Technical Council)
Purpose	Insight into and control of long-term IT costs	Insight into IT network costs	Insight into total IT costs	Definition and identification of IT worksite costs
Cost Categories	Hardware Software Management Support Development Communication End-users Down time	Hardware Software Personnel Communication Facilities	Applications Infrastructure Exploitation	Office space Hardware Software Local network Interconnection Management Telework Legislative costs

Source: R. Klompé, "IT-service als uitgangspunt voor kostenbeheer," *Informatie*, 2003.

strongly interrelated groups of activities involved in organizations: (1) product leadership, (2) customer intimacy, and (3) operational excellence.[26] Operational excellence is the focus of ABC.

The question of whether activities add value or not cannot be answered purely on the basis of ABC. In particular, we do not then account for the cost of the money necessary to perform the activities. The financial metric that does this is called Economic Value Added (EVA). In 1999, *Management Accounting* published a short article by Robin Cooper that explained the integration of ABC and EVA.[27]

Real Economic Value

It can be stated emphatically that ABC, portfolio management, and governance must be firmly linked to the ultimate goal, which is the performance of the organization or specific elements in it, such as business units or processes. However, we have still not said anything concrete about this performance or performances, or about their real economic value. "Real economic value" is what remains for the risk takers. This boils down to Net Operational Profit after Taxes (NOPAT) minus the cost of capital procurement. This notion, known since Adam Smith, is presently designated as EVA. Because the risk takers in large corporations are often the shareholders, "shareholder value" is often used as a synonym for EVA. The EVA of IT investment is a particularly controversial issue. We will return to this topic in "Accountants Overlook IT Value" in Chapter 9.

Nowadays, financial management is a tangle of rules, guidelines, and procedures. Thus strategic plans are often based on growth in turnover or market share. Individual products or "lines of business" are calculated in terms of gross margin or cash flow. Business units are represented in terms of Return on Assets (ROA), which does not take the costs of capital procurement into account or pay attention to budgeted profit levels. Financial departments evaluate capital investments mostly in terms of NPV, but they nevertheless regard intended acquisitions in terms of the prognosticated contribution to turnover. In brief, metrics and objectives are incomparable, as a result of which confusion and conflicts are created in organizations. Performance indicators frequently have little to do with business value, a situation that leads smart managers to do stupid things. Moreover, the bonuses for line managers and business-unit managers are mostly established on a yearly basis by means of a profit table. Because their bonuses are thus indirectly linked to their performances, a good incentive has not been established. Conversely, EVA provides a single consistent focus and makes sure that all decisions are modeled, monitored, communicated, and evaluated in precisely the same terms.

This may all be true, but what does EVA actually mean for IT? It ultimately means that the ROI outcome is fairer because the costs of capital procurement are discounted. A simple calculation will make this clear:

EXAMPLE: A SIMPLE CALCULATION

Let us say that we acquire €50,000 in hardware. If this investment has a net yield of €8,000, the ROI is then 16 percent. However, if we also include the cost of procuring the €50,000—say 12 percent—the actual profit (EVA) comes to €2,000, and thus the actual ROI is 4 percent. After all, 12 percent of 50,000 is 6,000; we have to deduct this from our 8,000, and the remaining 2,000 is only 4 percent of 50,000.

This cost of capital procurement can even mean that if one has two products, both costing €30, one may add value and the other may produce a loss, such as is the case in the following example.

EXAMPLE: IDENTICAL ABC COSTS BUT ONLY ONE PRODUCT GENERATES VALUE

Two products are entered into the ABC system as costing €30. Both are sold for €100. Consequently, a profit of €70 is made. However, they only remain equally profitable if we have to attract equal amounts of money to manufacture them. Let us say that we had to have €100 to make one product and €1,000 for the other and that we had to pay 10 percent interest on the money; this produces an EVA of €60 for one (70 – 10 percent × 100) and an EVA of minus €30 for the other (70 – 10 percent × 1,000). Hence, the first product adds value and the second does not.

Now, a low or negative initial EVA need not be a problem when the payback period remains within limits. One way of increasing EVA involves removing IT capital goods from the equation by means of outsourcing. The success of EVA is, among other things, revealed by the fact that companies like Goldman Sachs and Credit Suisse First Boston have adopted EVA as the most important benchmark for the value of businesses. Other organizations from around the world have followed this example. Even institutional investors are currently looking more at EVA performance.

According to *CIO*, "one in three finance managers uses EVA to help make technology investment decisions. And 15 percent use EVA as their primary finance metric for evaluating IT projects."[28]

EVAngelism

EVA is not only a measure that furnishes insight into the actual financial performance of an organization. The first EVAngelists—Joel Stern and Bennett Stewart—were determined to position EVA on a much grander scale. Linked to ABC and the Balanced Scorecard, the financial EVA metric grows, so to speak, into the greater EVA (see Exhibit 5.12)—into a profit-creation strategy for the company and the shareholders in particular. EVA, ABC, and the Balanced Scorecard are the three basic ingredients for making IT portfolio management work. They share the value orientation and focus on measurement of results. IT portfolio management needs all three elements that we need to build into a value-oriented system for IT management.

What is finally left for the risk takers is the profit of the operation after taxes (Net Operation Profit after Taxes) minus the cost of capital procurement; this reduced profit, pruned down in such a manner,

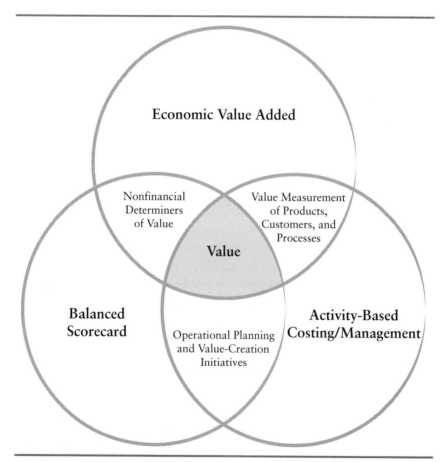

EXHIBIT 5.12   Three Core Ingredients of Portfolio Management

is the shareholder value. The EVA metric, or so it is claimed, makes it possible to institute a revised system of priorities and behaviors throughout the entire organization. EVA can be used as a practical means of focusing efforts on shareholder value and thus bring all the organization objectives into harmony. This is a solid basis for success in any organization, as well as for its individual employees.

Accordingly, the complete EVA package is nothing more or less than a method of implementing full-cycle governance. What is clearly lacking is the portfolio input. If we add this along with some extra support and statistics, we then arrive at what is roughly equivalent to Applied Information Economics, which we will discuss a little later in this chapter.

In the EVA system, the management is motivated by linking bonuses to EVA performance. All of this is supported by the following four instruments:

1. **EVA reporting infrastructure.** Views of EVA over time for each division, region, project, process, customer, and product.
2. **Integrated EVA scorecard.** The Balanced Scorecard along with EVA values and plans to communicate the value strategy of the organization.
3. **EVA business modeling.** The instrument that combines ABC/M and EVA.
4. **Online training for the basic principles of EVA planning and forecasting.**

SOME CRITICAL REMARKS

If we combined ABC and the Balanced Scorecard with a salary structure and massage of the complete body of thought, EVA could indeed become a new EVAngelism—or, as stated on the Stern Stewart website:

EVAngelism Is a Universal Success

EVA is a return to basics, a rediscovery of the most fundamental elements of business management that brings a lasting change in a company's priorities, systems and culture. EVA has been proven to work virtually everywhere because it is the right approach for all companies in all times and in all environments.[29]

We would like to add a few critical remarks to qualify this comment. To begin with, let us be fair; when using ABC, we work in fact with a Balanced Scorecard; whoever already has a Balanced Scorecard will use it when implementing ABC. However, as already mentioned, ABC is still in its infancy in terms of IT. Besides, the implementation of a Balanced Scorecard is no sinecure.

In an e-mail correspondence, Michael Bitterman, founder of the IT Performance Management Group (ITPMG) and former Vice President of Gartner, where he designed activities in the areas of IT Transformation and IT Performance Management, makes it crystal clear that IT organizations still have other things on their mind than the "soft benefits," e.g., the value of IT, so often given lip service. They are "usually" concerned about IT operations, services, and cost reduction, as well as the achievement of customer satisfaction in the most direct manner possible. IT organizations are evaluated in terms of these specific criteria. A confrontation with the issue of the business value of IT—in accordance with Forrester's fervent wish—does not seem to lie far off.

Michael Bitterman on the Balanced Scorecard, the "Value of IT," and the Measurement of Appropriate Things:

I spent a good deal of time trying to "fit" IT into the BSC [Balanced Scorecard]. It was like trying to put a size 10 foot into a size 8 shoe, it wouldn't go easily and if you did get it on it was very uncomfortable and you couldn't go anywhere in it. This experience gave rise to what we now call the IT scorecard. We maintained many of the aspects of the BSC, e.g. balance metrics in order not to skew behavior, cascading throughout the organization, linkage to causal factors, etcetera, but threw out the notion of having to create and maintain a strategy map and staying within the confines of the four perspectives.

The result of these changes was a much easier and closer fit to the IT organization's function and focus. Further, because of the departure from the BSC we were able to train the IT organization on how to build the right set of Key Performance Indicators (KPIs) for the organization. While many CIOs talked about wanting KPIs that reflected and communicated the "soft" benefits, e.g., Value of IT, when it came time to create the metrics they almost always focused on IT operations and services. This was/is not surprising in that most IT organizations still need to reduce cost, increase customer satisfaction and execute on projects and initiatives. Once they get good at all these things they can begin to focus their KPIs on the "softer" areas of measurement.

We also developed a very specific process for establishing an IT performance management program, which can include or exclude the actual IT scorecard. At some point you stop banging your head against the wall in trying to convince the CIO that they need the scorecard and simply establish the KPIs as a reporting mechanism without the features of the scorecard as cited above.

...

It is our belief that you can purchase and implement Business Intelligence software or Portfolio Management software, but if the process that established the metrics or selected the projects is flawed, all that you are doing is automating a flawed system.

In other words, the relation between a certain customer satisfaction and a certain business interest is mostly a set value. Hopefully, this value will be verified at some time, but there is the chance that it is only inferred. In both cases, actuality might have overtaken the validity of IT's business value, as was known and described at that time.

However, we must still head in this direction—toward this "real" value of IT. Otherwise, portfolio management makes little sense. The Balanced Scorecard has a large role to play as an orientation tool, even though it is trimmed down and not immediately linked to this or that strategic road map, nor exclusively confined to the four original Balanced Scorecard categories: financial, business processes, learning and growth, and customer (see Exhibit 4.10). This is what Bitterman's message boils down to.

Value Puzzle

The determination of IT's value, as we have seen above, is an exceedingly difficult matter (see Exhibit 5.13). The 1999 report "ROI and the Value Puzzle"[30] documents the processes involved in making such determinations, the use of metrics (NPV, EVA, IRR, and so on), and the methods to be employed. (The article "Quantifying the Value of IT-Investments" also throws some clearer light on the subject.[31]) One of these methods, Applied Information Economics, is the subject of the following section.

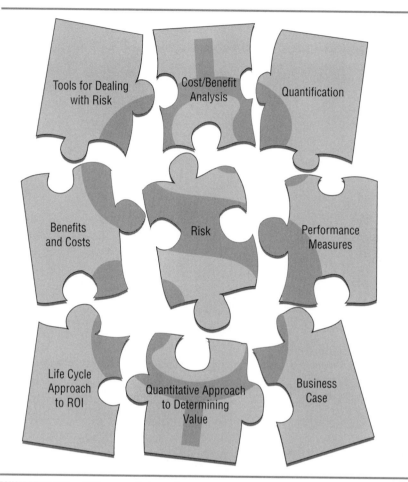

EXHIBIT 5.13   Whoever Solves the Puzzle Will See the Form of a Dollar Sign
Source: CIO Council, 1999.

APPLIED INFORMATION ECONOMICS

A shift of attention took place from the cost of IT to its benefits (because of the interdependence of IT and business and because of the value claims from the BPR and, subsequently, the e-business sectors), explicitly combined (on the expressed basis of business goals) with a consideration of risks, prioritization, and flexibility. This shift began to attain a more permanent form in 1995. Doug Hubbard, father of Applied Information Economics (AIE), was then still affiliated with

DHS & Associates in Chicago. AIE, which he developed at DHS, is now used by Hubbard in his own practice under license from his former employer.[32] AIE is meant to make definitive evaluations using purely financial cost/benefit analyses along with weighted-score methodologies, such as the Balanced Scorecard. AIE regards the financial cost/benefit analysis as insufficiently broad (and deep) and the divergent weighted-score methodologies as too unprofessional to furnish a sound basis for responsible decisions about IT investment. Instead of these two practices, AIE is meant to be an integrated method with thorough normalizations in all specialist areas that are rooted in science, statistics, and mathematics. Exhibit 5.14 shows the different disciplines that AIE brings together.

AIE is completely clear about the status of its own combination of initiatives. From the perspective of AIE, a purely financial cost/benefit analysis is only better than nothing, and weighted-score methods are illusory. AIE is supposedly the only approach that is scientifically and economically justifiable. Exhibit 5.15 shows this tripartite distinction.

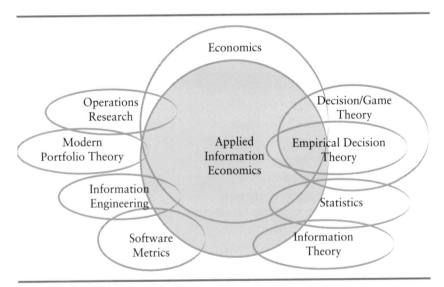

EXHIBIT 5.14   Disciplines Brought Together by Applied Information Economics

EXHIBIT 5.15 Supposed Superior Virtue of Applied Information Economics

	Better than Nothing	Illusory: No Measurably Better Investments	Scientifically and Economically Justifiable
	Purely Financial Cost Analysis	Weighted Score Methods	Applied Information Economics (AIE)
Financial Base Scales	NPV, ROI, EVA (proven financial scales of measurement).	Implicit or not present. The "scores" cannot be (easily) related to financial accounts.	NPV, ROI, EVA (proven financial scales of measurement).
Intangibles	Mostly disregarded.	Ambiguity not eliminated. In fact, the subjective scores increase ambiguity.	Means to banish ambiguity with properly specified definitions.
Uncertainty of Estimates	Decimal estimate. Distinguishes only on the basis of the ambiguous "hard" and "soft." Does not take differences in uncertainty levels any further into account.	No specific methods. Subjective scores only increase uncertainly.	Proven mathematical methods from actuarial science, statistics and financial management theory.
Information Gathering	Seldom systematic. Mostly independent of individual evaluation.	Seldom uses real measurement techniques.	Scientific information gathering. Also examines whether a decision is, in fact, sufficiently supported.

AIE is not only extolled by a self-assured Doug Hubbard, it is also praised by Gartner, Giga Information Group, META Group (now part of Gartner), and Marshall Van Alstyne, a professor at the University of Michigan School of Information:

Praise for Applied Information Economics

Quantifying the risk and comparing its risk/return with other investments sets AIE apart from other methodologies. It can substantially assist in financially justifying a project—especially projects that promise significant intangible benefits.

(Gartner)

AIE represents a rigorous, quantitative approach to improving IT investment decision making. This investment will return multiples by enabling much better decision making. Giga recommends that IT executives learn more about AIE and begin to adopt its tools and methodologies, especially for large IT projects.

(Giga Information Group)

AIE-like methods must become the standard way to make [IT] investment decisions.

(Forrester Research)

We believe that by year end 2000, 20%–30% of the Global 2000 companies will use AIE processes. CIOs will see the value of AIE to improve cost/benefit analysis to support IT investment decisions, develop financial-based QA metrics to validate IT efficacy, and compile and use the AIE data for strategic planning input to identify the best return on investment/value (RIO/V) for both new and enhanced information systems.

(META Group, now part of Gartner)

The theory of Applied Information Economics is right on target. People that don't use these methods will be missing a lot of opportunities.

(Marshall Van Alstyne)

Are we now dealing with the magical insights of Doug Hubbard? Well no... it is just common sense! Hubbard has undoubtedly conjured up a vision of the precise manner in which we might ultimately like to arrange things. If we consider how the scientifically and economically justified main AIE model pulls together the divergent elements of very relevant disciplines, not much can be said against this ambition. Once more, it is just a question of going ahead and trying it out, both in theory and in practice.

THE HUMAN MEASURE OF AMBITION AND LIMITATIONS

In the context of (quantitative) IT portfolio management, a good cost structure and net value is, at present, quickly gaining in importance. The way has already been prepared, especially by Activity-Based Costing, Economic Value Added, the Balanced Scorecard, and combinations of these tools, such as EVA.[33]

Full-cycle governance ideally means that the desirability of behaviors is actually understood, that they are mutually coordinated throughout the entire organization, and that the desirable behavior is adequately stimulated and, of course, put into practice across the organization, over time and in all budget cycles. Such a practice is not yet sufficiently developed. This certainly applies to IT and, because of the interpenetration of IT as well as its high investment costs, to the business operation as well.

Moreover, desirable behavior in information- and IT-related activities must be optimized, as such behavior is an important ingredient for good performance, the basis for such fundamental things as Activity-Based Costing, and therefore crucial for both full-cycle governance and portfolio management. One way of producing such behavior involves the Information-Orientation approach of Donald Marchand (see "Information Orientation and the Importance of Desirable Behavior" in Chapter 9). It still remains to be seen whether such an adjustment would be sufficient.

The generally accepted "bounded rationality" insights of Nobel prize winner Herbert Simon do not make us feel positive. These insights specifically reveal how limited we humans are; we use all kinds of rational constructs, such as full-cycle governance, portfolio management, and even ABC, to set what are nearly superhuman goals for ourselves. Anything that exceeds the human dimension is counterproductive, as history has demonstrated more than once. It is easy to build Towers of Babel, along with all the misunderstanding, miscalculation, and misfortune involved in them. Their construction, in fact, requires hardly any effort.

ABC, EVA, and AIE are examples of such overreaching constructs. When we regard them from a historical and philosophical perspective, all three are revealed to be Towers of Babel: too conceptual and not concrete enough—at least in terms of a translation into IT. Chapter 4 revealed that organizations need a great deal of extra help to determine and manage in a concrete fashion which IT investments actually contribute to business goals.

With IT portfolio management, we are trying to handle the situation in a different way. Given its full-cycle attention to costs, benefits, risks, and prioritization in relation to business objectives, IT portfolio management is perhaps still more conceptual than ABC, EVA, and AEI, but simultaneously we are also consciously attempting, for the first time, to keep everything related to IT completely concrete. Of course, we are "just" making use of ABC, EVA, and AEI, but now without taking note of it. Also, step by step, extra help is forthcoming from such tools as the investment process model (see "Maturity and IT Portfolio Management" in Chapter 4). Despite all the problems and obstacles, this gradual portfolio approach appears to be better suited to the human measure of ambition and limitation.

ENDNOTES

1. For a summary of financial performance measurement and management methods for everyone involved with IT, see T. Pisello and P.A. Strassmann, "IT Value Chain Management—Maximizing the ROI from IT Investments. Performance Metrics and Management Methodologies Every IT Stakeholder Should Know," 2003. *www.alinean. com/roiarchives/roiresources.asp*
2. R.S. Kaplan and R. Cooper, *Cost & Effect: Using Integrated Cost Systems to Drive Profitability and Performance,* Cambridge, Harvard Business School Press, 1998.
3. P. Drucker, *Practice of Management,* New York, Harper & Row, 1954.
4. R.S. Kaplan, "Yesterday's Accounting Undermines Production," *Harvard Business Review,* 1984.
5. R. Cooper and R.S. Kaplan, "Measure Cost Right: Make the Right Decisions," *Harvard Business Review,* September/October 1988.
6. N. Raffish, "How Much Does That Product Really Cost?" *Journal of Management Accounting* 72, pp. 36-39, 1991.
7. D. Brown, et al., "Organizational Influences, Ownership, and the Adoption of Activity-Based Costing in Australian Firms," University of Technology, Sydney, School of Accounting, Working Paper No. 46, June 2001.
8. D.T. Hicks, *Activity-Based Costing: Making It Work for Small and Mid-Size Companies,* Hoboken, John Wiley and Sons, 1999.
9. M. Smith, "Managing Your ABC System," *Journal of Management Accounting,* April 1994.
10. See note 5.
11. A. Rafiq and A. Garg, "Activity-Based Costing and Financial Institutions: Old Wine in New Bottles or Corporate Panacea?"

2002. *www.ey.com/global/content.nsf/International/Issues_&_ Perspectives_-_Activity_Based_Costing*

12. T. Pryor, "Simplify Your ABC." *www.icms.net/news-21.htm*
13. Ibid.
14. T. Pryor, "Productivity Rebels." *www.icms.net/rebels.htm*
15. Department of Defense, "ABC Guidebook: Guidebook for Using and Understanding Activity-Based Costing," 1995. *www.defenselink.mil/c3i/bpr/bprcd/0201.htm*
16. Results-Based Management Lexicon. *twiki.org/p/pub/Main/ RandyLegault/LexiconFINALFOMATTEDEnglish.10p.doc*
17. Canadian International Development Agency (CIDA), "RBM Handbook on Developing Results Chains: The Basics of RBM as Applied to 100 Project Examples," 2000. *www.acdi-cida.gc.ca/ cida_ind.nsf/0/D321E7D06CB2A65885256C62001B1B6C? OpenDocument*
18. J. Thorp, *The Information Paradox: Realizing the Business Benefits of Information Technology*, New York, McGraw-Hill, 1998. *www.acs.org.au/nsw/articles/1999062.htm*
19. A. Rafiq and A. Garg, "Activity-Based Costing and Financial Institutions: Old Wine in New Bottles or Corporate Panacea?" 2002. *www.ey.com/global/content.nsf/International/Issues_&_ Perspectives_-_Activity_Based_Costing*
20. Ibid.
21. C. Ness and T. Cucuzza, "Tapping the Full Potential of Activity-Based Costing," *Harvard Business Review*, July/August, 1995.
22. D. Cagwin and M.P. Bauman, "The Association between Activity-Based Costing and Improvement in Financial Performance," *Management Accounting Research*, 2002. *http://papers.ssrn .com/sol3/papers.cfm?abstract_id=298419*
23. W. Vercouteren, "Bezuinigingsmethoden kunnen slecht uit-pakken voor ICT," *Automatisering Gids*, May 2003.
24. H. van Maanen, "Total Cost of Ownership. ICT-kosten vanuit een informaticaperspectief," 2000, Thesis, Technical University of Delft.
25. R. Klompé, "IT-service als uitgangspunt voor kostenbeheer," *Informatie*, March 2003. *www.informatie.nl/artikelen/2003/03/ iTserviceAlsUitgangspuntVo.html*
26. M. Treacy and F. Wiersema, *The Discipline of Market Leaders: Choose Your Customers, Narrow Your Focus, Dominate Your Market*, New York, Perseus Books, 1995.

27. R. Cooper, "Integrating Activity-Based Costing and Economic Value Added," *Management Accounting*, January 1999.

28. J. Berry, "How to Apply EVA to IT," *CIO*, January 15, 2003. *www.cio. com/archive/011503/eva.html*

29. A. Ehrbar, "EVA: The Real Key to Creating Wealth," Hoboken, NJ, John Wiley & Sons, 1998. *www.sternstewart.com/pubs/ eva_excerpt.php*

30. Capital Planning and IT Investment Committee Federal CIO Council, "ROI and the Value Puzzle," 1999. *www.oit.state.ar.us/ Downloads/ITPlan/ROIPuzzle.pdf*

31. C. Verhoef, "Quantifying the Value of IT-Investments," 2003. *www.cs.vu.nl/~x/val/val.pdf*

32. Applied Information Economics. *www.hubbardresearch.com; www.infoeconomics.biz*

33. Stern Stewart. *www.sternstewart.com*

Supervision: Stimulating Desirable Behavior

Part One: Management

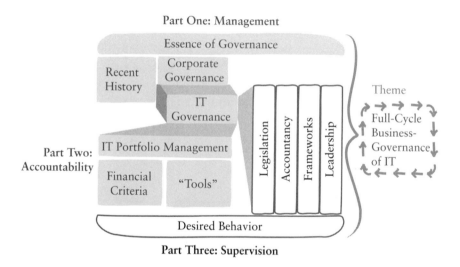

Part Three: Supervision

GETTING THINGS OFF THE GROUND

Part Three involves the supervision of behavior: Do things decided on actually occur? Do we get everyone on board? To what extent do we have to strictly enforce decisions from the top down to the bottom, and how do we cope with bottom-up forces? A limited number of organizations are currently busy with this manner of providing direction. We are also confronted with the challenge of winning over all employees, which does not happen by itself; it is useful to arrange matters so that we all willingly and enthusiastically do our bit.

FOUR FACTORS

In Chapters 6, 7, and 8, we explore four factors that are important for such implementation: leadership, legislation, frameworks, and accounting (the financial justification according to certain rules). The last three concern the "stricter" forms of supervision and direction. However, we must also deal with the weight that alternative forms of authority can and must place in the balance. In particular, we pursue the question of leadership. We will see that this trait is not linked to one person; leadership can be practiced by everyone functioning in his or her own capacity. Leadership must primarily be understood as the deliberate and clear performance of our roles in the appropriate relationship with the roles of others. If everyone is sufficiently aware of his or her role and of its place within the whole, leadership then furnishes an organic type of encouragement for other colleagues. Legislation, frameworks, and accounting can help to support leadership and vice versa.

BEHAVIOR

Chapter 6 focuses on human behavior. For a description of the conditions under which management mechanisms best flourish, we revert to two business-economic theories that penetrate the core of governance. They are organizational behavior theory and transaction cost theory. We offset them against the naive rational vision of humanity propagated by neoclassical economists. In this way, we come to the heart of the question of why supervision is necessary and to an insight into the degree of supervision that is permissible.

CHAPTER 6

Take Action When Necessary

Economically Justified Governance

Full-cycle business governance is used to provide a balanced treatment of the business objectives and behaviors that we wish to realize in the organization. We need goals and strategies on the one hand and successful action in line with our purposes on the other. Such action displays desirable behavior. In our full-cycle IT governance mechanism, supervision of this behavior and action at the right time are crucial. When do we intervene? When is supervision necessary? When do we let things go? The flag bearer of the modern business economy, Oliver Williamson, approaches this issue from the financial point of view. His "economics of governance" is an important current in business economics. Modern business economic theories are now beginning to insert the reality of human behavior into their models. Governance is not a kind of simple calculation, as some economists would have it—the "economics of governance" teaches managers to understand better how supervision should occur, especially in terms of the deliberations that precede intervention.

The Business, Ourselves, Our Department

What moves people to deviate from overarching organizational interests? The answer is simple: miscommunication or a chain of subgoals that are insufficiently linked. Even if both communication and the coordination of subgoals do occur, departments may persist in striving for their own specific aims. "Subgoal pursuit" is simply a part of any organization. Thus supervision must first of all involve surveillance of intentions, as well as the ability to communicate that these intentions must be channeled in the right direction.

We Cannot Do Everything at Once, Right Now

IT is a wish that is father to a thought. We think or would like to think that humans are hyperrational machines capable of absorbing any information and making only the right decisions. A Rational Economic Man, as identified by neoclassical economists, can scrape out everything that has been put into an enterprise. However, the reality is that we are capable of less than we think and that our competences are limited. We need to be aware of this fact. It is an undeniable part of the human dimension.

■ ■ ■

DESIRABLE BEHAVIOR AS A BLIND SPOT

Practical accounts of the effects of management are familiar; human beings and their conduct can be seen as if they were taken from a cartoon featuring Dilbert. In "academic" treatments, we encounter far fewer situations that appear to be taken from daily life. Academic observations have other merits; they supply the structures and concepts that are necessary to formulate our goals clearly and to support them. Structures and concepts are used to persuade others and thus allow us to establish indicators—at least, that is what we think. However, every conceptual abstraction downgrades cultural differences and the fickleness of concrete behaviors, so that these elements are given secondary consideration, even though they represent an important key to success.

We need both the clarity of structures and concepts and the anecdotes produced by concrete accounts (which frequently involve absurdities). Because anecdotal evidence cannot always be taken seriously and because it is difficult to predict fickle concrete behaviors, cultural differences and capricious behaviors are left out of consideration, for the sake of convenience. However, success can be achieved by focusing on behaviors, whereas too great a focus on structures and concepts represents a narrowing of vision. The danger is that theoretical constructs become dominant, causing behavior to be abstracted away. We overexpose the constructs and overlook what is really happening, as shown by the following story:

Here I at Least Have Enough Light

A policeman sees a man on his hands and knees looking for something under a lamp post.
"What are you looking for?" asks the policeman.
"My keys," the man replies.
"And they are lying here somewhere under the lamp post?" asks the police officer. "Not exactly," says the man, "I lost them over there," and he waves his hand in the direction of the darkness.
"But why are you searching for them here?" inquires the flabbergasted officer.
"Here I at least have enough light..."[1]

This joke is cited in the introduction to *The Support Economy*, by Shoshana Zuboff and James Maxmin, who emphasize that we can no longer manage with structures and concepts alone. Management concepts do not create the solutions for our problems. We need to search for other ways to deal with those problems. When you search where the light shines you will find concepts, but you really need to search in the dark to find the real answers you need. We will return to this point in Chapter 7, in which we will discuss the "apocalypse" that Zuboff and Maxmin predict. They feel that current organizations will fail because of their misunderstanding of individual interest and behaviors. Our changing society, they claim, will lead to a complete reorganization of businesses and new governance structures. In the future, organizations will flourish on the basis of the value that individuals create.

Interest in behavioral issues is increasing from various points of view. As a part of this trend, company strategy and business value are becoming linked to desirable behavior. This approach is different from that used in the familiar business/IT alignment; here business processes, information, and IT are the key factors. Such practices omit the relationship with concrete activities or at least underexpose it. No wonder that IT solutions do not produce the intended results.

The full-cycle business governance of IT places business value and desirable behavior on the same level. Such mechanisms as portfolio management and the Economic Value Added approach are indispensable concepts for establishing the boundary conditions. However, they only demonstrate their benefits when they are supported by the concrete actions of the people who make such instruments successful.

ECONOMICS OF GOVERNANCE

Modern business economists are heading in the right direction when they incorporate human behavior into their models. In this chapter, we examine the business economic approach to supervision, which we will categorize in the chapter's final section. We will see that these categories display a great deal of agreement with what we will have to say about leadership in Chapter 7. The economy of governance involves the cost of mistrust, ignorance, self-interest, frustration, learning, and thinking that you know best. The balance calculated at the end of the chapter summarizes which costs are incurred by each form of management in the organization. For a long time business economists did not dare to venture opinions about the financial consequences of controlling human beings in organizations.

From Transaction Cost Economy to the Economy of Management

In contrast to the neoclassical models, modern business economic theories explicitly attempt to find expression for the role of humans in organizations. In the first half of the 20th century, the guideline for relating our behavior to the cost of governance was provided by Ronald Coase and Friedrich Hayek's transaction cost theory. Although Coase and Hayek were the originators of this theory, the person who placed the relationship between transaction cost theory and governance on the map was Oliver Williamson, the standard bearer for modern business economics.

Transaction Costs Constitute a Key Economic Concept

Without the concept of transaction costs, which is largely absent from current economic theory, it is my contention that it is impossible to understand the working of the economic system, to analyze many of its problems in a useful way, or to have a basis for determining policy.[2]

The transaction cost theory states that internal projects and programs exist because it is cheaper to work within an organization than to make use of the free market.

Transaction costs consist of three elements:[3]

1. Search and information costs
2. Negotiation and decision-making costs
3. Costs involved in establishing and enforcing regulations.

All three are related to governance, the manner in which things have to be organized in order to keep costs as low as possible. In addition, cost savings may be gained in all three cases by clever use of information and IT. For example, when we are directly connected to the information systems of suppliers, our purchases can be made in a more substantial and effective manner. IT can therefore make market participation more attractive, with the partial or total disintegration of vertically integrated enterprises as a possible consequence.

Any decision to build and maintain cheaper IT systems depends on the costs we must incur in negotiating a good price on the market or, for example, on the price we must pay to remain up to date with the IT developments that are important to us. Can the market accomplish such things for less than what we would pay? And would there have to be another order and governance structure as a result?

Williamson took the step from "transaction cost economics" to "economics of governance."[4] He also reformulated the key question from "Do we do it ourselves or do we invoke the market?" to "How do we do it best ourselves and what can we do in-house to hold down costs?" Williamson and his followers have been reproached for perpetuating old-style economics and being too strongly wedded to classical notions of hierarchy and authority to appreciate properly the social relations in and between businesses.

Insufficiently Predictive and too "Inhuman"

Despite the claim of being predictive, transaction cost economics is still very retrospective and like economics assumes that everything has an economic value. Williamson ascribes too much influence to hierarchical authority and minimizes the importance of social relationships between and within firms.[5]

Although, as Mortensen suggests in this quote, economic approaches may be somewhat out of date, their findings can have a sobering effect. We assume that organizations will eventually be able to operate more efficiently as a result of IT. Research into how transaction costs have been developing indicates, however, that this expectation has not yet been fulfilled. Among others, Paul Strassmann suggests that the value of IT investments must be reflected in falling transaction costs.[6] He examined the development of transaction costs in more than 4,000 businesses from 1996 to 2002 but did not detect any decreases. According to Strassmann, this occurs because of rampaging IT departments (which had to be reined in), training costs, developments in software, reconstruction of legacy, and so on. With automation, we did indeed realize savings, but at the same time we incurred new transaction costs.

The other criticism of this economic approach, which Mortensen also mentions, is that it assumes everything is measurable; the importance of social relations in and between organizations is minimized. Although this is accepted by (neo)classical economists, it is not accepted by the new behavioral economists. However, economists like Oliver Williamson, Kristen Foss, and Nicolai Foss have brought transaction cost theory into the area of human behavior. In the following sections, their ideas will be given further consideration, and we will also discuss the work of Herbert Simon, who has put the human dimension into his theories.

SUPERVISION: A LOT OR A LITTLE?

When do we intervene and when do we allow a situation to run its course? In formulating an answer, we bump into the supervision paradox of Oliver Williamson. It is necessary to supervise so that it becomes possible to intervene when things go wrong. However, intervention gives rise to the chance that the person involved will be demotivated. What does that cost and what does it produce? Obviously, no simple answer can be given. Managers cannot spend the whole day watching their staff. Nevertheless, supervision is sometimes extremely necessary.

Kristen and Nicolai Foss, the former a professor and the latter an associate professor at the Copenhagen Business School, belong to the same school as Williamson. In their working paper "Authority and Discretion," they describe the deliberations involved in considering whether or not to take action in terms of transaction costs.[7] Authority is the central issue in this relationship. Can employees decide for themselves what they are to do or does intervention from higher up belong to the possibilities available at any moment? Foss and Foss have this to say:

We Do not Intervene

...when We Want Mistakes to Be Made

We do not interfere when we want a person to learn from his or her mistakes. Of course, we must determine whether the mistake that someone makes involves more learning output or whether it causes greater damage. Our first inclination, however, is to intervene when we see that things are going wrong.

...when We Wish to Prevent Frustration

Not being allowed to make independent decisions about ourselves and about the necessary resources can result in demotivated employees. The curtailment of freedom depends on a subjective estimate of what is good and what is not. However, blunders can also cause a great deal of damage.

...when the Other Knows Better

The question of who is right does not arise when people are experts. Supervision then makes little sense; an expert knows best what must be done in his or her area of specialty.

...when Everything Becomes too Difficult

Finally, Foss and Foss discuss "distributed decision making." Various studies reveal that distributed decision making is better than a top-down decision process in complex situations. When difficult issues arise, various departments and echelons must be seen to contribute their bit to the decision-making process. In IT, we are continuously encountering such circumstances. The infiltration of IT into a little bit of everything in an organization makes it especially difficult to undertake such a democratic practice properly. It is also often unclear who we must approach about the matter. Sometimes reorganizations make the practice untenable. Knowledge simplifies the situation enormously. The suggestion that clearer employer-employee or boss-subordinate relations should exist does not apply to IT. In this complex situation, supervision does not get us very far. Another form of interaction is the only solution: speaking with each other, sitting together around a table, and adopting a bottom-up manner of making decisions. Foss and Foss support the notion of distributed decision making by citing from Managerial Dilemmas by Gary Miller: "Dictatorship may do very poorly when the problem is one of making collective judgements about difficult problems."[8]

We will now turn away from these four reasons not to intervene, not to provide supervision, and to leave matters up to the employees. Now we wish to pose the complementary question: which cases require us to take action? We will proceed according to the views expressed in behaviorist theories.

GOOD MORES OR GOOD LAWS?

Sometimes a pertinent intervention is necessary, and in Chapter 2, we explored some examples. The enormous misappropriations threatened to frighten investors even further after the end of the Internet age. With the WorldCom scandal, the limit was reached; the U.S. government intervened with a law intended to restore trust in the management of organizations as quickly as possible. A law is comparable to an organizational directive presented to an employee.

The question is not whether we require supervision and control but the extent and the point at which the marginal return from extra supervision begins to dip. A trade-off exists between supervision and simply trusting that things will work out all right. In this respect, Francis Fukuyama makes a distinction between a high-trust and a low-trust society.[9] Jan Jooste, a partner in the American law firm of Huges and Hubbard, has a strong opinion on the differences in the levels of trust between the United States and his home country, the Netherlands. He is tried and tested when it comes to dealing with control mechanisms in big organizations. He writes the following about the differences between American and Dutch society:

In the Netherlands, There Is Still Social Control

The Dutch even have a tendency to economize on the apparatuses of control ... The Dutch have a completely different idea about ethics than Americans do. In the Netherlands, there is little relationship with lawmaking, but there are very clear rules and social pressure compelling you to behave correctly.[10]

Differences in morality are of course subject to dispute. It would be too simplistic to write off Americans as untrustworthy and regard the Dutch as social do-gooders.

Less supervision is necessary in the Netherlands because social processes act as a sufficient control apparatus. However, supervision and control do not involve ethics alone. Even when everyone is acting with the best intentions, control remains necessary, because supervision is especially concerned with competences. And since the Netherlands got acquainted with their own Ahold scandal, they have become aware that bad mores are not reserved to American organizations only. Laws and mandates are needed, even if we would assume that certain societies have stronger ethics because of social processes.

OUR LIMITATIONS

The need for supervision involves two factors applicable to every organization. The first is that everything done in an organization is the work of human beings. The second is that an organization is made up of departments, each with its own set of objectives. The more elements involved in a diversified order, beginning with the atomic individual, the more objectives and interests there are, and the greater the coordination that is necessary. The governance cycle operates in this context. Supervision is necessary because it can control and provide responsibility for all sorts of subgoals that contribute nothing or too little to the overriding goals of the organization. These entities were identified for the first time in *Behavioral Theory of the Firm*.[11]

This standard work, written by Richard Cyert and James March in 1963, as well as *Organizations*,[12] written by James March and Herbert Simon in 1958, has had a great influence on our thinking about the ways organizations function. No subsequent theories have taken the place of those presented by these authors. Sometimes we encounter situations in which it is difficult to predict organizational behavior; behavioral theory has not offered us much help here, and we run into difficulties.

The real limitation may lie in our inability to regard human conduct in terms of predictive, scientifically valid models. In our active lives, we encounter the most bizarre situations, which do not conform with the logic of our familiar theoretical concepts. We know, for example, that we act in the interests of the business by doing A, but certain circumstances have resulted in B being done. In following the path of least resistance, we sometimes deceive ourselves that we are acting in the only appropriate manner. These sorts of psychosocial mechanisms can have immense influence but have not yet been represented in workable, widely accepted models.

The Fallible Human Being

When Herbert Simon received the Nobel Prize in 1978, it was primarily for his pioneering work on the decision process in organizations. Simon has even characterized himself as someone who was monomaniacally fixed on decision making. His work was especially important because he adopted human limitation as his starting point. For a long time, it was more usual to portray individuals as capable of everything (omnicompetent). Simon introduced the fallible human being with limited competences. In his Nobel Memorial Lecture, we read the following:

> *... and it is now clear that elaborate organizations that human beings have constructed in the modern world to carry out the work of production and government can only be understood as a machinery for coping with the limits of man's abilities to comprehend and compute in the face of uncertainty. Responses to environmental events can no longer be predicted simply by analysing the "requirements of the situation" but depend on the specific decision processes that the firm employs.*[13]

In Simon's view, organizations can only be understood if we recognize the mechanism that has to compensate for human limitation. That people have limitations cannot be denied, even if it is difficult to admit one's own inadequacies. Fundamental human fallibility was, however, completely denied by the important thinkers we have come to label the neoclassicists. In their theoretical models and studies, they assume an idealized notion of humanity: the *homo economicus*.

Homo Economicus Rationalis

"Rational economic man" is the focus of neoclassicist business economic models. He has the capacity to make the appropriate prognosis on the basis of information. He knows his way to all sources of information, absorbs them, and understands them. There are no secrets. He can compare the outcomes of these prognoses with each other so that he can select the most optimal alternative. He is also constantly seeking the maximum return. All of these also contribute directly to the higher business goals. Finally, economic man is also, once and for all, completely honest in his activities and objectives.

This rational economic man plays a large role in Western thought. Our information society deluges us with facts, opinions, and advice, as if the adage "more is better" applies. However, the opposite is true: all the production around us does not make us correspondingly more productive. We are overburdened and can no longer keep up with the overload. Our focus is paradoxically shifting to information and IT production, while we neglect the problem of our incapacity to apply this production in a meaningful manner.

Why do organizations obstinately continue to embrace the illusion of an ideal economic world? The answer is twofold. First, it is obvious that not everyone is interested in the individuals who work at a particular organization. It is therefore easier to entertain a simplified view of humanity, one that is additionally in step with any given theory: Theoretical logic cannot be limited by an individual. In brief, this is the ideal individual. Second, (and we immediately run into the most important criticism against a behaviorist like Herbert Simon), how are we ever to practice science, obtain reproducible research results, or establish models when a fundamental human capriciousness is constantly throwing a monkey wrench into the works? For the sake of convenience, we therefore assume that human behavior is known and remains constant, which is to say that we ignore the behavioral factor.

OUR INTENTIONS

Rational economic man is thus the virtual superman that we have introduced for the sake of convenience. Herbert Simon has criticized this hyperrationality, introducing his concept of *bounded rationality*. The rationality of an organization is bounded by the rationality of the people who work there. They are individuals with limited memories and finite capacities who often cannot foresee where their deeds lead. The neoclassical notion of decision making is therefore an illusion. Simon's views have now gained broad support from nearly all contemporary thinkers concerned with the management of organizations. When we are making choices, we lack the mental capacity to calculate all the outcomes of all the alternatives. We resolve the situation by "satisfying," a good-is-good-enough principle that is determined by the level at which we find ourselves to be satisfied and that provides an alternative to optimization.

Various Views of Humanity

The story does not stop here. In addition to the limitations that Simon describes, we see another human quality in all newer organization theories: opportunism.[14] Simon presents a view of humanity in which human beings have limitations but also work on automatic pilot in realizing business objectives. In Simon's original theory, people are do-gooders for the organization. These "benevolents" are only inhibited by their imperfect capacities.[15]

Then other views were introduced, such as the one depicting individuals who allow self-interest to prevail. What constitutes personal interest can also intersect with the interests of the organization and its departments. This is not only short-sighted personal interest; it is aimed at short-term profit. A quick grab for the cash indeed yields direct profit but also runs counter to the organization's interest for which we are appropriately paid as employees. People fall in and out of step with the organization through the manner in which their pay interacts with standards and values. For example, we see employees choosing to join a department and an organization.

The egotist was described as early as 1776 by Adam Smith in *An Inquiry into the Nature and Causes of the Wealth of Nations*.[16] Smith does not regard egotism as a factor that has to be compensated for by supervision and pay but as the foundation of the economy; the entire society benefits from it. Egotism helps specialization to develop: the baker bakes bread the best and the accountant calculates the best. Self-interest is therefore not always necessarily negative.

What consequences does this have for supervision in the IT context? How does this affect our trust, as well as the manner in which employees are able to deal with complexity? If employees can do everything and if they do not pursue self-interest, supervision is then undoubtedly superfluous (see Exhibit 6.1).

EXHIBIT 6.1 From Mr. Spock to the Operator

Vision of humanity	Supervision
Mr. Spock (hyperrational machine)	No supervisory mechanism Complexity is no problem Trust goes without saying
The Pushover (limited and kind person)	Simple supervisory mechanisms Complexity leads to simplification We mistrust only capabilities
The Flip-Flopper (egotistic limited individual)	Simple supervisory mechanisms Complexity leads to simplification We mistrust both capabilities and intentions
The Operator (opportunistic strategist)	Complex supervisory mechanisms Control for misuse of machinery Synergy between business interests and self-interest

Mr. Spock and others who think very logically and base decisions on facts only exist in the Star Trek tales, but the pushover, the flip-flopper, and the operator can be found all over. For the opportunist and operator types, self-interest and politics will have a role to play. Of course, people cannot be stuffed into boxes and certainly not just these three. We have to establish adequate systems of pay, standards, and values that correspond with these types of people. When we do this, people are motivated by loyalty and insight to display the desired conduct. Of course, we are presupposing that these people are competent enough to perform their tasks.

The lessons offered us by Herbert Simon are especially pertinent to discussions concerning the construction of information systems. Humans have limited capacities to deal with information, and egotism is not foreign to any of us. The opportunist out for his or her own self-interest lurks in every person, and our governance structures should demonstrate awareness of this fact. In contrast, we are not entirely depraved; we also feel for others and would normally like to do everything well. Just like opportunistic behavior, one person may have a greater tendency to behave altruistically than others do. This remains true at all layers of an organization.

ARGUMENTS AND MISUNDERSTANDINGS

To allocate tasks efficiently to various specializations, organizations have departments. In so doing, we are also involved with separate sets of subgoals, rules, and regulations. Every department has, as it were, its own "language," whose words, processes, and conventions become second nature to the business. An extensive study has been done on the conflicts that arise as a consequence of the differing expectations, goals, and customs involved in various interdepartmental relations. These even have an impact on the collaborative relationship between business and IT. It is not uncommon for the IT decision-making process to be accompanied by arguments and misunderstandings, because these types of decisions involve distinct frames of reference and different conceptions about the course of affairs.

Oliver Williamson concludes that governance must ensure that the win-win situations in organizations are not disturbed by conflicts. Governance must produce an order in which problems are avoided, as Williamson says in his paper "The Theory of the Firm as a Governance Structure."[17] According to Williamson, conflicts, order, and shared interest are the three cornerstones of any organization. Governance must lead the way in recognizing the shared interests of departments, employees groups, individual employees, and the organization. Governance must bring the opportunistic individual and the organization together but also prevent departments from overshooting the mark in realizing its own goals. Governance has to create order and promote shared interests, so that goals can be achieved more easily and transaction costs reduced.

KEEP IT GOVERNANCE SIMPLE AND MAKE GOALS APPARENT

Rational economic man is not a conception against which we wish to fight; it is as if we would like to see our employees as all-capable (omnicompetent) individuals always acting honorably in the interest of the organization. However, an organization is simply not a kind of paradise but a construct in which interests will necessarily collide. The manner of controlling the organization, its divisions, and its people ranges from the gentle-handed approach to vigorous interference. First we extinguish small fires and smooth things over here and there. If things continue to run "rough," there are more consultations, and if the interests collide too severely, then the organizational structure might have to be adjusted.

Herbert Simon has made it clear that conventional management practices are inadequate. Intentions and competences can cause the feelings aroused by arguments and misunderstandings to become strongly entrenched. If we could ask Simon for two tips on IT governance, he would certainly give the following:

1. Keep It Simple

Taking our own limited capabilities into account and considering the complexity that is now inherent in every organization, we need to keep the managerial mechanisms, containing rules and processes, as simple as possible. Adequate pay and shared goals, standards, and values are instruments that can help stimulate desirable behavior from the bottom up throughout the organization.

2. Continuously Bring Higher Goals to Mind

*Divergent organizational and departmental interests make gover-
nance necessary. Making objectives apparent is therefore very
important.[18] We must keep talking and continue to douse fires.
Maintaining and adjusting supervision in this way is necessary to
allow the subgoals of individuals and departments to make their
supple and optimum contribution to the business objective of the
organization.*

The insights of Simon and the behaviorists are abstract, but,
given the constant battle that we fight about the relevance of IT, they
are eminently applicable to this field.

THE BALANCE OF SUPERVISION AND INTERVENTION

Behavioral elements have long been left out of IT discussions. We are
referring here to Enterprise Resource Planning, Customer Relationship
Management, and other business-related IT concepts. Full-cycle business governance must integrate the stated business goals with the
desirable behavior (see Exhibit 6.2); our arguments, misunderstanding, intentions, and limitations are also involved.

The interesting (and also tiresome) thing is that we all (must) act
on the basis of money and all our actions must be expressed in terms
of value. When we make governance a question of dollars and cents,
we have an objective reference. However, the translation of behavior
into monetary value is extremely difficult. What value must we
attribute to motivation and which costs to frustration? Because it is
so difficult to quantify behavior, the "hard" side of governance automatically receives more attention, and we feel unjustifiably satisfied
with what we achieve there. We continue to look where the light is
shining, while we know perfectly well that the key to the issue lies
somewhere in the darkness.

This question concerns what we must continue to supervise and
whether such supervision is necessary. Perhaps in some cases "non-
governance" is cheaper. If we draw up a balance sheet summarizing
what Williamson, Foss and Foss, and Simon teach us, we arrive at the
choices shown in Exhibit 6.3.

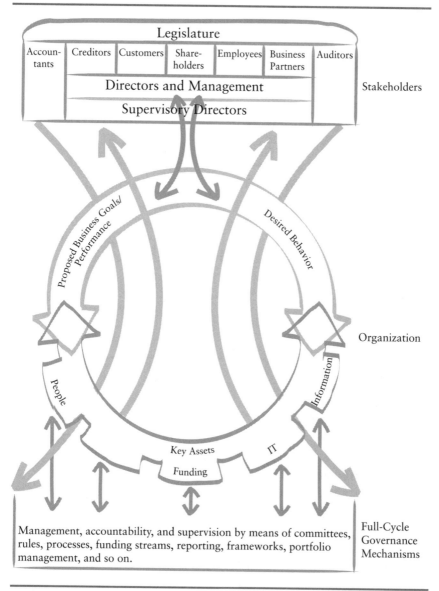

EXHIBIT 6.2 The *Perpetuum Mobile* of Stakeholders, Organizations, and Full-Cycle Governance

EXHIBIT 6.3   When and When Not to Intervene

To Intervene	Not to Intervene
Something really has to change: altered perceptions or circumstances	**Someone else knows better:** expert knowledge
Self-interest of employees: extremely opportunistic behavior, mistrust	**Avoid frustration:** intrinsic motivation
Disputes between departments: "subgoal pursuit" carried too far	**Deliberately allow mistakes to be made:** learning effects
Limited capabilities: "bounded rationality"	**Complex problems:** distributed decision making
	People are to be trusted: altruism

If we relate these choices to IT governance, the challenges confronting the leaders in our organizations become clear, taking us right into Chapter 7, which deals with leadership and how to preside over the changes in the field of tension involving supervision and intervention. Leaders are confronted with the task of uniting all the entries in the balance sheet in an accountable manner.

ENDNOTES

1. S. Zuboff and J. Maxmin, *The Support Economy: Why Corporations Are Failing Individuals and the Next Episode of Capitalism,* New York, Viking Adult, 2002.
2. R. Coase, *The Firm, the Market, and the Law,* Chicago, The University of Chicago Press, 1988.
3. C.J. Dahlman, "The Problem of Externality," *Journal of Law and Economics,* Vol 22, 1997. *www.sp.uconn.edu/~wwwciom/Dahlman.pdf*
4. O.E. Williamson, *The Economics of Governance: Framework and Implications,* 1984. In R.N. Langlois, ed., *Economics as a Process: Essays in the New Institutional Economics,* Cambridge, Cambridge University Press.
5. M. Mortensen, "Marks Org Theory Website," 2002. *www.stanford.edu/~mmorten/orgweb/summaries/mse/content/Williamson.html*
6. P. Strassmann, "Squeezing More Value out of the IT Budget," *Information Economics Journal,* 2003.

7. K. Foss, N. Foss, "Authority and Discretion: Tensions, Credible Delegation, and Implications for New Organizational Forms," 2002.

8. G.J. Miller, *Managerial Dilemmas: The Political Economy of Hierarchy*, Cambridge, Cambridge University Press, 1992.

9. F. Fukuyama, *Trust: The Social Virtues and the Creation of Prosperity*, New York, Free Press, 1995.

10. J. Ansink, "Vertrouw nooit een Amerikaan," *Fem Business*, 2003.

11. R.M. Cyert and J.G. March, *A Behavioral Theory of the Firm*, New Jersey, Prentice-Hall, 1963.

12. J. March and H. Simon, *Organizations*, Hoboken, Wiley, 1958.

13. H. A. Simon, "Rational Decision Making in Business Organizations," 1979. *www.nobel.se/economics/laureates/1978/simon-lecture.pdf*

14. O.E. Williamson, "Human Actors and Economic Organization," 1999. *www.econ-pol.unisi.it/quaderni/247.pdf*

15. O.E. Williamson, "Herbert Simon and the Theory of the Firm," 2001. *www.haas.berkeley.edu/bpp/oew/herbertsimon.pdf*

16. A. Smith, *An Inquiry into the Nature and Causes of the Wealth of Nations*, 1776. *www.bibliomania.com/2/1/65/112/frameset.html*

17. O.E. Williamson, "The Theory of the Firm as Governance Structure: From Choice to Contract," 2002. *groups.haas.berkeley.edu/bpp/oew/choicetocontract.pdf*

18. J.G. March and H.A. Simon, *Organizations*, Hoboken, John Wiley & Sons, 1958.

Leadership: Overseeing Change

Toward Better Management

Traditional leadership is inadequate, a fact that has immediate consequences for IT governance. Today simple top-down managerial practices no longer get us very far. The alternative is a combination of distributed leadership, genuine trust, and cooperation. These elements point the way to the management improvements necessary to restore the credibility of IT. To begin with, we will show the role that leadership plays according to a number of prominent authorities in the field of IT governance.

IT Leadership Is for All of Us

IT leadership is faced with the challenge of "guiding" the organization toward a state in which IT makes a larger contribution to business performance. This leadership is confronted with the need for an exemplary fulfillment of the roles that help to realize this change. IT leadership must furthermore provide the set of personality characteristics necessary to undertake the appropriate deliberations if authoritative task-assignment relationships should disappear. These characteristics do not apply to anyone in particular but to all of us working in the business-IT field in general. For this reason, we end up with distributed leadership. Finally, and most important, IT leadership is tasked with delivering the goods by converting words into actions. In displaying IT leadership, we ensure that we are getting the job done—that is, that we are getting IT portfolio management off the ground.

■   ■   ■

IT GOVERNANCE AND LEADERSHIP

If we can believe the journals, statistics, and studies, leadership is extremely important. Anyone who looks at the archives of the magazine *CIO* quickly sees the current topics: "The Utility of Humility," "Leadership from Below," "Advanced Leadership Learning," "True Leadership," "How to Say No to the CEO," and so on. For IT bosses, leadership is an important phenomenon, an essential ingredient in the spectrum leading to meaningful IT initiatives.

The fact that leadership adds to IT governance has also been demonstrated in our own research, the results of which are in line with the insights and findings of the IT Governance Institute and the European Foundation for Quality Management (EFQM).[1]

At the end of 2002, 237 IT decision-makers were asked what they felt had the greatest influence on the quality of IT decisions (see Exhibit 7.1). The respondents placed leadership at the top of the list. Four of every ten IT decision-makers included leadership in their top two, and nearly everyone mentioned leadership as an important factor. Business knowledge of IT and power sharing were in the second and third spots. Leadership seems to be an important (perhaps the most important) factor in the process of meaningful decision making.

The notion that leadership must be in the foreground of IT management is recognized by the IT Governance Institute, the originator of Control Objectives for Information and Related Technology (COBIT). The Institute gives the following definition of IT governance:

> *IT Governance is the responsibility of the board of directors and executive management. It is an integral part of enterprise governance and consists of the leadership and organizational structures and processes that ensure the organization's IT sustains and extends the organization's strategies and objectives.*[2]

EXHIBIT 7.1   According to IT Decision-Makers, the Leadership Factor
Has the Greatest Influence on the Nature and Quality of IT Decisions

Which factors have the greatest influence on the quality of IT decisions? (Multiple Answers Possible)		
1	Leadership in the organization	43%
2	The business knowledge of IT-ers	39%
3	The distribution of the authority (power) over IT	30%
4	The knowledge of IT possessed by the directors	26%
5	ROI calculations	20%
6	Internal political games	19%
7	The personal relationship between the directors and the CIO	5%
8	Recommendations of consultants	5%
9	Organization methods, such as Cobit, EFQM, ISO 9000	4%

Source: ViNT Study, 2002.

Seven years before the IT Governance Institute was established, the European Foundation for Quality Management launched its model for managing organizations. Leadership has a central position here also (see Exhibit 7.2).

According to many, leadership is important, but what it does is a little harder to identify. In the definition provided by the IT Governance Institute, there are three factors for ensuring that IT supports the business strategy and the business goals: leadership, organization structures, and processes. The Institute regards leadership as a business enabler, as does the EFQM model.

In terms of what leadership actually does in relation to governance, we are not made much wiser by the IT Governance Institute. The Institute's discussion stops at the observation that leadership is one of the three elements of governance. EFQM goes a little further: Leadership means the determination and realization of goals. To achieve this, personal skills are necessary, and these are what we identify as leadership. The skills make us capable of developing visions and plans and of getting people to implement these plans. According to EFQM, leadership becomes an especially crucial factor when turbulent waters are encountered. Leadership is two-sided: We can lead, but of course we also have to be followed. This is especially important when the organization is undergoing changes.

The ability to get people on our side is determined by their willingness to allow themselves to be led and the reasons why they will

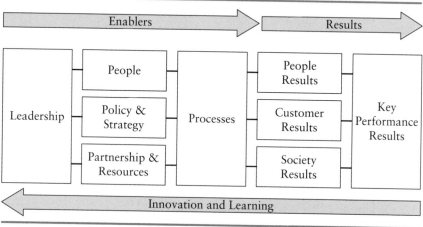

EXHIBIT 7.2   Excellence Model
Source: European Foundation for Quality Management.

allow themselves to be led. The latter issue has been researched by James Kouzes and Barry Posner for nearly a quarter of a century.[3] By examining which values are sought and admired in a leader, they have been able to compile a list of qualities. The ability to mobilize people is primarily determined by the extent to which people feel someone is honest, competent, far-sighted, and inspirational. Thousands of managers have now participated in this study. The results over the years have been highly consistent: What was important 15 years ago is still important today. Exhibit 7.3 shows what the order of desirable qualities was in 2002.[4]

EXHIBIT 7.3   What Followers Look for in Their Leaders (Multiple Answers Possible)

1	Honest	88%
2	Forward looking	71%
3	Competent	66%
4	Inspiring	65%
5	Intelligent	47%
6	Fair minded	42%
7	Broad minded	40%
8	Supportive	35%
9	Straightforward	34%
10	Dependable	33%

We seek someone who is honest, has some expertise, looks to the future, and inspires us. The extent to which we allow ourselves to be led is, however, subject to erosion. What attracts disciples to their leader may remain constant over the years, but our need to follow is not as stable.

FROM CONTROL TO DISTRIBUTED LEADERSHIP

If organizations would like to improve their IT management, a greater effort must be made than just distributing portfolio formats by e-mail. The challenges confronting IT leaders are great. In previous times, supervision and control could perhaps be fully contained in the organizational structure and rules, but this is no longer good enough. We still want to have our hands on the controls, but our actions often turn against us.

Claudio Ciborra describes this management paradox in the book *From Control to Drift.*[5] Forrester Research suggests that in the e-business age rigidly controlled hierarchical organizations are no longer suitable. However, when hierarchy disappears, what do we get instead? Leadership then becomes more important. In former times, all innovations and decisions moved much more frequently along hierarchical lines. Nowadays, everything runs together, or so it seems, exceeding the existing managerial capacities; thus we have a greater need for leadership. We suspect it is all becoming too complex.

Leadership is, above all, a set of personal characteristics that enables us to make the right decisions in complex situations. The information age has put a greater demand on these qualities, not only for people at the top but also for every member of the organization. We therefore have to rely more heavily on the judgment of others. Our trust in each other is also tested. Surrendering authority is fine, but we would like to be granted trust in exchange for it. We need to be able to trust that things will go well and that we are all acting in the interest of the organization. Work on establishing trust is therefore extremely important. This change in "organizational logic" is displayed in Exhibit 7.4.

The old way consists of allocating task assignments and exercising control on the basis of authority. The new way requires group

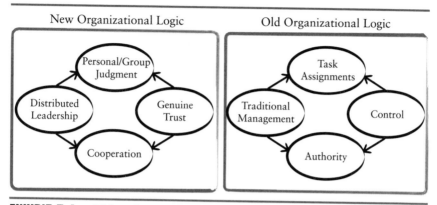

New Organizational Logic   Old Organizational Logic

EXHIBIT 7.4   Old and New Organizational Logic

and personal judgments, genuine trust (we will return to this subject; see the subsequent section "Cooperation instead of Coercion"), and cooperation. In his dissertation, Ryan Peterson says that we are dealing with a new organizational logic and that we must therefore work on competences, especially those competences involving new methods of decision making. In their book *The Support Economy*,[6] Shoshana Zuboff and James Maxmin discuss the new organizational logic comprehensively. According to them, we are involved in a new organizational form: distributed capitalism.

Shoshana Zuboff's Distributed Capitalism: The Apocalypse

Zuboff and Maxmin represent a new current of thought in organizational knowledge. Many scholars, organizational theorists, and practical experts note that the current cycles of supervision and intervention, control, and authority are no longer suitable. Zuboff and Maxmin's concepts are extreme in the sense that they forecast new organizational forms and do not believe in change from the inside out by the organization itself. They foresee a future with new types of organizations that produce value much more efficiently, based on the notion that these newly structured organizations will save, for example, on the costs of frustration caused by the mismatch between the organizational form and what intrinsically motivates people. When individuals have greater motivation, they will also serve the customer better. This organizational logic is more in tune with the wishes of the contemporary individual and consumer. Zuboff, the Harvard professor and Maxmin, the former CEO of Volvo UK, support their vision with a great deal of historical analysis. At the beginning of the book, they describe the coming apocalypse for our current forms of organization:

> *People have changed more than the business organizations upon which they depend. The last 50 years have seen the rise of a new breed of individuals, yet corporations continue to operate according to a logic invented at the time of their origin, a century ago. The chasm that now separates individuals and organizations is marked by frustration, mistrust, disappointment, and even rage. It also harbors the possibility of a new capitalism and a new era of wealth creation.[7]*

As outlined below, Zuboff and Maxmin predict an economic order of "distributed capitalism" in which everything concerning the individual will be organized. By cooperating with others, we arrive at maximized value creation. At the center of this support economy is "deep reconfigurable support by and for individuals."

Basic Premises of Distributed Capitalism

1. *All value is to be found in us as individuals. This value is realized in relationships meant to provide intense and sincere support ("deep support").*
2. *Because value is therefore shared, wide structures of production, ownership, and management are also necessary inside organizations.*
3. *In the new support economy, relationships based on devotion and trust are responsible for the creation of value.*
4. *Markets determine their own dynamics.*
5. *Intense, sincere support is the new denominator for economic activity.*
6. *Federative support networks are the new competitive parties.*
7. *All economic activity is geared to the individual.*
8. *Infrastructural convergence lowers costs enormously, as a result of which many more resources and services are made available to everyone.*
9. *Federations are repeatedly restructured.*

10. *New methods of valuation reflect the primacy of the individual.*
11. *The individualization of consumption implies new labor relations. Cooperation and coordination are key factors in this regard.*

Distributed capitalism is one extreme in the spectrum of organizational change. We remain somewhat closer to home with distributed leadership and will now explore what leadership can contribute to the transformation of organizations from inside out.

PEOPLE NO LONGER PUT UP WITH CONTROL

Het Financieele Dagblad cites a speech that Karel Noordzij, former president of Netherlands Railways, made to the association of interim managers entitled "On the Road to Another Type of Leadership." His slogan is: "people no longer put up with control." "People feel powerless and robotized," says Noordzij, "on the one hand, by the lack of attention to and respect for their workmanship, on the other hand, by the accumulation of rules and procedures. They have the feeling that they are not being listened to. Rules are made without me and about me. Along with this, business results are now under a great deal of pressure. Management often reacts misguidedly to this situation. It exercises still more control and introduces new rules that further inhibit the individual freedom of employees. Moreover, the focus on quarterly results causes the GPS of the managers to be misdirected. As a consequence, the clutch-and-grab culture at the top is increasingly distrusted."[8]

Noordzij sketches the situation in which we find ourselves. We want entrepreneurs: empowered persons who can direct events with daring; we don't want to be saddled with "scaredy-cats" or managers who are purely driven by Key Performance Indicators and who craftily combine self-interest and targets.

Just like Noordzij, Claudio Ciborra, professor of Information Management at the London School of Economics, is of the opinion that we are now in a spiral of increasing control that works contrary to intentions. Exhibit 7.5 is a simplification of the model from his book *From Control to Drift*,[9] in which he outlines this mechanism (see Appendix A for the complete diagram).

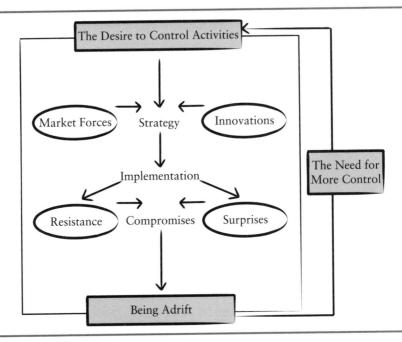

EXHIBIT 7.5   Ciborra's Management Paradox

From Control to Drift follows the development of infrastructure in six organizations for a lengthy period. Ciborra concludes that there is no such thing as orderly top-down decision making. Organizations with pyramid structures, hierarchical management lines, and mechanical decision processes are fabrications of positivist thinking. In practice, organizations do not work this way, as was already evident in our industrial past; in our current information society, such structures simply will not wash: "Although we can use technology to refine our governance, we also appear, with technology, to create a world that is resistant to control."[10]

Ciborra establishes a relationship between an aversion to control and the development of the technology that makes more information available to us. On the basis of his research into the implementation of IT systems, Ciborra comes to the conclusion that we lose our grip on matters by exercising greater control. Any strategy we formulate is influenced by market forces, cost reduction, and globalization. Even technological innovations influence strategy. Ultimately, a top-down strategic alignment gives rise to complex processes. Compromises are the result. A sort of bottom-up alignment is created, and we find ourselves "adrift." Management becomes aware of this and increases control; this is how the *perpetuum mobile* of ineffective management operates. Such ineffectiveness is caused by the complexity that arises in the entire strategic process and by the compromises we make when we subsequently wish to get the complex process up and running.

Complexity as a Side Effect of Strategy

Increasing globalization, cost pressure, and standardization are the most important influences on our business strategy. Technological innovation, which is important for the implementation of strategy, entails the introduction of new systems, the revision of business processes, and the use of new applications. Together, these lead to more complex IT, processes, and standards.

Compromises When We Implement

We must nevertheless take care to introduce the particular complexity into our operation, and we will be confronted by surprises when we do so. The surprises come from two directions. First, they come from technology, whenever it does not work exactly as predicted. Currently existing IT is one of the causes for such surprises. Second, we will run into resistance that will have to be overcome. During implementation, we can anticipate resistance by applying implementation tactics especially aimed at the groups from which the greatest resistance will probably come. These implementation tactics, along with the technological surprises, result in compromises and consequently a deviation from what the top executives might have intended or desired. Such drifting is a signal to intervene and to exercise more control.

Ciborra comes to two important conclusions. First, we must consider our IT from a different point of view. Only if we see IT as *bricolage*, as a patchwork of interdependent parts, can we arrive at improvements. Second, Ciborra makes an urgent plea for a "loosening of command:" "we should leave it to the practitioners." We need to leave it to the people who are involved in the work and who know something about it; we should not think that we can achieve better results with our management.

Control Drama

Noordzij talks about the "control drama" involving the rules and procedures to which we are bound in organizations. These are becoming increasingly more complex and wide ranging, a point that reiterates what we have just learned from Ciborra, who seeks the remedy in a letting-go of power, in delegation to others. Noordzij, however, looks closer to home for a solution:

> ...especially when we are under pressure. That's when we again control the details instead of the goals and strategy ... We, the managers, must begin with ourselves, not with the employees ... We can certainly go and read all the books on leadership, but that does not get you very far.[11]

Noordzij talks about the need to create a proper domain for the employees within which they have the freedom to work in their own way. Such a designated domain can be very threatening. "It places the responsibility on yourself, no matter if you are employee or manager."

The change that we have to undergo therefore involves both management and the people who are being managed. The commitment to realize the goals within one's own domain and to accept one's own responsibilities is a concern for everyone in the organization.

Leadership involves the overseeing of this transformation. It happens by allowing leeway, by setting up domains, and by stimulating self-reliance and personal responsibility.

Evolution of Leadership

In "Building eBusiness Leadership,"[12] Forrester Research describes its evolution, and brings leadership closer to the individual level. Everyone in the organization must display leadership. Leadership is thus not the exclusive right of management but a necessary quality that needs to be stimulated in every employee. Forrester speaks of "distributed leadership," which involves "a culture where employees at all levels make decisions and collectively exhibit leadership behavior consistent with company strategy."

In Forrester's model of distributed leadership (see Exhibit 7.6), traditional means of control are kept at a distance. Decisions are taken in a shared manner, and leadership is meant to stimulate further leadership throughout the entire organization (see Exhibit 7.7).

Noordzij, Ciborra, and Forrester all argue for a necessary transformation in corporate management. All three indicate that the individual must be granted more responsibility. This will not occur on its own; leaders are needed, individuals who have the supervisory task of ensuring that this change happens.

In "eLeadership for the Net Economy,"[13] Forrester describes the evolution of leadership as the transition of formal hierarchy, task

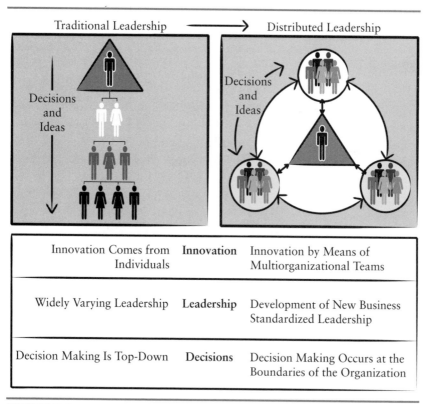

Innovation Comes from Individuals	**Innovation**	Innovation by Means of Multiorganizational Teams
Widely Varying Leadership	**Leadership**	Development of New Business Standardized Leadership
Decision Making Is Top-Down	**Decisions**	Decision Making Occurs at the Boundaries of the Organization

EXHIBIT 7.6   Distributed Leadership

Industrial Economy ⟶ Network Economy

Structure	Mechanical, Closed and Stable	E-Business Network with Fluid Borders
Control	Power and Information in a Limited Number of Hands	Power and Information Are Shared, Dialogue
Actions	Slow and Restrained, in Long Durations	Fast and Approximate, Iterative
Focus	Individual	Collective Tasks and Significance, Relation-Oriented

EXHIBIT 7.7   Evolution of Leadership

assignment, and leadership of an individual into leadership in networks, informal influence, and the capacity to enter into relationships. Employees who were initially told what to do by the boss must now make judgments and decisions either on their own or in teams. Wherever authority disappears, a need for the development and application of new skills comes into existence.

If we are to be controlled, let us control ourselves, and if we receive a leading role, how are we going to handle this freedom? Are we able to make the proper decisions on our own or in dialogue with others? Do we then have understanding of each other? Such issues become more important, and a close watch is kept on their interrelationship. It is not a question of just surrendering control. In Forrester's model of distributed leadership, decisions are made in teams. Innovations arise at several areas in the organization. Top-down is no longer the automatic pathway to change. Working on the required competences in order to understand each other and to arrive at good products that contribute to the essential relation with the business result is a necessary route we must all take together. Instead of performing only the task officially assigned to us, personal and group decisions need to be made.

This raises two questions. The first one concerns competences. When leadership is distributed throughout the entire organization, what qualities do we need in order to make good judgments? What does the "distributed leader" in each one of us look like? Second, when we make distributed decisions about IT, do we then have a number of IT governance instruments available to us in order to cultivate the necessary competences? We begin with the competences themselves.

EIGHT LEADERSHIP ROLES

Robert Quinn, who is a professor at the University of Michigan and who founded of the Wholonistics Leadership Group in 1998, is an authority on the subject of leadership. Key to his vision is the Competing Value Framework stemming from his 1988 book *Beyond Rational Management*.[14] In later books and publications, such as *Change the World*[15] and the somewhat older *Deep Change*,[16] Quinn constantly returns to this model.

The Competing Value Framework distinguishes eight leadership roles (see Exhibit 7.8), competences that are involved in various situations relating to our daily work. They affect how we process information and how we regard the world. Is this done because of the feeling we have for people, the goal that we wish to achieve, or the control that we want to exercise over the situation? Or is our mind open and, above all, outwardly directed? These four dimensions continue to build on the historical research into leadership roles.

Quinn distinguishes four modes of information processing that involve both the short and long term, our approach to risk (are we flexible or do we want control), and our internal or external orientation.

1. **Human Relations Model.** We deal with information from the perspective of people and process. The preference is for long timelines and little security; this model is internally oriented. Information is handled in a way that is sensitive to people as individuals. Collectivity is sought.

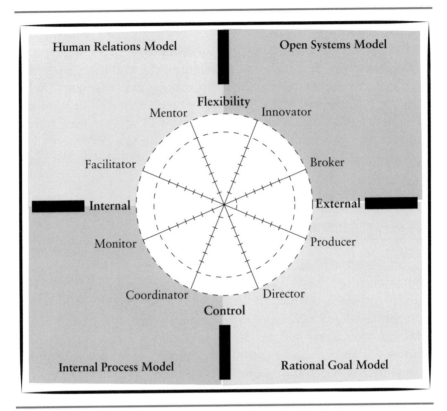

EXHIBIT 7.8   Information Processing and Leadership Roles
Source: R.E. Quinn, *Beyond Rational Management*, San Francisco, Jossey-Bass 1988.

> *Facilitator:* Team builder, someone who looks for cohesion and achieves it. This individual can manage interpersonal conflicts. He or she is focused on the process as a participatory leader.
>
> *Mentor:* This person is focused on feelings and emotions. He or she is able to allow people to develop themselves better, is helpful, sensitive, easily accessible, and honest, and also listens and supports.

2. **Open Systems Model.** This view of the world is from an idealistic perspective and is outwardly oriented. The preference is for short timelines and little security. We trust internally generated ideas and intuitions.

Innovator: He or she facilitates change and is strong at conceptualization. In contrast to the monitor, this person uses his or her creativity and is not really concerned with figures.

Broker: This person is persuasive and influential. Reputation is important. He or she is oriented toward the outside world and is expected to do business with the external world. This individual is a negotiator and representative.

3. **Rational Goal Model.** There is a preference for short timelines and a great deal of security, often with one goal in mind. Information is processed and tested in terms of its contribution to this goal.

   Producer: This individual is expected to be task oriented. He or she is resolutely focused on his or her work and is strongly motivated. Colleagues are urged to accept responsibility, fulfill tasks, and achieve goals.

   Director: This person sets goals, makes plans, and is decisive. He or she indicates problems and selects alternatives, defines roles and tasks, and determines the rules and evaluates them.

4. **Internal Process Model.** There is a preference for short timelines and high security. This person requires predictability and certainty, systematically investigates data that come from external sources, and is focused on one goal.

   Coordinator: This is a reliable person, independent of others. He or she maintains that which exists, protects continuity, and minimizes disruptions. This person is good at paper work, writing reports, and requesting budgets.

   Monitor: This individual knows what is going on in his or her business or unit, knows when people satisfy the norms, has a passion for detail, and is good at rational analyses.

"[Master] managers have the capacity to see problems from contradictory frames, to entertain and pursue alternative perspectives."[17] The dimensions in Quinn's model constitute a recognizable dynamic of "competing values": internal versus external orientation, as well as control versus flexibility. We must be both mentor and director. We must simultaneously coordinate and innovate, as well as be able to facilitate and produce. This is necessary in order to give some form to organizations in our complex society. Leadership is therefore not attached to a single role but to the ability to deal with the tension among various roles.

REALISTS AT THE HELM

Robert Quinn is not alone in his views about leadership. Peter Koestenbaum, a philosopher and, like Robert Quinn, an authority in the field of leadership, is of the same opinion: leadership involves the ability to deal with opposites to arrive at a well-considered judgment.

Koestenbaum has his own leadership institute (Philosophy in Business), has advised a number of multinationals, and has written a great many books on the subject. According to Koestenboem, "the central leadership attribute is the ability to manage polarity."[18] Koestenbaum's four categories are complementary to Quinn's four axes and eight roles. The four attributes that a leader must possess are vision, ethics, a sense of reality, and courage. Note that we are also dealing with the polarities in a field of tension (see Exhibit 7.9).

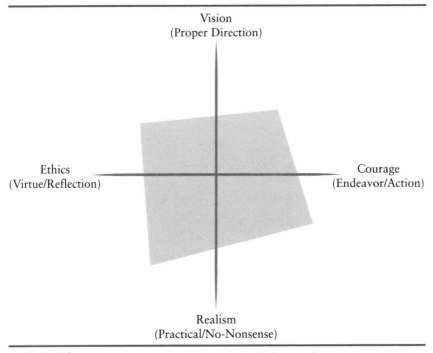

EXHIBIT 7.9   Koestenbaum's Categories and Their Polarities

In Forrester's distributed leadership model, we see that the importance of leadership throughout the entire organization has increased. In the organizational model that contrasts with this situation (the traditional hierarchy), the role of leadership is different and is reserved for a much more select group of individuals. In the new model, attention is paid to the further development of leadership characteristics (which is explored in the writings of Quinn and Koestenbaum). However, the distributed leadership model is concerned not only with the attributes of leaders but also, to an important extent, with the manner in which collaboration occurs. Certain mechanisms of collaboration provide some assistance in this regard.

(Self)Assessment

If you want to go more deeply into the subject of leadership, take a look at the work on leadership by the populist Stephen R. Covey[19] or dive into the more fundamental research that Saucier and Gouldberg[20] have done on the dimensions of personality. Indeed, there are many lists of leadership qualities, and you will see that many of them display strong similarities to the categories devised by Koestenbaum and Quinn. You can use Covey's "power tools" to test yourself in terms of the five characteristics generally acknowledged to be the ones by which personality is constructed.[21]

COOPERATION INSTEAD OF COERCION

Distributed leadership confronts us with the great challenge of making collaboration successful. Making decisions in teams and knowing what to do in cases of conflicting interests—this sort of teamwork does not occur on its own. In 1997, we might have thought that IT democracy was just the thing, but nothing was further from the truth. As mentioned in Chapter 3, effective collaboration requires something more. Bobby Cameron at Forrester Research recommends the following: Place the pot of gold in the middle; define IT initiatives in terms of added value for the business; estimate the possibilities; determine the risks; and prioritize. These are key aspects of IT portfolio management. A good collaboration is created by synchronizing money and interests.

In addition to this form of collaborative process, we would like to present a number of mechanisms that can be important in enabling IT to enhance business performance. Ryan Peterson, associate director of the Information Management Research Centre in Madrid, has conducted extensive research into the "soft" mechanisms for integrating business and IT.

Peterson does not much care for authoritative top-down IT management and the resulting forced collaboration. The person with whom one shares a room can, in fact, be more important than the person who is the boss. By using "soft" integration mechanisms to promote and improve the teamwork between IT and business, we can enhance the success of IT governance. In general, more attention is paid to hard mechanisms. Enough has been written on the subject of IT portfolio management, as well as on the centralized or decentralized control of IT activities. The interpersonal side of integration is fundamental but harder to grasp. For this reason, we hear less about it.

In his dissertation, "Information Governance," Peterson presents the mechanisms that lead to better teamwork (see Exhibit 7.10).[22] On the left side of the hexagon are participation, decision making, and coordination structures. IT governance is more successful when, among other things, we ensure that business management participates in IT projects, that IT and business jointly make decisions, and that structures are set up to coordinate activities. These coordination structures consist of architectural boards, steering committees, and other consultation platforms. On the right side of the framework are efforts to develop a shared understanding of IT, conflict resolution, and infrastructural coordination. Finally, there is infrastructural coordination, by which Peterson means the underlying communication structures that are decisive for effective collaboration. Job rotation or cross-training can result in better communication among all departments, for example. However, even the communication structure itself (e.g., accessibility to intranets) and collocation are important.

Peterson makes a plausible case for the fact that IT initiatives are much more successful when they are imbued with these mechanisms. Although less attention has been paid to this approach to IT management, evidence has been piling up that these integration mechanisms have important roles to play. Peterson provides a good survey of all the research on this topic.

Integration Mechanisms

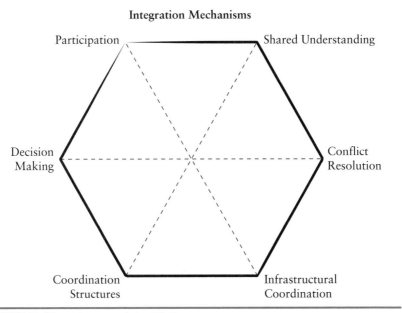

EXHIBIT 7.10   Teamwork in IT Governance

Source: R.R. Peterson, "Information Governance: An Empirical Investigation of the Differentiation and Integration of Decision Making for Information Technology in Financial Services," 2002.

Differences among countries are a good subject for study in the context of the mechanisms that Peterson identifies. Other cultures and their customs have an important effect on the manner in which collaborations occur, as well as on the ways in which they have to be undertaken. Many companies are devoting a great deal of effort to the centralization of IT, a policy that results in shared services that transgress national borders. Thus Dutch and U.S. employees of the same company must explain, for example, how IT services should be structured. The conflicts that occur in such cases often have little to do with a lack of knowledge in either of the two camps; instead, they arise because of the manner in which things are done. Manfred Kets de Vries, the Dutch leadership guru affiliated with the prestigious European Institute for Business Administration (INSEAD), speaks in this regard about "global leadership." His view about the need for multinationals to take national differences into account cannot be stated strongly enough.

NO PROSPECTS WITHOUT BUILDING TRUST

Maintaining supervision is only possible when the facts are at hand and the data are correct. Michael Jensen, professor emeritus at Harvard Business School, inveighs against the mechanisms in businesses that promote the tendency to manipulate data.

Gaming the System . . .

When the manipulation of budget targets becomes routine, moreover, it can undermine the integrity of an entire organization. Once managers see that it's okay to lie and to conceal information to enrich themselves or simply to hold on to their jobs, they soon begin to extend their dishonest behavior to all parts of the company's management system and even to its relationship with outside partners. . . . Moreover since managers are well aware that everyone is attempting to game the system for personal reasons, you create an organization rife with cynicism, suspicion, and mistrust.[23]

Full-cycle governance, in which the control and accountability of actions and policy are supported by corrective supervision, is only possible on the basis of a realistic presentation of matters. Clear facts and accurate figures are of crucial importance. Such a realistic depiction of IT is especially difficult, given one of its essential characteristics: the interpenetration of IT throughout the entire organization. We must realize that material risks and complexity pose an extra burden on the risks and complexity involved in the promotion of interests. Thus we must not only remain on course with our IT projects butwe must also ensure that we are not being hoodwinked, knowingly or unknowingly.

Herbert Simon has written about the element of "gaming the system"; people's intentions and competences can stand in the system's way, and departments strive to maximize their own performances. Consequently, supervision to ensure honesty of actions, accuracy of facts, and the mutual trustworthiness of departments and employees is an important managerial task.

Robert Galford (managing partner of the Center for Executive Development, which was founded in 1987 by a number of Harvard professors) and Anne Seibold Drapeau (HR manager at the Digitas marketing agency) have distinguished three levels of trust in their book *The Trusted Leader*.[24] The personal trust between people is the most essential. At least some personal trust must exist before we can speak of the second level, trust in the manner in which the organization functions. The third level is strategic trust, which can exist separately; an organization with a brilliant product or a unique position in the market can enjoy strategic trust without faith in the people who work there or the manner in which the work is done.

Galford and Seibold Drapeau have tried to define the meaning of trust by using the following formula:

$$T = \frac{C + R + I}{S}$$

Trust (T) is the sum of Credibility (C), Reliability (R), and Intimacy (I) divided by Self-Interest (S). An important element of trust is credibility, orknowing and understanding what a person is saying. Reliability relates to the trustworthiness of statements and commitments—arriving on time, fulfilling our agreements, that sort of thing. Finally, the intimacy with which we operate contributes to trust. Are we personally involved? Do we have a feeling for the situation? Do we have the empathic capacity to involve our colleagues personally? All this is divided by egocentrism. Higher egocentrism therefore leads to lower trust. The most trustworthy leader is the one who operates without much thought for him- or herself, who knows what he or she is doing, who lives up to agreements, and who has an empathic ability to involve others. Defining the trustworthy leader in an equation might suggest that there is a scientific quality to leadership, which is not the case, of course—but we can use the equation above as a springboard.

The foundation is honest collaboration. Such collaboration can be achieved when we use dependable facts about our IT projects, when we depict situations reliably (in order to build business cases), and when we fulfill the agreements to which we are committed. When trust built in this form is encouraged and supervised, our IT investments will indisputably bear better fruit.

According to Lao Tse, "A leader is most effective when people hardly know he is there. And less effective when people obey and applaud him. He is least effective when people despise him.... But about a good leader who speaks sparingly, when his work is done and aim fulfilled, they will all say: 'This we did ourselves.'"[25]

MANAGEMENT AS INSTITUTIONALIZED MISTRUST

In their book *Building Trust*, Solomon and Flores say that "management is institutionalized mistrust."[26] This viewpoint is quite useful, especially when we consider how to draw the line between responsible latitude and meaningful superintendence. Additionally, it should be emphasized again that whereas supervision does indeed cost money, the lack of it could cost even more, as shown by the slide in stock prices lasting until March 2000, which was caused by misplaced trust in accountants, the business community, banks, and IT.

When is trust misplaced and when is it justified? We need to explore justified trust further, to find the balance between supervision and latitude. Solomon and Flores suggest that genuine trust has to be cultivated and that misplaced trust has extremely damaging effects.

Genuine trust gives us something on which to build. Genuine trust provides a basis for the leader's supervision, as well as for the supervision of others.

The three categories of trust established by Solomon and Flores are as follows:

1. **Simple Trust.** Simple trust is trust that is unchallenged, untested, and undisturbed. It is an attitude, an assumption, and not a decision that is taken. Simple trust can be regarded as naive and optimistic, similar to the blind trust of children for their mother. This "infantile" trust is based on an ideal vision that does not exist in reality. Sometimes we simply have to trust people whom we do not know well. In retrospect, after our trust has been damaged, we realize that it was blind. We had simply not considered the possibility that we should *not* trust someone.
2. **Blind Trust.** Blind trust can be betrayed and abused. We dismiss or do not even acknowledge the evidence that such trust is ungrounded. Blind trust is the denial of the possibility that trust is unjustified. Blind trust is self-deceit. In the case of simple trust, doubt is never cast on the trust; blind trust involves the denial of

all possible counter evidence. This is thus a simple-minded sort of trust, which also has a courageous side to it. The denial of danger often leads to painful situations that we could have avoided.

3. **Genuine Trust.** Genuine trust is not blind and is based on the possibility that it could be damaged. It is a reasoned choice. Simple trust is not reflective, blind trust is self-deception, and genuine trust is both reflective and honest. The possibility of relying on others requires all these forms of trust. With blind and simple trust, everything is destroyed when the trust is damaged; in contrast, genuine trust does not end in a surprise or disaster. Solomon and Flores argue for a "finger-on-the-pulse" sort of trust, one that is built up gradually, that must be earned, and that is based on a strong sense of reality. The reality is that we are dealing with divergent interests, various intentions, and insufficient competences. If we adopt these as our starting points, which we can do when we invoke genuine trust, then we have a realistic view of damaged trust. People make mistakes, and we allow for this in calculating genuine trust. Blind and simple trust occur more frequently than one might think. When Alan Greenspan spoke of "irrational exuberance" in December 1996, we did not want to hear about it. The trust in IT and the Internet that set the agenda after this speech has been discussed in other parts of this book.

In the context of the various forms of trust, Solomon and Flores regard genuine trust as a better operational practice than the control drift that we often witness. As alternatives to trust, they identify fear, control, and power. When a leader holds people in an iron grip or intimidates them through fear, the prospects are not pleasant. Manfred Kets De Vries provides an alternative. He claims that successful organizations are systems in which people feel happy. The business organization is oriented to the team, the customer, and the performance; the individual is respected; there is openness to change and renewal of knowledge; it is possible to speak of pleasure and entrepreneurial spirit; and the atmosphere is filled with a trusting air. This last element is a basic ingredient for a successful business; once again, it depends on the extent to which our leaders are trusted. "Managers must present good examples," says Kets de Vries. "To do this, one has to communicate, which means having to listen and speak."[27]

BACK TO IT GOVERNANCE AND LEADERSHIP

To bring the measurement and control loops required for IT management into effective operation, we have to engage in control,
accountability, and supervision. We implement these three elements
in order to guarantee the essential relationship between IT and
business-economic performance. Leadership is assigned a large role
in this game, as we have learned from many thinkers, including the
IT Governance Institute. To get a well-running IT governance mechanism off the ground, all the pieces of the puzzle must be in their
proper place. People must be happy with it, and it must also be workable, i.e., able to attain our goal. Leadership has much to contribute
to this aim, but not everything. The entire weight of IT governance is
not borne by organizational leaders alone. What we can and must
expect from leadership is that it provide something to replace the
authoritarian control we have abandoned. What we can expect from
leadership is that a foundation for genuine trust be laid beneath the
organization. The idea that everyone has to develop leadership qualities and that we must make shared decisions does not imply a blind
trust that everything will continue to run smoothly. Put more
strongly, the area of freedom described by Noordzij must remain
readily measurable, manageable, and controllable.

In Part Two we identified a few essential items associated with
the relationship between IT management and business performances.
IT portfolio management is the most important item. Directly related
to it is the conversion from cost-oriented to revenue-oriented thinking. It is not just the IT leader, our CIO, who has to get this idea into
his or her head, but everyone in the organization using IT to do business, and that more or less means everybody. This is the only way to
get IT portfolio management up and running. What we can also
expect from leadership is that IT portfolio management be taken up
and transformed into actions. A leader does not sit and wait for the
starting shot from this or that manager; he or she simply walks into
the room and asks if we can do something together to get the ball
rolling. This is daring; this is realism. It immediately makes things
more concrete than they are in any general discussion about the
characteristics of leadership.

LEADERSHIP AND LANGUAGE

In many languages (Dutch being one of them), the notion of the leader is often associated with militarism, the cult of personality, and even totalitarian dictators, such as Hitler, Mussolini, and Franco. The Merriam-Webster Online Dictionary lists the military context as the first specialized usage of the term *leader* when it refers to a person. Other meanings involve qualified uses in such formulations as *project leader, team leader, party leader, spiritual leader,* and so forth. In terms of the negative connotations of the word, Manfred Kets de Vries has written a book on the subject of despotic leadership.[28]

Compared with *leader,* the notion of *leadership* (without further qualification) adds an extra dimension to our feelings of uneasiness. Overt displays of leadership can get under our skin, even though the expression *leadership qualities* is associated with the managerial skills that someone exercising authority independent of the cultural context must in fact possess. When, for example, things are not going well in a company based on a culture of consultation, it is perhaps healthy to appoint someone to act decisively and tear down a few roadblocks. The question immediately arises of whether such a crisis manager can be called a *leader.*

We see that the concepts of *leader* and *leadership* call up many questions. Often, the issues involve slavish acts of translation. Translations of U.S. management literature have caused terminology related to *leader* and *leadership* to spread throughout other languages, in which the negatives associated with leadership are much stronger (i.e., Dutch). In English, the two concepts, particularly in their qualified, "small l," usages have developed a wider range of uses than in other languages and have much less "suspect" meanings. Despotism, which makes us uneasy about the "large L" terms *Leader* and *Leadership,* now appears to be an abnormal variant.

In general, the less devious senses of leader and leadership involve "the provision of guidance and direction at a high level." English has no specific terms to label these activities and the people who perform them in all contexts. Out of expediency, the words *leader* or some form of *leadership* are often used.

For a good understanding of *leadership,* we must remember that it is a modern (post 1821) equivalent of the older term *headship,* which means "the office of the head (e.g., of a school or family)." In addition, *leadership* is often a synonym for *lead* when it concerns the state of "being in front" or "being ahead." *Technological leadership*, for example, can be best defined as "technological trend-setting," or something of that nature (see Exhibit 7.11).

As an extension of the religious sense of "(spiritual) leader," the term can be used in a weaker political sense, one closer to the notions of "mentor" or "guide." This sense is also mentioned in Webster's Internet edition.

THE CHARISMA AND LEADERSHIP PARADOX

We should not overlook a certain leadership quality that is much discussed: the capacity of (positively) influencing others. This quality is called "charisma."[29] We conclude this chapter with a discussion of this phenomenon, which is still little understood. In *The Wall Street Journal* Hall Lancaster said the following about Bill Gates:

> *Several years ago I spent a few days on the Microsoft campus and interviewed Mr. Gates, who certainly doesn't fit any conventional definition of charisma. During the interview, he rocked distractedly in his chair, rarely made eye contact and offered wordy, elliptical answers to questions. But Mr. Gates's vision of a world transformed by technology infected workers at the sprawling, Redmond, Washington, campus, like a computer virus. I remember being struck by how many people parroted the Gates mantra about wanting to change the world. It was the right message for the right audience and in that particular group, Mr. Gates was a charismatic icon.[30]*

The fact that Bill Gates might not have charismatic "looks" but appears throughout the world as a charismatic icon may have something to do with the paradox of leadership. Until we enjoy success and have proved ourselves to be right, it is difficult to attract others to our ideas. The improbable fame of the man who created Microsoft has resulted in his transformation into a hero. Therein lies the rub, namely, leadership is revealed and accepted retrospectively, but leadership is actually needed beforehand in order to arrive at the point when leadership is recognized. IT leadership is all that has been discussed in this chapter, but it is, above all, the transformation of words into deeds, deeds that lead to a better contribution of IT to

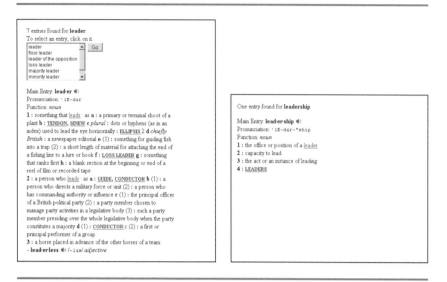

EXHIBIT 7.11 Definitions of *Leader* and *Leadership*
Source: The Merriam-Webster Online Dictionary (*www.webster.com*).

business performance. As has often been said, leadership is required at many more levels than the top.

We conclude with the words of Professor Peter Weill: "Don't just Lead, Govern!"[31] Leadership promises a great deal, but it is not everything. Weill says that IT governance is important because (among other things) leadership only has a certain bandwidth, which is of course true. IT governance involves an interplay of factors; IT leadership is only one of these, albeit an important one.

As in the case of IT itself, we only have leadership, when it permeates the organization as a quality of the people who are active there. It is precisely with such a powerful enabler as IT that we require this pervasiveness. The strong "invisible hand" with which we can make the best use of IT is what we call leadership, and the strongest "invisible hand" is present when power manifests in all our actions.

ENDNOTES

1. EFQM Excellence Model. *www.efqm.org*
2. IT Governance Institute. *www.itgi.org/overview.htm*

3. J. M. Kouzes and B.Z. Posner, "Follower-Oriented Leadership: A Chapter in the Encyclopedia of Leadership," 2003. *business. scu.edu/faculty/research/working_papers/pdf/posner_feb03.pdf*

4. Ibid.

5. C. Ciborra, et al., *From Control to Drift: The Dynamics of Corporate Information Infrastructures*, New York, Oxford University Press, 2000.

6. S. Zuboff and J. Maxmin, *The Support Economy: Why Corporations Are Failing Individuals and the Next Episode of Capitalism*, New York, Viking Adult, 2002.

7. Ibid.

8. J.F. van Wijnen, "Mensen pikken de controle niet meer," *Het Financieele Dagblad*, June 20, 2003.

9. See note 5.

10. See note 5.

11. J.F. van Wijnen, "Mensen pikken de controle niet meer," *Het Financieele Dagblad*, June 20, 2003.

12. T. Pohlmann, "Building eBusiness Leadership," Forrester Research, 2001. *www.forrester.com*

13. J.C. McCarthy, "eLeadership For The Net Economy," Forrester Research, 2000. *www forrester.com*

14. R. Quinn, *Beyond Rational Management: Mastering the Paradoxes of Competing Demands of High Performance*, San Francisco, Jossey-Bass, 1988.

15. R. Quinn, *Change the World*, San Francisco, Jossey-Bass, 2000.

16. R. Quinn, *Deep Change*, San Francisco, Jossey-Bass, 1996.

17. See note 14.

18. P. Koestenbaum, *Do You Have the Will to Lead?*, March 2002. *www.fastcompany.com/online/32/koestenbaum.html*

19. S.R. Covey, *The Seven Habits of Highly Effective People*, New York, Fireside, 1989.

20. G. Saucier and L.R. Goldberg, "What is Beyond the Big Five?," *Journal of Personality* 66, pp. 495-524, 1998.

21. To take the test yourself go to *www.time4talent.nl/detector/* or *www.outoffservice.com/cgi/psych.cgi.*

22. R.R. Peterson, "Information Governance: An Empirical Investigation of the Differentiation and Integration of Decision Making for Information Technology in Financial Service," 2000, Thesis, Tilburg University.

23. M.C. Jensen, "Corporate Budgeting is Broken-Let's Fix It," 2001. *http://papers.ssrn.com/sol3/papers.cfm?abstract_id=321520*

24. R. Galford and A. S. Drapeau, *The Trusted Leader*, New York, Simon and Schuster, 2002.

25. Lao-Tse (604–531 BC): *Te-Tao Ching*.

26. R. C. Solomon and R. Flores, *Building Trust in Business, Politics, Relationships and Life*, New York: Oxford University Press, 2001.

27. C. van Lotringen, "Leiderschap bepaalt of het bedrijf een goelag is," *Het Financieele Dagblad*, 2003.

28. M. Kets de Vries, *De Geest van Despotisme: Shaka Zoeloe en de Psychologie van Tirannieke Macht*, Amsterdam, Nieuwezijds, 2003.

29. T. Allessandra, *Charisma: Seven Keys to Developing the Magnetism that Leads to Success*, New York, Warner Books, 2000.

30. H. Lancaster, "Is a Lack of Charisma Holding You Back?," *Wall Street Journal*, August 20, 2002. *www.careerjournal.com/myc/climbingladder/20020820-careercorner.html*

31. P. Weill, "Don't Just Lead, Govern! Implementing Effective IT Governance," 2003. *www.csbs.org/pr/presentations/2003/AMC2003_Weill_DontJustLead-Govern.pdf*

CHAPTER 8

Issuing Rules Is Maintaining Supervision

The Long Arm of the U.S. Lawmaker

It is not our present intention to discuss exhaustively all the implications of national or international legislation. First we will examine the specific legislation concerning IT management based on the portfolio approach and then the law that sharpened reporting regulations immediately after the WorldCom fraud scandal. This legislation makes the directors of businesses liable for the accuracy of financial reports and has an effect on the reporting of IT. As was made clear in Chapter 1, this law applies to all businesses with large interests in the United States. Thus CFOs are going to make more stringent demands on the numerical data the CIO has to provide. We will also discuss developments in European legislation. These involve combinations of self-regulation based on codes of conduct and legislation that mandates some of these codes.

Regaining Trust

In Part One, we saw that accountants, managers, and banks knew who to call on when practicing improper business governance. This has inflicted deep wounds on business management, and stakeholder trust has fallen to a low point. Misunderstood IT was used and misused to provide predictions about future earnings that, in the end, were completely beyond the bounds of reality. Redressing the existing flaws by means of legislation is an absolute condition for restoring trust in IT and providing a better return on investment.

■ ■ ■

THE LEGISLATOR AS SUPERVISOR

To get "good corporate governance" back on the rails, a law was put through in the United States faster than any law had ever been passed: the Public Company Accounting Reform and Investor Protection Act (the Sarbanes-Oxley Act). Partly in response, Europe implemented an action plan based on a report by Jaap Winter, chairman of the High Level Group of Company Law Experts, professor of International Company Law at Erasmus University in Rotterdam, and a partner in De Brauw Blackstone Westbroek. The plan includes short- and medium-term measures running until 2008. The Netherlands wants to be the model student in the European class: In 2004 the 140 governance rules of the Tabaksblat Committee were already in place.

In Europe, a combination of self-regulation and legislation is being sought, using the principle of "comply or explain." A business is not required to observe the code, as long as it can explain to its shareholders why it is not doing so. Exceptionally heavy penalties for the provision of incorrect information will probably not be introduced in Europe. Anyone who is completely out of line will not be allowed to continue as a manager.

The legislation discussed in this chapter involves the measures needed to prohibit improper information from being given to shareholders and to regain the trust of financiers in the system of corporate governance. Our focus on IT governance provides us with two views of the matter. Both these views include the need for leaders to insist more strictly on the provision of correct data and the observance of codes and legislation. A number of non-U.S. businesses come under the jurisdiction of the U.S. law because of their financial dealings in the United States; in such cases, the reins will be held even more tightly, particularly by European business leaders.

That the world has become a global village is evident in this legislation. Globalization—one might even say "Americanization"—is visible if one cares to look.

In addition, these new measures will compel better estimating and accounting for the economic value than IT investments can deliver. Previously, we all trusted unconditionally in the profitability of IT, a state of mind that will never return. The current understanding, supported by legislation that repeatedly emphasizes the need to inform shareholders in a proper, transparent manner, supports the use of IT portfolio management, Activity-Based Costing, and Economic Value Added.

Finally, well functioning IT governance is unthinkable when the basis for corporate governance is weak. Repairing all the flaws in our corporate governance by means of national and international legislation—and through the tangible actions of management—is an absolute condition for a healthy and properly functioning full-cycle business governance of IT.

In addition to the legislation on corporate governance, some interesting IT governance legislation is in place that should be considered in greater detail. The IT Management Reform Act (Clinger-Cohen Act) was enacted by the U.S. Congress after extensive consultation with the U.S. business community. IT portfolio management and architecture are two practices addressed by this law.

However, the law that is most often in the news is Sarbanes-Oxley. Although Sarbanes-Oxley and Clinger-Cohen both focus on the supervision of investments, their objectives have little else in common. The Clinger-Cohen Act was devised to ensure the prudent investment of tax dollars in governmental organizations. Such supervision had to be set down in law, because people were concerned about the great number of expensive IT projects that were going astray. Sarbanes-Oxley, however, monitors the intentions of people and protects shareholders' interests. This law comes down hard on the misuse of managerial power.

The Clinger-Cohen Act perhaps provides the best overview of everything that a CIO must keep in mind. Because this act applies to the investment of tax dollars in the U.S. government, it also applies to more than 6 percent of the total worldwide IT expense. The IT budget of the U.S. government in 2003 amounted to $52 billion,[1] of a total worldwide budget of $852 billion.[2] Because of the enormity of U.S. government IT spending, Clinger-Cohen was enacted to ensure more effective surveillance of the returns of IT investments for U.S. taxpayers.

THE IT MANAGEMENT REFORM ACT OF 1996 (CLINGER-COHEN ACT)

The Clinger-Cohen Act is a serious attempt to stipulate the role and tasks of the highest executives responsible for IT. In the 1990s, when the strategic role of information and IT began to be delineated more sharply and also when many IT projects were on the rocks, the tasks and authority of the Chief Information Officer (CIO) were laid down by law. The Clinger-Cohen Act, the content of which was drafted in dialogue with the business community, applies to government organizations and has as its primary purpose the proper accounting of expended tax money.

Clinger-Cohen is viewed as a response to the call for IT leadership and fiscal responsibility. With the appearance of the CIO, IT found a place at the boardroom level; the CIO became a peer among other organization leaders, such as the Chief Financial Officer (CFO) and the Chief Executive Officer (CEO).

Portfolio Thinking and Activity

An advisory report from the U.S. Federal Government General Accounting Office (GAO) lays the foundation for a great many of the directives in Clinger-Cohen.[3] The report was based on case studies of organizations that had taken a lead in IT governance and that were deeply concerned with the question of IT performance. American Airlines, Kodak, The Royal Bank of Canada, United Services Automobile Organization, and Xerox shared their best practices with the GAO. The report also mentions portfolio management as an instrument for accomplishing substantially better control over IT.

In Clinger-Cohen, we do not find the expression "IT portfolio management," but the description of management principles in the act allow for no uncertainty about the connection:

- Establish an IT management process ensuring that the value of IT is maximized, and thoroughly examine the risks.
- Integrate the IT management process with the budgeting processes, the financial processes, and the decision making in program management.

- Stipulate goals for the improvement of the business operation's efficiency and effectiveness, and, when necessary, set goals for service provision resulting from the effective use of IT.
- Make sure that there are prescribed ways in which the results of IT are to be measured and that they provide insight into the contribution made to the organization's program.

Because most companies attach great importance to the performance measurement of projects and programs, the CIO should be responsible for conducting such measurements vis-à-vis IT projects and programs. In this effort, the CIO has a controlling and advisory task. The most important tasks and responsibilities, as established in Clinger-Cohen, are as follows:

- Responsibilities of the CIO
  - Advising and supporting the CEO and other senior management so that information and IT mesh with policy, procedure, and priorities
  - Developing, maintaining, and facilitating clear and integrated IT architecture (which has now become extended so that it encompasses enterprise architecture)
  - Making the functioning and development of all large information management processes (as well as any improvements to the work processes) more effective and efficient
- Tasks of the CIO
  - The management of information sources, the CIO's most important task.
  - Monitoring and evaluating the performance of IT programs and advising the CEO on the continuation, adjustment, or termination of a program or project
  - As part of the strategic planning process, conducting an annual survey to assess whether the knowledge and skill requirements of IT personnel are still adequate for information source management
  - Determining whether the upper and second tiers of the organization still satisfy these requirements
  - Developing strategies and plans for hiring people, training, and professional development, if it is established that the organization cannot satisfy the stipulated requirements

- Reporting to the CEO about the progress recorded in the improvement of information source management.

The Clinger-Cohen Act distinguishes three CIO roles: a *monitor role* for the quality of IT initiatives in the organization, an *advisory role* for advising the CEO, and a *personal responsibility role* for the development of architecture, the purchase of resources, and the improvement of work processes and information management.

Does This Law Work?

At the end of 2000, a special government committee (the Thompson Committee), headed by Senator Fred Thompson (R-Tennessee) and Senator Joseph Lieberman (D-Connecticut), was set up to determine whether the Clinger-Cohen Act was yielding fruit. The unavoidable conclusion was that matters were moving too slowly.

For the most important task (the management of resources), government organizations received an extremely low (failing) grade. The statistics used for decision making have not been made available. However, among the causes for failure, two factors catch the eye immediately:

1. The turnover of CIOs was very high. Over the period from 1996 to 2000, all government authorities gave IT command to new CIOs three or four times. Hence, the average CIO job life expectancy was little more than a year.
2. The powers that the CIO had to provide supervision were too limited.

The report offered 12 arguments that CIOs should be given more authority. Whereas they were charged with the task of providing proper supervision and assigning responsibility, they lacked the authority to realize these commissions. A good judgment of the effects of the law can only be made when the existing IT management is made capable of transforming its words into actions.

Not only do the recommendations provide good insight into where things are going wrong, they also reveal what the Committee considered the difficulties in exercising effective control of IT. Their advice on how to get a better grip on IT expenditure through better management is appropriate for any organization, public or private.

The Committee recommended that government organizations must strongly endeavor to:

- Reexamine whether they indeed have the appropriate mechanisms in place that would allow full application of the policies, procedures, and daily practices necessary to comply with the Clinger-Cohen Act.
- Clearly indicate how the various roles are to be shared and how the relationships are represented in reports.
- Give the CIO the authority to exercise control over IT budgets and investment processes.
- Improve the quality of budget planning and the control over investment practices; make sure that all data about costs and revenues relating to investment decisions are accurate and complete.
- Set up clear procedures concerning the manner in which CIO and program managers communicate information about the status and progress of large IT projects.
- Prevent deadlines from being exceeded and costs from getting out of hand; put milestones in place for IT decision making.
- Effectively identify IT projects that seriously deviate in terms of costs, planning, or quality.
- Improve the abilities of employees to manage projects and to make estimates.
- Provide better data about the contribution of IT investments to government programs.
- Develop IT management plans that provide different insights into the results, progress, and areas requiring attention.
- Clarify the requirements for process development in budget plans as well as the procedures concerning the control of investment.
- In constructing and acquiring information systems, make greater use of modular contracts.

The Committee also recommended that the high turnover of CIOs must be halted. This has led a number of high civil servants to argue that IT professionals working for the government should be paid better; relatively low pay appears to be one element causing this turnover.[4]

PUBLIC COMPANY ACCOUNTING REFORM AND INVESTOR PROTECTION ACT OF 2002 (SARBANES-OXLEY)

At present, Sarbanes-Oxley is in the spotlight; at the annual Gartner Conference held in October 2003 in Orlando, Florida, there was an entire Sarbanes-Oxley pavilion. All businesses that have $10 million in shares in the United States or 500 shareholders of whom 60 percent are American are affected by this law. Also, all companies listed on American exchanges are under its jurisdiction. Sarbanes-Oxley therefore applies to most public companies. Foreign-based firms are finding they must comply with Sarbanes-Oxley, if they wish to continue listing financial instruments for trading on U.S. exchanges or if they intend to do so in the future.

The Dutch company VNU now has some doubts about applying to be listed on a U.S. exchange,[5] and Rijkman Groenink, chairman of the Board of Directors at ABN AMRO, has noted that a real option is the disintegration of large organizations into a number of smaller ones, thereby avoiding the qualifying provisions of the law, now that the U.S. legal system has caused foreign-based companies to bear this added responsibility.

Groenink says that "If the management of our American companies must be undertaken in accordance with American metrics for corporate governance using American supervisors, then it could be that we no longer have anything left to say, even when we hold 100 percent of the stock."[6]

Groenink is not happy about this intrusion and views it as U.S. meddling. He specifically names Sarbanes-Oxley as evidence of the one-sidedness of the United States, which could ultimately lead to regionalization, with the financial world broken up into market fragments.

Sarbanes-Oxley has provisions that apply to the top managers of an organization, its accountants, its auditors, and the business itself. Organizations are required to appoint an independent "audit committee" to monitor the accountants, who would no longer report directly to management. Furthermore, stringent requirements have been established to guarantee the independence of the accountants, and managers are made principally responsible for reporting.

Sections 800 and 900 of Sarbanes-Oxley contain the measures that make managers directly accountable for the provision of information to shareholders.

The CEO and CFO Must Personally Sign for Reports

Each periodic report containing financial statements filed by an issuer with the Securities and Exchange Commission . . . shall be accompanied by a written statement by the chief executive officer and chief financial officer (or equivalent thereof) of the issuer. (Subsection 906)

Up to 10 Years for Inconsistent Reporting

Whoever . . . certifies any statement . . . knowing that the periodic report accompanying the statement does not comport with all the requirements . . . shall be fined not more than $1,000,000 or imprisoned not more than 10 years, or both. (Subsection 906)

Up to 20 Years if This Is Done Willfully and Deliberately

[Whoever] willfully certifies any statement . . . knowing that the periodic report accompanying the statement does not comport with all the requirements set forth in this section shall be fined not more than $5,000,000, or imprisoned not more than 20 years, or both. (Subsection 906)

Tinkering with Documents Also Punishable by up to 20 Years

Whoever knowingly alters, destroys, mutilates, conceals, covers up, falsifies, or makes a false entry in any record, document, or tangible object with the intent to impede, obstruct, or influence the investigation or proper administration of any matter within the jurisdiction of any department or agency of the United States or any case filed under title 11, or in relation to or contemplation of any such matter or case, shall be fined under this title, imprisoned not more than 20 years, or both. (Subsection 802)

EUROPEAN LEGISLATION: COMPLY OR EXPLAIN

Because of Sarbanes-Oxley, entrenched domestic business practices in foreign countries, such as the Dutch model of change through consultation (the "polder model"), are now no longer workable, especially for the 40 Dutch companies listed on the U.S. exchanges.

What is Europe doing to deal with the fall-out of Sarbanes-Oxley? At the head of the European clean-up operation is European Commissioner Frits Bolkestein. In May 2003, he presented ten priorities for accountant control,[7] based on the report "A Modern Regulatory Framework for Company Law in Europe" by the High Level Group of Company Law Experts.[8] This is familiarly called the Winter Report, after the chairman of the group, Jaap Winter.

With these ten priorities, Europe bares its teeth at the United States. Bolkestein states: "I want European solutions that are tailored to our needs, respect our divergent traditions and enjoy the support of European professional groups. I also cannot accept that our offices have U.S. standards imposed on them, and the European Union strongly opposes the registration of EU accounting offices at the Public Company Accounting Oversight Board (PCAOB) of the United States. The EU will itself exercise supervision over its businesses."[9]

This prickliness is part of a long series of European-U.S. conflicts.[10] Such conflicts began with the Kyoto agreement and extend to what has been identified by Bolkestein as the imposition of rules on Europe by the PCAOB; they also involve the international politics of trade, the Basel-II Accord (which is specifically applicable to banks), and policy imposed by the International Monetary Fund (IMF).

To some Europeans, the United States appears to be going its own way, establishing policies and laws with growing significance for companies that deal with the U.S. market. Whether this will lead to a fragmentation of organizations, as Rijkman Groenink suggests, remains unclear and is difficult to predict with any degree of accuracy.

Although Europe has not gone as far as the United States in mandating behavior, it has not stood still. The Winter Report outlines current European policy.

There Will Be No European Governance Code

A European code for corporate governance will not be established. Europe will take a coordinated route to better corporate governance. The Winter Group puts it as follows:

> *The Group is of the opinion that a European code concerning corporate governance does not have any substantial added value but is only an extra level inserted between international principles and national codes. The approach involving self-regulation based only on nonbinding recommendations is equally insufficient to guarantee good corporate governance. Given the increasing integration of the European capital markets, the EU must establish a common policy containing a few essential rules, and it must ensure good coordination of the national codes pertaining to corporate governance.*[11]

The following five initiatives are regarded by the Winter Group as the most urgent:

1. "Introduction of annual statements concerning corporate governance ('Annual Corporate Governance Statement'). Businesses listed on stock exchanges must be required to include a coherent written statement of the most important features of their corporate government structures and practices in their annual reports.
2. Development of a legal context to help shareholders exercise their various rights (for example, by posing questions, introducing resolutions, voting in absentia, participating in general meetings by means of electronic aids). These facilities need to be offered to shareholders in the entire EU, and there is an urgent need to resolve specific problems relating to cross-border voting.
3. Acceptance of a recommendation to promote the role of independent authorities ('supervisory directors') and officials not involved in day-to-day management activities ('non-executive directors'). At the European level, minimum standards have to be set for the establishment, composition and roles of appointment, remuneration and audit committees. These need to be maintained by member states, at least on the basis of 'comply or explain.'
4. Acceptance of a recommendation concerning the amounts paid to managers. The member states must quickly attempt to introduce a

suitable legal regulation offering shareholders more transparency and influence, and requiring detailed disclosure of individual salaries.

5. Establishment of a European Corporate Governance Forum to promote the coordination and convergence of national codes and the manners of maintaining and supervising the observance of them." [12]

Whereas the United States has chosen simple, straightforward legislation applicable to everyone, Europe has gone for "comply or explain" and for regulations in each country. This may appear somewhat artificial, but it is possibly the fastest way to use orderly government practices to legislate stricter controls. Europe is currently not unified enough. We will have to await the work of the yet-to-be established European Corporate Governance Forum to harmonize all the existing codes. Appendix C presents the different European definitions of corporate governance.

A EUROPEAN EXAMPLE: DUTCH LEGISLATION

As one of the leading trading nations of Europe, with a number of its principal publicly traded companies deeply involved in the U.S. market, The Netherlands has undertaken some governance initiatives of its own.

Going back to 1997, however, the 40 recommendations of the Peters Committee (the first corporate governance committee in the Netherlands)never got out of the starting gate. At the end of 2003, the Dutch Corporate Governance Code was given its definitive form, consisting of 21 principles, 113 best practices, and 15 recommendations. The code is called *Code Tabaksblat* after chairman Morris Tabaksblat. Does the Tabaksblat Code really provide something new that companies are going to embrace, or will companies choose to ignore it? The answer to that question will only come in time.

Following are some of the key tenets of the Tabaksblat Code that illustrate what, the Dutch are doing in response to the approach of the United States toward the now global need for more effective IT governance:

- Tabaksblat is anything but content with the current state of corporate governance. The decision by the U.S. pension fund CalPHERS to stop investing in Dutch businesses was repeatedly mentioned by Morris Tabaksblat when he presented the draft report in July 2003. CalPHERS has little faith in the transparency of Dutch businesses. The sudden loss of KPNQuest and Baan, along with the problems at Ahold, which also came as a complete surprise, is anathema to investors.

- To ward off suspicion, the Tabaksblat Committee has now published a new code for healthier corporate governance, one that provides the desired insights into the businesses in which investments are being made.

- The comments on the proposals are positive, but there is a strong refusal to make commitments. The recommendations of the Peters Committee were ignored; if words are not transformed into actions, the Tabaksblat Code might well end up on the legislative shelf.

- The possibility that corporate governance codes will be shelved depends on what politicians will do with the recommendations. The first recommendation is to include a "comply-or-explain" principle in Book 2 of the Dutch Civil Code. Businesses may deviate from the rules but must provide an explanation for doing so.

- The report expresses the essence of good corporate governance as follows:

  > "Good entrepreneurship, including honest and transparent actions by management, and good supervision, including the attribution of responsibility for performed controls, are essential for restoring stakeholder trust in management and supervision. These are the two cornerstones on which corporate governance must rest and to which this code applies."[13]

Guaranteeing Trust and Removing Temptation

The Tabaksblat Code is bulging with rules of conduct intended to guarantee the integrity of management. Every possible effort is made to remove temptations not to act honestly in the best interests of the organization. Thus a director may not, for example, "demand or accept any (material) gifts for him or herself, his or her spouse, registered partner or other type of living companion, foster child, blood relative or in-law until the second remove." Rules of conduct are stipulated for the Board of Directors, the Supervisory Directors, the accountants, and the shareholders. Shareholders can only profit from the measures, for the rules are meant to protect them.

In Jail or out of Work

If the last of the recommendations are adopted by Dutch lawmakers, directors and supervisors will lose their jobs if they publish misleading financial information. Moreover, they will not be allowed to represent other European businesses. This proposal appears on the agenda of the European Commission to be enacted between 2006 and 2008. In the United States, a violator of the law will be imprisoned if convicted; in Europe, banishment appears to be the penalty.

ENDNOTES

1. CIO Council, "A Summary of First Practices and Lessons Learned in Information Technology Portfolio Management," 2002. *www.cio.gov/documents/BPC_portfolio_final.pdf*
2. IDC, "Worldwide Total IT Spending Forecast, 2003–2007: Preliminary Outlook," 2003. *www.amazon.com/exec/obidos/tg/detail/-/B00008WHQK/104-1935646-0403934?v=glance&vi=contents*
3. General Accounting Office, "Executive Guide: Improving Mission Performance through Strategic Information Management," 1994. *www.gao.gov/special. pubs/ai94115. pdf*
4. "Investigative Report of Senator Fred Thompson on Federal Agency Compliance with the Clinger-Cohen Act," 2000. *www.senate.gov/~gov_affairs/101900_table.htm*
5. M. Houben and J. Wester, "Regels ordenen ook polder," *NRC Handelsblad*, August 14, 2002.
6. Koelewijn, J. "Europa biedt Bush te weinig tegenwicht," *NRC Handelsblad,* April 12, 2003.

7. European Commission, "Audit of Company Accounts: Commission Sets Out Ten Priorities to Improve Quality and Protect Investors," 2003. *europa.eu.int/rapid/start/cgi/guesten. ksh?p_action.gettxt=gt&doc=IP/03/715|0|RAPID&lg=EN& display=*

8. High Level Group of Company Law Experts, "A Modern Regulatory Framework for Company Law in Europe: A Consultative Document of the High Level Group of Company Law Experts," 2002. *europa.eu.int/comm/internal_market/en/ company/company/modern/consult/consult_en.pdf*

9. European Commission, "Company Law and Corporate Governance. Commission Presents Action Plan," 2003. *europa.eu.int/rapid/start/cgi/guesten.ksh?p_action.gettxt= gt&doc=IP/03/716|0|RAPID&lg=EN&display=*

10. M. Schinkel, "Ook wereldeconomie voelt macht van VS," *NRC Handelsblad,* April 5, 2003.

11. See note 8.

12. See note 8.

13. Corporate Governance Committee, "De Nederlandse corporate governance code. Beginselen van goede corporate governance bepalingen en best practice bepalingen," 2003. *www.corpgov.nl*

CHAPTER **9**

Frameworks and Accountants as Means of Supervision

Frameworks Provide a Helping Hand

A number of frameworks can provide support to the supervision of the desired IT behavior. On the basis of performance indicators and controls, such frameworks make it possible to observe what is happening. We will discuss Control Objectives for Information and Related Technology (COBIT) in detail, as it is the most extensively elaborated governance framework for information and IT. In addition, we will examine a number of other frameworks that operate on the same strategic level of "governance." Operational approaches such as the IT Infrastructure Library (ITIL) will not be covered in this book.

In addition, we will investigate the specific roles that accountants play. The question we will ask concerns the extent to which accountants and the rules of accountancy help us to determine the concrete values that information and IT have for business processes. In this regard, we will examine the attention that both receive in reports.

Financial metrics can contribute a great deal toward the clarification of business value of IT if they are used in a strategically and operationally responsible manner. As seen in Chapters 4 and 5, financial systems of measurement must chart costs and benefits and are linked to instruments representing the business goals, the organizational processes, and the human dimension. In addition to financial yardsticks, we need adequately formulated and monitored processes that incorporate Key Performance Indicators (KPIs) in a manner based on clear performance standards. COBIT, Six Sigma, the

Balanced Scorecard, and the somewhat less well-known Information Orientation (an approach that emphasizes the information and IT behavior of employees) are all available for use. By practicing IT governance within a consistent framework that covers all the risks and examines all the necessary connections, a logical whole is generated. The logic must provide support for our management of information and IT, because the complexity, interdependence, and (financial) interests exceed normal management capacities.

COBIT as the World Standard

The IT Governance Institute—the group of individuals who are the most prominent guardians of integrity, the auditors—presents COBIT as a worldwide standard for IT governance. This is not just a vain pretension; nearly all large accountancy organizations have rallied behind COBIT. Such support has become so great that COBIT is now a de facto standard. The sober reality is, however, that since its origins in 1998, COBIT has only been implemented in bits and pieces. Perhaps the "IT Control Objective for Sarbanes-Oxley" will bring about some change here.[1]

■ ■ ■

MANAGEMENT GOALS FOR INFORMATION AND IT

Anyone who doubts that everything is fine with IT accountability must get hold of the COBIT document and conduct an audit. We can say that COBIT outlines the most fundamental and detailed descriptions of the tasks and responsibilities that need to be considered in IT. The individuals who prepared COBIT will not thank us if we deal with their method as an audit tool. COBIT was meant to show us how to piece things together from the ground up without overlooking anything and to specify where and how measurements should be made to determine whether the objectives set are in fact achieved. This is a different activity than conducting an audit.

In its short existence, COBIT has clearly made a name for itself. COBIT comes from the auditing field. The relationship is as follows:

The Information Systems Audit and Control Association (ISACA) established the IT Governance Institute (ITGI) in 1998. ISACA is an overarching organization for those who are involved with audits. The auditor blood was transmitted to the subsidiary organization ITGI, albeit in a somewhat refined and modified manner. ISACA's original "control objectives" changed at ITGI into management objectives. COBIT defines *control* as follows: "The policies, procedures, practices and organisational structures designed to provide reasonable assurance that business objectives will be achieved and that undesired events will be prevented or detected and corrected."[2]

The definition has therefore been derived from the standards that laid the foundations for COBIT.

It is not clear whether COBIT is making enough noise to allow it to occupy the central location in the management of IT that it claims for itself. The most important power that COBIT possesses is its ability to disclose responsibilities, making it possible to monitor these responsibilities.

Many Other Standards in Addition to COBIT

There are other Business Control Models out there, such as the Internal Control-Integrated Framework from the Committee of Sponsoring Organizations of the Treadway Commission (COSO), the British Cadbury model, the Canadian CoCo model, and the King model from South Africa. A number of other systems are more concerned with IT: the British Security Code of Conduct, the Canadian Information Technology Control Guidelines, and the American Security Handbook. The ones most closely related to COBIT are the Systrust Principles and the Criteria for Systems Reliability. Systrust is an initiative of the American Assurance Service Executive Committee and the Canadian Assurance Service Development Board. Systrust benefits managers, customers, and business partners by improving the security, integrity, and maintainability of the systems and processes that support business operations. The fact that there are various methods of evaluation, such as the security standards ITSEC, TCSEC, and ISO 9000, while a single generally applicable method does not exist, limits usability. It is the ambition of COBIT to become the one universally accepted methodology.

How Is COBIT Put Together?

COBIT is a multistage framework that places processes at the center of IT and information management. COBIT consists of 4 main processes and 34 subprocesses, which together include 318 management goals. The main processes are as follows:

1. Planning and organization
2. Acquisition and implementation
3. Delivery and support
4. Monitoring

Exhibit 9.1 shows the subprocesses of the IT Governance framework of COBIT. Business objectives give direction to these processes.

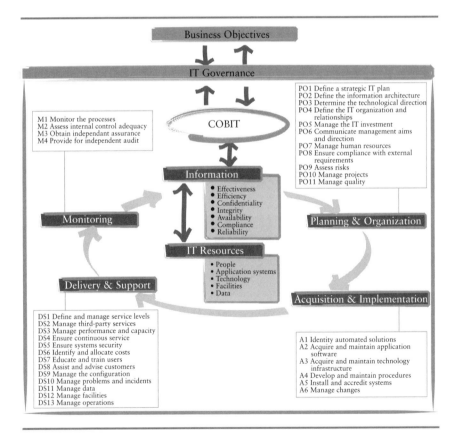

EXHIBIT 9.1   The COBIT Framework
Source: ISACA, 2001

To give an impression of how COBIT works, we will explore one arbitrarily chosen line of management: the line that leads to the hiring and promotion of personnel.

This is one of the nine goals involving the Human Resources Management (HRM) subprocess. HRM is a component of the "planning and organization" main process. From the top down, the "reasoning" behind the COBIT framework is, in this case, as follows: to empower the proper performance of the IT component of HRM (see point 4 below), we have to know what we wish to achieve with HRM in a business sense (3), that is, how to attract and keep highly motivated and competent personnel capable of making the maximum contribution to information and IT processes. For this reason, sound, honest, and transparent processes are necessary to support the whole organizational "life cycle" of the employees (2). Recruitment and promotion constitute one of the nine elements (1) that COBIT distinguishes in this regard.

4 Control over the IT process of managing human resources

3 that satisfies the business requirement to acquire and maintain a highly motivated and competent workforce and to maximize personnel contributions to the IT processes

2 is enabled by sound, fair, and transparent personnel management practices to recruit, line, vet, compensate, train, appraise, promote, and dismiss

1 and takes into consideration
- recruitment and promotion
- training and qualification requirements
- awareness building
- cross-training and job rotation
- hiring, vetting, and dismissal procedures
- objective and measurable performance evaluation
- responsiveness to technical and market changes
- properly balancing internal and external resources
- a succession plan for key positions.

Personnel Recruitment and Promotion Control Objective: Management should implement and regularly assess the processes needed to ensure that personnel recruiting and promotion practices are based on objective criteria and consider education, experience, and responsibility. These processes should be in line with the overall organization's policies and procedures in this regard.

COBIT WILL DO THIS, BUT...?

The Meta Group (now part of Gartner Group) predicted in mid-July 2000 that COBIT and COBIT-related instruments will do all that was discussed above.

> We believe by 2002/03, more than 30%–40% of Global 2000 companies deploying new technologies and entering new markets with e-products and services will have adopted a COBIT-like risk assessment and balanced risk/reward process.[3]

COBIT has not yet reached this point. The elasticity of this statement derives from the term "COBIT-like." Anyone who is familiar with the success stories on the COBIT website will not be overcome with awe. Things have not progressed very far since 1998 apart, of course, from the COBIT subset known as the "IT Control Objectives for Sarbanes-Oxley," which are available from the IT Governance Institute's website. In contrast, IT portfolio management is currently shining in the spotlight. The distinguishing factor is probably that COBIT is geared to processes and not directly to investments.

To access an easy-to-use method, we would be well advised to go to the ezCOBIT website (pronounced easy COBIT). For a fee, we can obtain some helpful tools, such as those found in Methodware. The simplicity of the maturity model (Appendix B) and the COBIT self-assessment of ISACA (Appendix C) is also promising. Thus a number of initiatives exist that can help us translate the method into a particular situation. COBIT is strong in its implementation of process management, so that a set of performance indicators are generated, which supervisors can use concretely.

COBIT AND THE BALANCED SCORECARD

At the end of the 1980s, the need grew for an organization's financial management to supplement and test customer perception, business processes, and quality. Schneiderman explains on his website how the Balanced Scorecard was consequently developed (*www.schneiderman.com/scorecard.htm*). Kaplan and Norton made the Balanced Scorecard famous. The four domains through which organizations should steer their operations are internal business processes, customer satisfaction, finances, and learning and growth.

Given their interdependence with business, information and IT are not directed at financial performances alone. This is why the Balanced Scorecard is so extensive. (Further and more elaborate information on this subject can be found in "The Portfolio Approach as an Aggregation of the Balanced Scorecard, Activity-Based Costing, and Economic Value Added" in Chapter 4.)

In the report "Board Briefing on IT Governance,"[4] the IT Governance Institute gives a detailed explanation of the role of the Balanced Scorecard in IT management. This is the same vision that Wim van Grembergen, professor at the University of Antwerp, explores in his article "The Balanced Scorecard and IT Governance."[5] COBIT and the Balanced Scorecard supplement each other nicely. Exhibit 9.2 shows how van Grembergen establishes the relationship between IT Balanced Scorecards and the Business Balanced Scorecard.

Exhibit 9.2 shows that IT scorecards are derived from the business scorecard and that there are various IT scorecards. Performance indicators can be established at the strategic, operational, and IT developmental levels and used to help steer the organization. The productivity of programmers can be one such indicator. We then measure progress, for example, in terms of a number of monthly job indicators for each employee. The number of training days for each employee in the IT department is another such indicator. Van Grembergen translated the original four-part division into comparable goals on each of the IT scorecards, such as those illustrated in Exhibit 9.2.

SIX SIGMA: PLUS OR MINUS THREE TIMES THE STANDARD DEVIATION

Six Sigma is a methodology for performing the measurements that lead to improvements. COBIT and the Balanced Scorecard share the fact that they center on process. Everything in Six Sigma is measured against the customer. For this reason, Six Sigma is viewed as the

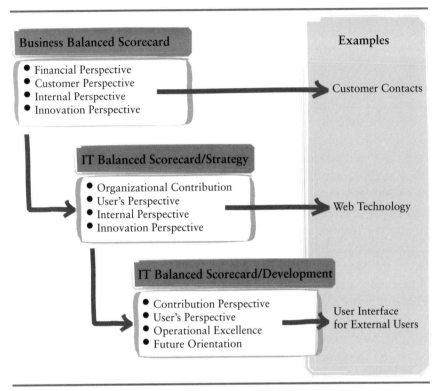

EXHIBIT 9.2   A Business Balanced Scorecard and Two IT Balanced Scorecards

ultimate instrument for generating customer satisfaction and quality. Information and IT are also concerned with these factors.

The father of Six Sigma is Carl Frederick Gauss (1777–1855), who devised the standard curve, a manner of expressing deviations from the mean in units. In 1920, Walther Stewart formulated the theorem that three units away from the mean, i.e., three above or below, is where the critical boundary exists. Given such a deviation, you would then have to intervene in order to adjust the process. Two times three is six, and the standard deviation is represented by the Greek letter sigma; this explains the name Six Sigma, a name whose origin is attributed to Bill Smith at Motorola. Six Sigma can therefore be regarded as a technical instrument for keeping processes on the right path.

Motorola has enhanced the reputation of Six Sigma. In 1991, the trade name Six Sigma was registered by Motorola with the U.S.

Patent and Trademark Office. From the "two-times-three-times-the-deviation" of 200 years ago, we have now arrived at programs with black- and green-belt practitioners, and a top-to-bottom elaborated vision of how an organization can be best governed.

DMAIC and DMADV

Define Measure Analyze Improve Control (DMAIC) and Design Measure Analyze Design Verify (DMADV): Such is the Six Sigma terminology. We have learned this jargon from Kaizen, Deming, Total Quality Management (TQM), and ISO 9000. Even within Six Sigma the plan/do/check/act circle is key. It entails making policy, implementing improvements, measuring, and verifying—all actions taken as a coherent whole. DMAIC and DMADV are instruments that are used in Six Sigma, just like failure-cost estimates, Pareto analyses, and the statistical analysis ANOVA calculations.

The methodology even emphasizes the centrality of the process and requires an external view. The optimization of the processes to a level of perfection is the key. The failure costs inextricably linked with the mistakes made in the processes are charged to the organization. Motorola, Honeywell, and General Electric are the success stories of Six Sigma. They claim to have saved hundreds of millions to billions of dollars. Based on research into the annual figures of these three businesses, a cost saving is forecast amounting to 1.2 to 4.5 percent of annual turnover. The point is therefore to reduce costs by refining processes. Everything is measured in terms of the customer, for the customer does not notice the average but only the deviation; such is the Six Sigma maxim.

INFORMATION ORIENTATION AND THE IMPORTANCE OF DESIRABLE BEHAVIOR

Donald Marchand, professor of information management and strategy at the Institute for Management Development in Lausanne, has developed a promising approach called Information Orientation. In contrast to COBIT and other frameworks, methods, and philosophies, Marchand focuses on the information behavior of employees.

As do similar other approaches, Marchand works with goals and dashboards. Information Orientation measures a business's capacity to use and manage information effectively. Information Orientation hooks on to existing KPI systems that ideally arise from Balanced Scorecard exercises.

Marchand has extensively investigated a group of more than 1,000 senior managers. Based on his research, he identifies 15 competences that are regarded as important for the effective use and management of information. As described in such books as *Making the Invisible Visible* and *Information Orientation: The Link To Business Performance*,[6] as well as in an article in *Sloan Management Review*,[7] these competences are classified into the three cornerstones of Information Orientation:

1. **Information Behaviors and Values.** For example, the capacity of a business to promote and enforce appropriate attitudes to information is important. Included among these are integrity, formality, control, transparency, sharing of information, and proactivity.
2. **Information Management Practices.** This involves the capacity of a business to manage information effectively during the entire life cycle of use. This involves issues such as the discernment of information, as well as the collection, processing, and maintenance of this information. An example is the capacity of an organization to dig up important market information, to analyze it, and to ensure that something is done with it.
3. **Information Technology Practices.** IT practices involve the capacity of a business to manage IT applications and infrastructure effectively so that they support business processes, innovation, and decision making. This involves the relationship between the technology (hardware, software, and telecommunications) and the support for all the tasks in an organization, from top to bottom, from production work to strategy analyses by the directorship.

Marchand's most important claim is that a relationship between Information Orientation and business performance has been demonstrated. Such an assertion implies that businesses subjected to Marchand's system of rules and measures know how they are performing and what they should do to improve business performance by way of improvements in the orientation of information.

All sorts of supplementary views, such as Information Orientation Strategy Scan and Snapshot, help the organization to gain and maintain some insight into the desired information behavior. The Information Orientation Scorecard, intended for organizations that participate in the program of the enterpriseIQ company—the business in which Marchand has lodged the commercial spin-off of his research—can be fed KPI data from existing systems of analysis. It then becomes possible to benchmark in terms of other companies.

A "Passion" for Information Orientation: A Missing Link?

To do business successfully with information and IT, a sort of hierarchy is gradually created from various standards and structures. We are then not dealing with frameworks alone, such as COBIT, but also with more operational approaches like ITIL. However, the identification of various layers and the relationships between them is still insufficiently clear. To be sure, these and other systems have a high common-sense quotient, but they remain conceptually inspired. There is therefore room for a bottom-up developed and organically applicable system of categories and recommendations that can help to realize the "higher goals" adequately.

It is tempting to examine what is not offered by other frameworks, once we have been made aware of Donald Marchand's approach. What Marchand does is put information behavior in the spotlight. This immediately raises the question of whether other frameworks do similar things. After all, it is logical that we can only obtain value from our IT when information behavior is directed in the way that we wish it to be. With full-cycle governance, we would specifically like that a reliable link be established between planning and behavior. This is precisely the potential of Marchand's method. In other frameworks, this connection is much less explicit than it is in Information Orientation.

According to Marchand, Information Orientation is an empirically based and soundly validated "measurement and control system" that functions as a missing link. Information Orientation is unique of its kind in terms of its foundations. The claim is that the method makes the invisible (the crucial "soft" side of information and IT) visible and that it can easily be parachuted into the daily practices of organizations and can function well there. Such claims are explained in the book *Making the Invisible Visible.*[8]

> *This book tracks winning companies in diverse industries globally pursuing a passion—yes, that's the right word—for managing how information and IT are effectively used by their people each day to create outstanding business value.*
> (Matti Alahuhta, President of NOKIA Mobile Phones)

Eleven important points taken from Marchand's consulting practice are as follows:

1. After all the debacles, emphasis now falls on a positive Return on Investment (ROI) and Economic Value Added (EVA) for IT investments. We must never, however, make the mistake of becoming content about this necessity. The real use of IT involves the adequate application of information. This purpose must always be dominant.

2. Mostly, we tacitly assume that information processing skills at work will flourish. Collecting and structuring data do not, however, constitute inspiring activities. Therefore, they have to be compensated, and their importance needs to be emphasized.

3. Allowing for mistakes is essential for every learning organization. Therefore, requiring employees to share problems with management can sanction such behavior.

4. We should continue to promote all chosen actions and associated values actively and to develop them further from the top of the organization down. Senior management has a large role to play.

5. The IO categories of integrity, formalism, control, and openness form the basis of the trust that enables information to be shared.

6. All the IO cornerstones and categories are refined in an empirical-statistical manner from the observations of senior (business) management and can, therefore, be translated into decisive action.

7. IT must involve collaboration or be abandoned: "Do IT together or don't do IT at all."

8. Guarantee that information continues to be of the highest quality throughout its entire life cycle.

9. The greatest challenge for Information Orientation is its realization and measurement.
10. Effectiveness is a journey without a destination.
11. Trust and integrity are key factors.

But Do We Have any Proof That It Works?

Marchand's claim is strong, but the question remains of whether his system works. At present, we may be optimistic about the empirical and statistic anchorage of Information Orientation. The method and the various benchmarks that are made possible by such tools as Marchand's expanding database have proved valuable for Dell, Heineken, Hilti, IKEA, NOKIA, Ritz Carlton, Sony, ABN AMRO, and other banks, as well as for Wal-Mart. However, for most medium and small players, specific, difficult-to-predict situational factors probably play a decisive role. More than 30 businesses have now altered their approach. In addition to the top man from Nokia, many others speak approvingly of Information Orientation. The judgment of Mario Corti, the CFO of Nestlé, gives a good example of Marchand's intentions:

> We at Nestlé have often said *"people are more important than systems"* in seeking to improve information use in our company. The merit of this book is to have attacked with method the hidden complexity of our common sense formulas. This book helps managers understand the effective use of information in the dynamics of our business world.
>
> *(Mario Corti, Executive VP and CFO)*

Marchand's book can therefore help everyone to open their eyes to the behavior orientation involved in the application of information and IT. This is certainly valuable.

ACCOUNTANTS OVERLOOK IT VALUE

Would it be useful if we were assisted by accountancy standards in our efforts to use portfolio management and EVA? We could then base management reports on what we must already include in our external reports. In this section, we will first explore the extent to which external supervisors direct their attention to IT and then consider the specific issue of how IT must be entered in our books and annual reports, namely, neither as an expense nor as a potential value for the organization.

The relationship between IT and corporate governance is an issue raised by several writers, including Boer and Van Sommeren.[9] At the time they were writing, the topic of corporate governance had received a great deal of attention, but the extremely important IT resources had hardly surfaced. Such was the situation in 2000. The two KPMG-ers felt that a change was coming. In particular, IT would have to be given a place in reporting. Especially relevant key topics were the concrete objectives of IT, the information on the basis of which management can determine whether the objectives are achieved, and the manner in which the management and administration of IT can be measured.

Open any annual report. The chances are small that you will find anything meaningful about IT. Research done a few years ago on the degree to which businesses listed on the stock exchange reported on thorny IT issues in their annual reports revealed that the millennium problem was prominent. This 1997 analysis of 434 annual reports showed only that enormous differences were present, related to the nature and size of the company. Nothing more could be concluded.[10] During an exploratory study by ViNT into what Amsterdam Exchange (AEX)-listed businesses revealed about IT in their 2001 annual reports, it quickly became evident that nearly nothing was said about it. Evidently the subject had become too emotionally charged after the Internet, IT, and telecom hype.

The most concrete governance regulations are the so-called Guidelines for Annual Reports. These are specifically meant to make the financial aspects of businesses intelligible and comparable. Software falls under what is labeled "immaterial production resources." Baruch Lev, professor at New York University and an authority in the area of the valuation and reporting of information and IT, has an outspoken opinion on this subject. He feels that the greatest problem of our current bookkeeping systems and standards arises because such systems are still based on transactions, such as sales:

This difference, between how the accounting system is handling value created and is handling investments into value creation, is the major reason for growing the disconnect between market values and financial information.[11]

Enormous differences exist between the market value of a business and the published financial information. This can only be resolved when we make every effort to develop the skills and applications for establishing and communicating the value of intangible assets, such as IT. This is in the immediate interest of investors.

It is remarkable that, in the computer age, information about buildings and machines still dominates financial reports. Since the beginning of the 1990s, more and more business processes have been incorporating large information systems. Because of this technological transformation, the relative importance of knowledge and information compared with products has been increasing rapidly. Large portions of a business's value are currently left off the balance sheets. In sectors with a large body of knowledge and information, the differences are so great that a growing number of people want to abandon accepted bookkeeping principles.

However, accountancy rules (such as "conservatism") and legal provisions currently prevent IT from being expressed in terms of value instead of costs. On July 1, 1999, the European standard for reporting on intangible production resources came into effect. International Accounting Standard 38 also applies to "software." This software must only be expressed as a cost item, ignoring the possibility that such a practice could cause incorrect information to be provided to the shareholder, as Lev asserts. Both U.S. and European accounting standards strictly maintain the old-school methods of valuing IT.

Lev suggests that we immediately begin to appraise our IT in terms of the value we expect it to deliver and that managers develop the skills to do this. Thus this view is in line with what the champions of IT portfolio management and those adept at EVA also advise.

Such methods of accounting for information and IT are of immediate importance for the revision of reporting on intangible resources, of which IT applications constitute an important element. (We also need to recognize that this is a difficult process, as Verhoef demonstrates in "Quantifying the Value of IT Investments."[12]) At the beginning of the 1980s, we could still discern 60 percent of the market value of a business in the books, but just before the millennium, this had fallen to 20 percent, which is unacceptable. We need to obtain and provide better insight into our value-generating processes. The iValue company has put it nicely: "Creating shareholder value from information technology."[13]All investments whose yields are clear—at least within certain limits—should be included in the reports made to financial backers. Amortization can begin from the first moment that an investment has generated its initial revenue. If this practice were ensconced in the bookkeeping rules, as Baruch Lev and others would argue, then the accuracy of reporting in principle could be sanctioned through new rules, which would be backed up by legislation, namely the Public Company Accounting Reform and Investor Protection Act (Sarbanes-Oxley Act).

WHICH FRAMEWORK SHOULD WE CHOOSE?

Choosing a framework and trying to fathom the concepts that underlie it is more inspiring work than selecting a methodology with which to begin.

It is characteristic of frameworks that they stimulate thought; the basic principles are often recognizable. Once we begin to work with frameworks, we often have the tendency to stray onto a level at which either no one understands what is actually involved or no one wants to participate. Then we lapse back into old patterns and familiar behaviors. However, what makes frameworks so attractive despite this criticism is that they speak a specific language capable of reverberating throughout the entire organization. Everyone understands what the subject is, what we mean, and why we are doing things in a particular way. Of course, this can only occur if we are successful in adapting a given framework to suit ourselves.

In our opinion, frameworks can fail because of all the factors reviewed in this book. If we follow Claudio Ciborra, our position must be that frameworks fail because we are striving for the wrong goal; our goal should be to obtain more value from our IT. We sometimes select frameworks only to exercise more control, and Ciborra has revealed what happens then. We go astray and find ourselves in a downward spiral: "from control to drift." When we listen to Herbert Simon, it becomes clear that frameworks constructed with too much complexity (which can easily happen) are way off target. From other behaviorists, we have learned that "gaming the system" is a human quality familiar to everyone. A good framework must therefore be able to withstand the corruption test. After all, the goal remains the realization of value through IT and not the maximum yield measured by an organization's own KPIs.

A fundamental problem is that companies can select frameworks with the capacity to carry out the wrong activities in the best possible way. Therefore Forrester Research suggests that we test each framework to determine how much money is strategically spent on it. At this point, portfolio management again raises its head, for this is the intention of portfolio management: first, make the right choices.

The ideal framework must be directed at the right target (more value from IT), must help to set the appropriate priorities, must be easy to use without requiring people to manipulate the system, must link strategy to desirable behavior, and must fit inside your complete organizational management. This might be Marchand's method, ezCOBIT with simple scorecards, or portfolio management alone with support from financial tools such as Activity-Based Costing, and combined with Lean Six Sigma, for example. In short, your framework can be tailor made to fit your wish list for an ideal framework that will best help you attain your goals.

Whatever we choose, there is a great deal of work to be done; given the ever growing opportunities provided by IT as well as the increasing expenditures, your efforts will quickly prove to be more than worthwhile. We conclude this book with a slide that Marc C. Paulk from the Software Engineering Institute has been using for years (see Exhibit 9.3). Although it deals with a specific discipline, it clearly has general validity. It reads: "We must continue to use our heads! Keep it simple and respect the human dimension. Sink your teeth into it and keep at it." For something as complex as the full-cycle business governance of information and IT, such strictures represent basic guidelines.

Picking a Framework

Any model or standard can be helpful; all models and standards must be used with intelligence and common sense.

The best known and most widely used "quality standard" for general use is ISO 9001 (plus 9004).

The best known and most widely used model for software process improvements is the Software CMM.

Some models and standards may be more relevant to your environment, e.g., Trillium for telecom.

Models and standards are not necessary for effective improvement.

EXHIBIT 9.3   We Must Continue to Use Our Heads!

ENDNOTES

1. IT Governance Institute, "IT Control Objectives for Sarbanes-Oxley," 2003. *www.itgi.org*
2. Committee of Sponsoring Organisations of the Treadway Commission (COSO), "Internal Control-Integrated Framework," 1992 and "Systems Auditability and Control Report (SAC)," 1994.
3. A. Passori, "Risk without Remorse," Meta Group, 2000. *www .isaca.org/ctmeta.htm*
4. IT Governance Institute (ITGI), "Board Briefing on IT Governance," 2001. *www.itgi.org/template_ITGI.cfm?template=/ ContentManagement/ContentDisplay.cfm&ContentID=6679*
5. W. van Grembergen, "The Balanced Scorecard and IT Governance," 2001. *www.itgi.org/balscorecard.pdf*
6. D. Marchand, et al., *Information Orientation: The Link to Business Performance*, New York, Oxford University Press, 2000.
7. D. Marchand, et al. "Information Orientation: People Technology and the Bottom Line," *Sloan Management Review*, 2000. *www2 .bus.oregonstate.edu/students/b/blada097/group1/Information% 20Orientation.pdf*

8. D. Marchand, et al., *Making the Invisible Visible: How Companies Win with the Right Information, People and IT,* Hoboken: John Wiley & Sons, 2001.
9. J.C. de Boer and E.R. van Sommeren, "Corporate Governance: de relatie naar ICT," 2000. *www.kpmg.nl/Docs/Information_ Risk_Management/Publications/2000303Compact00-3-Boe.pdf*
10. S.M. Williams, "Disclosure, Anorexia, or Legitimization in the Face of IT Problems", 2001. *www.haskayne.ucalgary.ca/ research/media/2001_ 15.pdf*
11. J. Daum, "Accounting, Reporting and Intangible Assets," Interview with Baruch Lev, 2002. *www.juergendaum.com*
12. Verhoef, "Quantifying the Value of IT Investments," *Science of Computer Programming,* 2005. *www.cs.vu.nl/~x/val/val.pdf*
13. iValue Company. *www.ivalueinstitute.com*

From Control to Drift

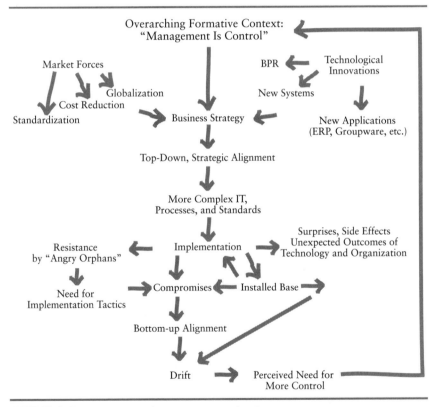

EXHIBIT A.1   Mapping the Dynamics of Infrastructure

The COBIT IT Governance Maturity Model*

This is a model of governance over IT and its processes with the business goal of adding value, while balancing risk versus return.

0 NONEXISTENT

There is a complete lack of any recognizable IT governance process. The organization has not even recognized that an issue needs to be addressed and hence there is no communication about the issue.

1 INITIAL/AD HOC

There is evidence that the organization has recognized that IT governance issues exist and need to be addressed. However, no standardized processes have been put into place; instead, ad hoc approaches are applied on an individual or case-by-case basis. Management's approach is chaotic, and communication on issues and approaches to address them are sporadic or nonconsistent. The importance of capturing the value of IT in the outcome-oriented performance of related enterprise processes may be acknowledged. No standard assessment process

---

*Source: The Board Briefing on IT Governance. *www.itgovernanceinstitute.org/boardbriefing.pdf*

exists. IT monitoring is only implemented in reaction to an incident that has caused some loss or embarrassment to the organization.

2 REPEATABLE BUT INTUITIVE

There is global awareness of IT governance issues. IT governance activities and performance indicators are under development, including IT planning, delivery, and monitoring processes. As part of this effort, IT governance activities have been formally established in the organization's change management process, with active senior management involvement and oversight. Selected IT processes have been identified for improving and/or controlling core enterprise processes, are effectively planned and monitored as investments, and are derived within the context of a defined IT architectural framework. Management has identified basic IT governance measurements and assessment methods and techniques; however, the process has not been adopted across the organization. No formal training is in place, and communications on governance standards and responsibilities are left to the individual. Individuals drive the governance processes within various IT projects and processes. Limited governance tools are chosen and implemented for gathering governance metrics, but they may not be used to their full capacity because of a lack of expertise in their functionality.

3 DEFINED PROCESS

The need to act with respect to IT governance is understood and accepted. A baseline set of IT governance indicators has been developed, whereby linkages between outcome measures and performance drivers are defined, documented, and integrated into strategic and operational planning and monitoring processes. Procedures have been standardized, documented, and implemented. Management has communicated standardized procedures, and informal training has been established. Performance indicators over all IT governance activities are being recorded and tracked, leading to enterprise-wide improvements. Although procedures are measurable, they are not sophisticated, but rather are the formalization of existing practices.

Tools have been standardized, using currently available techniques. IT Balanced Business Scorecard ideas are being adopted. It is, however, left to the individual to get training, to follow the standards, and to apply them. Root cause analysis is only occasionally applied. Most processes are monitored against some (baseline) metrics, but any deviation (mostly acted on by individual initiative) would probably remain undetected by management. Nevertheless, overall accountability of key process performance is clear, and management is rewarded based on key performance measures.

4 MANAGED AND MEASURABLE

There is full understanding of IT governance issues at all levels, supported by formal training. There is a clear understanding of who the customer is, and responsibilities are defined and monitored through service-level agreements. Responsibilities are clear, and process ownership has been established. IT processes are aligned with the business and with the IT strategy. Improvement in IT processes is based primarily on a quantitative understanding, and it is possible to monitor and measure compliance with procedures and process metrics. All process stakeholders are aware of risks, the importance of IT, and the opportunities it can offer. Management has defined tolerances under which processes must operate. Action is taken in many (but not all) cases in which processes do not appear to be working effectively or efficiently. Processes are occasionally improved, and best internal practices are enforced. Root cause analysis is being standardized. Continuous improvement is beginning to be addressed. Technology is being used, although on a limited, primarily tactical, level, based on mature techniques and enforced standard tools. All required internal domain experts are involved. IT governance is evolving into an enterprise-wide process. IT governance activities are becoming integrated with the enterprise governance process.

5 OPTIMIZED

There is advanced and forward-looking understanding of IT governance issues and solutions. Training and communication are supported by leading-edge concepts and techniques. Processes have been refined to a level of external best practice, based on the results of continuous improvement and maturity modeling with other organizations. The implementation of these policies has led to an organization, to people, and to processes that are quick to adapt and fully support IT governance requirements. All problems and deviations are analyzed by root cause, and efficient action is expediently identified and initiated. IT is used in an extensive, integrated, and optimized manner to automate the workflow and provide tools to improve quality and effectiveness. The risks and returns of the IT processes are defined, balanced, and communicated across the enterprise. External experts are leveraged, and benchmarks are used for guidance. Monitoring, self-assessment, and communication about governance expectations are pervasive within the organization, and the use of technology is optimal to support measurement, analysis, communication, and training. Enterprise governance and IT governance are strategically linked, leveraging technology and human and financial resources to increase the competitive advantage of the enterprise.

Ten Definitions of Corporate Governance in the European Member States[*]

1. Corporate governance is the system by which companies are directed and controlled.
   (Cadbury Report, United Kingdom)
2. Corporate governance refers to the set of rules applicable to the direction and control of a company.
   (Cardon Report, Belgium)
3. Corporate governance is the organization of the administration and management of companies.
   (Recommendations of the Federation of Belgian Companies)
4. Corporate governance comprises the goals according to which a company is managed, as well as the major principles and frameworks that regulate the interactions among the company's managerial bodies, the owners, and other parties who are directly influenced by the company's dispositions and business (in this context jointly referred to as the company's stakeholders). Stakeholders include employees, creditors, suppliers, customers, and the local community.
   (Nørby Report & Recommendations, Denmark)

---

[*]*Source:* Comparative Study of Corporate Governance Codes Relevant to the European Union and Its Member States (2002). *www.usc.es/cde/a_Docs/ Comparat_Corp_Gov_Codes_UE.pdf*; Corporate Governance in the ECE Region: *www.unece.org/ead/pub/031/031_c4.pdf*

5. Corporate governance describes the legal and factual regulatory framework for managing and supervising a company.
   (Berlin Initiative Code, Preamble)
6. Corporate governance, in the sense of the set of rules according to which firms are managed and controlled, is the result of norms, traditions, and patterns of behavior developed by each economic and legal system.
   (Preda Report, Italy)
7. The concept of corporate governance has been understood to mean a code of conduct for those associated with the company ... consisting of a set of rules for sound management and proper supervision and for a division of duties and responsibilities and powers effecting the satisfactory balance of influence of all the stakeholders.
   (Peters Report, The Netherlands)
8. Corporate governance is used to describe the system of rules and procedures employed in the conduct and control of listed companies.
   (Securities Market Commission Recommendations, Portugal)
9. Corporate governance ... involves a set of relationships among a company's management, its board, its shareholders, and other stakeholders. Corporate governance also provides the structure through which the objectives of the company are set and the means by which the attaining of those objectives and monitoring performance are determined.
   (OECD Principles)
10. Corporate governance comprehends that structure of relationships and corresponding responsibilities among a core group consisting of shareholders, [supervisory] board members, and managers designed to best foster the competitive performance required to achieve the corporation's primary objective.
    (Millstein Report on the OECD)

KIMBIA, the Portfolio Model of Rabobank Nederland: Management/Business ICT Alignment Implementation Chains

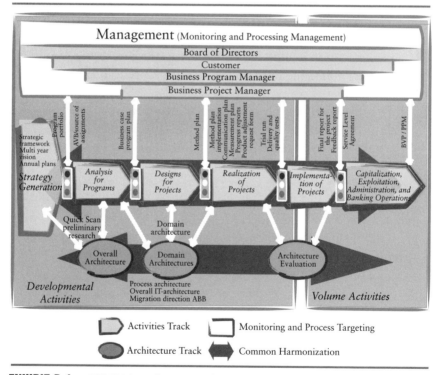

EXHIBIT D.1 KIMBIA Definitions of Management (Monitoring and Process Management)

- **Strategy:** A strategy consists of all the policy intentions that direct the development of the Rabobank group and/or its divisions.
  - Concrete objectives (SMART) are established for these policy intentions.
  - The latter are realized by portfolios constituting a cohesive whole comprising programs, projects, and regular (volume) activities.
- **Portfolio:** A portfolio is a cohesive whole consisting of programs, projects, and volume activities that are meant to achieve and fulfill a formulated strategy or portion thereof. A portfolio has a dynamic composition and can be adjusted in an ad hoc manner.
- **Domain:** A domain is an interrelated collection of processes and/or functionalities that can be coherently organized. There are two types of domains:
  1. Process domains: related business processes
  2. Application domains: interconnected ICT functionalities
- **Program:** A program is an interrelated collection of projects and supporting activities that are intended to achieve a formulated strategy or portion thereof.
  - A program is temporary and goal oriented.
  - Various disciplines are involved in realizing a program.
  - The activities (improvisations, routines, and so on) are undertaken to manage and execute the programs.
- **Project:** A project is a coherent whole comprised of activities performed to achieve an unambiguous, preformulated result.
  - A project is limited and directed at a result.
  - A project consists of activities from several disciplines (marketing, HRM, Organization, ICT, and so on).
  - A project is composed of phases and is approved on a phase-by-phase basis.

Index